COMPELLING STORIES
FROM WORLD HISTORY

SCOTT ALLSOP

Published by L & E Books

www.mrallsophistory.com   www.historypod.net

ISBN: 978-0-9956809-1-3

For Alice
with whom every day is significant

PREFACE

The past is enormous. People and societies have since interpreted the past in a myriad of different ways, resulting in a complex tapestry of world history that is as fascinating to study as it is confusing.

We live in a world swathed in this tapestry, where dates and historical events act as vital cultural waymarkers. The celebration and commemoration of anniversaries draws on and shapes our social identity, but against a bulwark of 'headline history' other people and events have been lost to the sands of time. Through researching and writing this book I have sought to remind us all that something worth remembering happened somewhere and to somebody on every day of the year.

366 Days purposefully contains a disparate range of events from the worlds of politics, economics, religion, science, technology, society, and the arts. Although the decision over which event to include on any given date is arbitrary, I have provided contextual details in an attempt to outline each one's historical significance. These explanations have been greatly influenced by various educationalists who have developed ways to classify factors that contribute to historical significance. I consequently owe a great debt to the work of Christine Counsell, Rob Phillips and Ian Dawson as well as many others in shaping my approach.

I have endeavoured to ensure historical accuracy and objectivity, but the differing claims of 'truth' in both contemporary and secondary sources have made this a challenge. Even some supposedly straightforward facts do not always agree. I have therefore sought to indicate issues over which commentators have differing views, but have avoided extensive exploration of such interpretations for the sake of a what I hope is an engaging narrative.

I am very grateful to those people who listen and subscribe to my HistoryPod podcast. Without their encouragement to research, write, record and publish a daily 'on this day' podcast this book would not exist.

JANUARY

JANUARY

1

1942

The Declaration by the United Nations was agreed and signed by the representatives of four major Allied nations during the Second World War.

The original signatories – United States President Franklin D. Roosevelt, British Prime Minister Winston Churchill, the USSR's Ambassador to the US Maxim Litvinov, and Chinese Minister of Foreign Affairs T. V. Soong – were joined the next day by a further 24 nations.

Having been drafted by Churchill, Roosevelt, and Roosevelt's aide Harry Hopkins, the short declaration was linked to acceptance of the principles of the Atlantic Charter of 1941. The document also provided a foundation for the later establishment of the UN itself, but was firmly rooted in the political and military situation of the time. All signatories agreed to apply themselves fully to 'a common struggle against savage and brutal forces seeking to subjugate the world'. Referring to these forces under the umbrella term 'Hitlerism', it is clear that the Allied leaders did not differentiate between the different regimes against which they were fighting.

The declaration also presented the intended conclusion of the war. Rather than accept an armistice as had happened at the conclusion of the First World War, the signatories agreed that 'complete victory over their enemies is essential'. This meant that the Allies would only accept the unconditional surrender of their enemies. Furthermore, they agreed to cooperate with every other signatory in the ongoing war and therefore not pursue a separate peace for their own nation's advantage.

By the time the war ended in 1945, a further 21 countries had signed the declaration.

Serial killer Peter Sutcliffe, who is better known as the Yorkshire Ripper, was arrested by police.

Sutcliffe was found guilty of murdering 13 women over a six-year period, and of attempting to murder a further seven. He was sentenced to life imprisonment in May 1981. In 2010 the High Court issued him with a whole life tariff which means that he is likely to stay in jail until his death.

Although Sutcliffe first assaulted a woman in 1969, his famous series of attacks began in 1975. Many theories exist regarding his motive, with some focusing on a hatred of prostitutes after he was conned out of money by one.

Despite the connection between Sutcliffe and prostitutes, not all his victims were sex workers. However, it was after police stopped him with a prostitute in his car on 2 January 1981 that he was finally arrested. He was taken into custody due to his car having false number plates, but while in Dewsbury Police Station the similarities between him and the Yorkshire Ripper's profile led him to be questioned about the case.

Sutcliffe admitted to being the Ripper two days later, on 4 January, and while in custody claimed that he heard the voice of God commanding him to kill prostitutes. The prosecution wanted to accept his plea of diminished responsibility after four expert psychiatrists diagnosed him with paranoid schizophrenia. However, the judge rejected the plea and therefore the case went to full trial.

Since Sutcliffe had already admitted his guilt as part of his plea of diminished responsibility, the members of the jury were only asked to determine his mental state rather than his guilt.

JANUARY
3
1961

The United States of America severed its diplomatic relationship with Cuba and closed its embassy in Havana.

The move came in the wake of the nationalisation of industries in Cuba that were owned by US citizens. The number of nationalisations increased as the American government gradually introduced a trade embargo.

The earlier overthrow of President Fulgencio Batista by Fidel Castro's 26th of July Movement in 1959 had brought about a dramatic change in US-Cuban relations. American President Dwight D. Eisenhower initially recognised the new socialist government, but the situation quickly deteriorated as Cuba introduced agrarian reforms and nationalised US-owned interests.

In response the USA stopped buying Cuban sugar and banned the sale of oil, so Castro's government turned to the USSR for economic assistance. This led to a further deterioration of relations with America. However, a complete trade embargo only came about after Cuba nationalised the three American-owned oil refineries in the country in October 1960.

Further nationalisations over the next three months – including that of private property owned by Americans – led the Eisenhower administration to cut all diplomatic ties with Cuba on 3 January. Meanwhile a group of Cuban exiles in the USA, known as Brigade 2506, were trained by the CIA to overthrow Castro's government. This plan, which resulted in the failed Bay of Pigs invasion, was followed through by John F. Kennedy after he became the 35th President of the USA less than three weeks after the closure the embassy. Diplomatic relations between Cuba and the US were restored on 20 July 2015, although the trade embargo continued.

Charles I of England attempted to arrest the Five Members of Parliament, prompting the English Civil War and his own eventual execution for treason.

Charles ascended to the throne in 1625, but as a believer in the divine right of kings ruled without Parliament for the eleven years of what is known as his personal rule. During this time his policies, particular those regarding taxation and religion, were met with hostility from his subjects.

Charles' religious policies towards Scotland were so badly received that they led to the outbreak of the Bishops' Wars in 1639, which saw a Scottish army invade England in August 1640. The King became convinced that the Scots had been encouraged in some way by the Five Members: John Pym, John Hampden, Denzil Holles, Arthur Haselrig and William Strode. Charles was afraid of them turning the London mob against him and, having heard rumours of a plan to impeach the Queen, charged them with treason.

The Five Members failed to respond to a summons on 3 January. Therefore the next afternoon Charles himself entered the House of Commons chamber – an act that was a huge violation of Parliamentary privilege – and sat in the Speaker's chair to demand the men be handed over to him.

The Five Members had already left the building for safety. When asked for their whereabouts, the Speaker announced that he wouldn't tell Charles their location as he was a servant of Parliament, not the crown. Exclaiming that 'the birds have flown,' Charles soon left the capital and began to assemble his forces. The English Civil War began just a few months later.

JANUARY

5

1968

The Prague Spring began when Alexander Dubček became the new First Secretary of the Communist Party of Czechoslovakia.

Dubček was a committed communist, and had been First Secretary of the Communist Party of Slovakia since 1963 although he struggled to work with Antonín Novotný, the President of Czechoslovakia. Under Novotný's control the country had experienced a slow and uneasy move towards de-Stalinisation while suffering a huge economic downturn.

Frustrated by the President's failure to effectively restructure the country, Dubček and other reformists challenged him at a meeting of the Central Committee in October 1967. In response Novotný secretly invited the Soviet leader Leonid Brezhnev to visit Czechoslovakia to secure his support. However, this plan backfired when Brezhnev learned just how unpopular Novotný was and instead gave his support to those who wished to remove him from power.

Dubček replaced Novotný as the leader of Czechoslovakia on 5 January 1968 and quickly began to introduce a series of political and economic reforms. Known as 'socialism with a human face' this programme was intended to keep the Communist Party in control of the government while allowing some mild democratisation and political liberalisation.

As the reforms took hold, the government was faced with public demands to go even further. At the same time, the USSR and its allies in the Warsaw Pact began pressuring Dubček to bring what had become known as the Prague Spring under control. On 20 August the countries of the Warsaw Pact took matters in to their own hands and moved their armed forces into Czechoslovakia.

JANUARY
6
1066

Harold Godwinson was crowned king of England. Harold II was the last Anglo-Saxon king of England.

Edward the Confessor died had died the previous day, having suffered a series of strokes in late 1065 and lain in a coma for much of the remainder of his life. Edward died without an heir, and this sparked a succession crisis that culminated in the Norman invasion of England later that year.

The Normans claimed that Edward had promised the throne of England to William of Normandy. This is reported by various Norman chroniclers, and the Bayeux Tapestry even shows Harold swearing an oath on sacred relics to support William's claim to the English throne after he was shipwrecked in 1064. The reliability of the Tapestry's account is debated by historians, especially since it goes against the English tradition that the new king would be chosen by the Witenagemot – the 'meeting of wise men'.

Whatever the truth of Edward's promise and Harold's meeting with William, Edward apparently regained consciousness and entrusted his kingdom to Harold for 'protection' shortly before he died. When the Witenagemot met on 6 January they elected Harold to be the new king, and his coronation took place the same day. Historians generally believe that this took place in Westminster Abbey, which had been built by Edward and was consecrated just a few days earlier on 28 December 1065.

Hearing of Harold's accession to the English throne, William of Normandy soon began preparing to invade. Harold reigned for barely nine months before being killed at the Battle of Hastings on 14 October by the Norman invaders.

JANUARY

7

1979

Pol Pot, the Cambodian revolutionary and General Secretary of the Central Committee of the Communist Party of Kampuchea, was overthrown when Vietnamese forces captured the capital city Phnom Penh.

Pol Pot was leader of the Cambodian communist group the Khmer Rouge who were formed in 1968. Areas of Cambodia were already being used by Vietnamese communists as bases, which led to American carpet bombing campaigns in Cambodia. Although the significance of this campaign on the rise of the Khmer Rouge is debated by historians, the Khmer Rouge were able to seize power in 1975. They renamed the country Democratic Kampuchea and set about introducing a form of radical communism that aimed to eradicate all Western and modern influences and create a purely agrarian society.

This upheaval saw the closure of schools, hospitals, and factories. Banking, finance, and currency were abolished. Intellectuals were killed in enormous numbers, while others were sent on long forced marches into the countryside where they were subjected to forced labour on collective farms. Millions of people died.

Although both countries were communist, relations between Cambodia and Vietnam declined by the end of 1978 as a result of border clashes and differing ideologies. Consequently, on 25 December, Vietnamese armed forces launched an invasion of Cambodia supported by the newly-formed Kampuchean United Front for National Salvation. The latter consisted of Cambodian communists who had defected from the Khmer Rouge. After they captured Phnom Penh on 7 January 1979, Pol Pot's Khmer Rouge forces fled into the jungle.

United States President Woodrow Wilson made a speech to Congress in which he outlined his principles for world peace, known as the Fourteen Points.

Three days earlier, on 5 January, the British Prime Minister David Lloyd George had outlined British war aims at the Caxton Hall conference of the Trades Union Congress. It was the first time any of the Allies had shared their post-war intentions and, as a result, Woodrow Wilson considered abandoning his own speech since many of the points were similar. However, he was persuaded to deliver the speech anyway. Keen to distance the United States from nationalistic disputes that fuelled European rivalries, he sought a lasting peace by securing terms that avoided selfish ambitions of the victors.

Wilson's Fourteen Points were greeted with some reluctance from France in particular. Georges Clemenceau, the French Prime Minister, is said to have remarked that, 'The good Lord only had ten!' as a comparison to the Ten Commandments.

Wilson's speech led to the Fourteen Points becoming an instrument of propaganda that was widely circulated within Germany. Consequently it later served as a basis for the German armistice that was signed later that year.

France's vastly different intentions meant that, when the Paris Peace Conference began on 18 January 1919, there were significant tensions between the negotiators. The fact that Wilson himself was physically ill meant that he was less able to argue for his preferred peace terms against Clemenceau, who was nicknamed the Tiger, and his demands to cripple Germany. Consequently many Germans felt incredible anger over the final terms of the Treaty.

JANUARY

9

1799

Modern income tax was introduced for the first time.

The British Prime Minister, William Pitt the Younger, announced the introduction of income tax in December 1798 as a way to pay for the wars against France. The tax stayed in place until 1802, at which point the Peace of Amiens secured a temporary break from hostilities. Income tax was reintroduced in 1803 after the war recommenced.

Britain had become involved in the French Revolutionary Wars in 1792 and, by 1799, almost continuous conflict had seriously weakened the country's finances. For much of this time the French had been better organised than the forces of the First and Second Coalitions, and Britain had found itself needing to offer financial support to other coalition members in order to maintain the size of force necessary to take on the French military.

Britain's financial commitment to the war ran up a huge national debt, and attempts to reduce the cost of the military had led to starvation in the army and a mutiny in the navy. Pitt the Younger, who held the joint positions of Prime Minister and Chancellor of the Exchequer, consequently introduced his 'graduated' or progressive income tax as 'aid and contribution for the prosecution of the war'. The tax rate gradually increased from less than 1% for people on incomes of £60 up to 10% of incomes of £200 and was only intended to be a temporary measure to pay for the war. Although it was abolished in 1802 it was reinstated and repealed another two times before being made permanent.

Interestingly, war also led the United States federal government to introduce its first income tax on 5 August 1861, which helped to pay for the American Civil War.

The Treaty of Versailles came into effect.

Although the Treaty had been signed in June the previous year, the terms weren't activated until 10 January. As well as instigating the punishment of Germany, this meant that the League of Nations was officially founded as the Covenant of the League was now in operation.

The League was set up on the urging of US President Woodrow Wilson, who included it as one of his Fourteen Points. His desire was to create 'a general association of nations formed under specific covenants for the purpose of affording mutual guarantees of political independence and territorial integrity to great and small states alike.' The League was therefore the first worldwide organisation established with the explicit aim of securing world peace. It intended to do this through collective security, disarmament, the promotion of international trade, and the improvement of social conditions.

Six days after its establishment, the League's first Council meeting took place. The United States was notably absent, as opposition in the Senate meant the USA did not ratify the Treaty of Versailles. Although there were many reasons for not ratifying the Treaty, a key factor was opposition to Article X of the Covenant which stated that League members would come to each other's defence if they were attacked.

The League therefore began with 42 members, of which 23 remained until the League was dissolved in 1946. It was replaced by the United Nations which, coincidentally, held its first General Assembly on 10 January 1946.

JANUARY

11

1923

French and Belgian troops marched into Germany and occupied the industrial Ruhr area.

France and Belgium had grown increasingly frustrated by Germany frequently defaulting on the reparations that had been agreed in the Treaty of Versailles. The occupation was met with passive resistance, which was only called off on 26 September as rampant hyperinflation crippled the German economy.

Although the French leader Raymond Poincaré was initially reluctant to occupy the Ruhr, he had grown increasingly exasperated by Germany's regular defaults and the lack of international support for sanctions as a way to persuade the government to pay. He argued that the reparations themselves were not the issue, but rather that allowing Germany to defy this part of the Treaty of Versailles could lead to further attempts to undermine the Treaty at a later date.

It was Germany's failure to provide the full quota of coal and timber in December 1922 that provided France and Belgium with the excuse to occupy the Ruhr on 11 January 1923. They established the Inter-Allied Mission for Control of Factories and Mines to ensure that goods payments were made, but the Germans responded with a campaign of passive resistance that stopped production. Tensions were high between the occupiers and Ruhr locals and, by the time Gustav Stresemann's new government called off the strikes in September, approximately 130 German civilians had been killed by the occupying armies.

The occupation enabled France and Belgium to extract reparations, but it was Germany that won international sympathy. The last occupying French troops finally left the Ruhr on 25 August 1925.

The National Trust was founded by Octavia Hill, Sir Robert Hunter and Hardwicke Rawnsley.

Describing itself as 'a charity that works to preserve and protect historic places and spaces – for ever, for everyone' the National Trust is one of the largest landowners in the United Kingdom. It is therefore able to protect numerous beauty spots, historic houses and gardens, industrial monuments, and social history sites.

Octavia Hill, arguably the leading founder of the trust, spent much of her life developing social housing. Her time within London's housing estates led her to seek protection for the capital's remaining green spaces for 'the enjoyment, refreshment, and rest of those who have no country house.' This inspired her to take a role in setting up the National Trust.

The National Trust now controls over 985 square miles of Britain. This accounts for nearly 1.5% of the total land mass of England, Wales and Northern Ireland and it has the right to impose bylaws that apply to anybody visiting the land. These statutory powers were granted through six separate Acts of Parliament between 1907 and 1971 that are collectively known as the National Trust Acts.

The National Trust is an independent charity, and many of its country houses and gardens were donated by their owners in lieu of death duties. It is supported by a huge team of over 61,000 volunteers and gets most of its income from annual subscriptions, which allow members to access all the trust's properties for free.

With a membership of around 4 million, it is the largest membership organisation in the United Kingdom.

JANUARY

13

1935

The Territory of the Saar Basin voted to reunite with Germany.

In 1918 the Saar Basin was a heavily industrialised area that boasted a large number of coal mines. Following the Treaty of Versailles the area was occupied and governed by France and Britain under the auspices of the League of Nations. France was also given exclusive control of the area's rich coal mines as part of the reparations agreement. The Treaty called for a plebiscite to decide the long-term future of the Saar region after a period of fifteen years.

By the time of the plebiscite Adolf Hitler had secured his position as the supreme leader of Germany. This had caused a number of people who opposed Nazi policies to move to the Saar Basin since it was the only part of Germany free from their rule. These people were keen for the area to remain under the League's administration, but maintaining the status quo was unpopular with many other Germans in the area.

The Nazis launched an intensive pro-Germany campaign in the area that was led by propaganda chief Joseph Goebbels. As early as 1933, complaints that the Nazi campaign amounted to a 'reign of terror' had been noted by American political scientist Sarah Wambaugh who was one of the members of the commission sent to oversee the plebiscite. Although the Nazis did restrain their tactics by the end of 1934, the League of Nations still provided a peacekeeping force to monitor the plebiscite.

Voter turnout was 98% of all eligible voters, and 90.8% of them chose to re-join the German Reich. The overwhelming result surprised many observers, and acted as powerful propaganda for the Nazi Party.

The Casablanca Conference began in Morocco.

The conference saw the Combined Chiefs of Staff join American President Franklin D. Roosevelt and British Prime Minister Winston Churchill to discuss the future strategy for fighting the Second World War. Representing the Free French forces, Generals Charles de Gaulle and Henri Giraud were also in attendance although they took a minor role in the discussions.

Roosevelt's attendance at the conference marked the first time a President had left American soil during wartime. Meanwhile, Joseph Stalin did not attend as he felt his presence was needed at home during the ongoing Battle of Stalingrad.

The Casablanca Conference saw the national leaders agree to invade Sicily after the completion of the North African Campaign. This was intended to divert Axis forces away from mainland Europe and weaken the German defence ahead of a later Allied invasion of France. In return, Churchill agreed to send more troops to the Pacific to help in the fight against the Japanese. The leaders also agreed to launch combined bombing missions against Germany and to destroy German U-boats in the Atlantic.

Details of the conference were kept from the public until the participants left Casablanca, although a number of journalists had been invited to a press conference on 24 January where vague details of the discussions were announced by Roosevelt.

Coming as a surprise to Churchill, Roosevelt announced his demand for the 'unconditional surrender' of the Axis powers. This had been discussed at the conference, but had not been fully embraced by the British Prime Minister.

JANUARY
15
1919

Rosa Luxemburg and Karl Liebknecht were killed by members of the Freikorps.

The two German socialists were joint-founders of the Spartacist League and the Communist Party of Germany, and were captured following the Spartacist uprising that began on 4 January.

Luxemburg and Liebknecht had originally been members of the Social Democratic Party of Germany. Frustrated by the wider SPD's support for Germany's declaration of war in 1914, they and other leftists created a separate organisation known as the *Spartakusbund* or Spartacus League. Named after the leader of the Roman Republic's largest slave rebellion, the Spartacus League actively opposed the ongoing war. In 1916, both Luxemburg and Liebknecht were found guilty of high treason and imprisoned after they organised an anti-war demonstration.

They were released in 1918 and, in December, renamed the Spartacist League the Communist Party of Germany. The abdication of Kaiser Wilhelm II had led to a post-war revolution. Friedrich Ebert, a centrist member of the SPD, had assumed the position of Chancellor but struggled to maintain control of the country amidst the uprisings. His government had begun to side with conservatives, while the left sought the establishment of a government based on workers' councils.

On 5 January thousands of people swarmed into the Berlin streets and began occupying government and press offices. Two days later around half a million people began a general strike. By this point, however, Ebert had hired Freikorps to crush the revolt. They did so quickly and violently. On 15 January Luxemburg and Liebknecht were arrested, tortured, interrogated and executed.

The Roman Senate granted Octavian the titles *Augustus* and *Princeps*.

The title *Augustus* is understood to translate as 'the illustrious one' and, although the title did not grant him political authority, many historians see this as the point at which Augustus' rule as first Roman Emperor began.

Octavian's rise to power, and his position as Emperor, was achieved over a long period of time. Julius Caesar was his great-uncle and, in Caesar's will, was declared his adopted son and heir. Consequently Octavian inherited Caesar's property and lineage, along with a number of titles and offices that had been bestowed upon his adoptive father. Octavian had already proved himself a formidable military general, but his position as Caesar's heir won him further support from many veteran legionnaires.

His assumption of the role of an Emperor was achieved by collecting a further range of powers as *Princeps Civitatis*, which translates as 'First Citizen of the State'. These powers were voluntarily granted to him for life by the Senate. When he appeared before them in 27 BCE to return the powers he had already accumulated, the Senate requested he remain in position. They even extended his authority. Consequently his position was in keeping with the traditions of the Republic as his powers came from the Senate, but in practice he wielded exclusive political authority.

Furthermore, having been granted control of the more problematic provinces of the empire, the Senate had effectively given Augustus control of the vast majority of the Roman army, which further guaranteed his dominance of Roman politics.

JANUARY
17
1991

The combat phase of the Gulf War began when Operation Desert Storm was launched.

Operation Desert Storm was intended to destroy Iraq's military and civilian infrastructure through an aerial bombing campaign. Over 2,250 coalition aircraft flew in excess of 1,000 sorties a day for five weeks, after which a ground campaign to force Iraqi troops from Kuwait began.

The trigger for the Gulf War was Iraq's invasion of Kuwait on 2 August 1990. Driven by a desire to seize Kuwait's vast oil reserves and relieve Iraq of crippling debts accrued during the Iran-Iraq War, the invasion was completed within just three days. International condemnation of Iraq was immediate and far-reaching. The UN began by imposing complete economic sanctions and, on 29 November 1990, gave Iraq an ultimatum: withdraw from Kuwait by the 15 January 1991 or face military action. In preparation, US Secretary of State James Baker secured support from 34 separate countries for a multi-national coalition force.

Meanwhile over 500,000 troops were sent to defend Saudi Arabia in Operation Desert Shield in case Iraq chose to attack. Despite this growing pressure, Saddam continued to refuse to withdraw from Kuwait.

Operation Desert Storm began shortly after midnight on 17 January. Just a few hours later, Saddam Hussein appeared on state radio saying that 'the great duel, the mother of all battles has begun. The dawn of victory nears as this great showdown begins'. His optimism was ill-placed. Following five weeks of aerial bombardment, the Coalition's ground assault forced the Iraqi army from Kuwait in just four days.

Wilhelm I of Prussia was proclaimed the first German Emperor.

Wilhelm had been made the President of the North German Confederation on its formation in 1867, and during the Franco-Prussian War took a leading role in the command of the combined German forces. Amidst the patriotic fervour that followed the successful German advance, in November 1870 the remaining states south of the river Main joined the North German Confederation.

On 10 December the Reichstag of the Confederation renamed itself the German Empire. Wilhelm was formally declared the German Emperor in the Hall of Mirrors at the Palace of Versailles on 18 January. The title was accepted grudgingly by Wilhelm who would have preferred 'Emperor of Germany' rather than 'German Emperor', but Bismarck warned that this would be dangerous as it suggested he had a claim to other Germanic lands such as Austria, Luxembourg and Switzerland. He also refused to be titled 'Emperor of the Germans', since this would have suggested he ruled with permission from the German people rather than by 'the grace of God'. As a believer in divine right, this suggestion was unacceptable to him.

Three months later, on 14 April, the Reichstag adopted the German Constitution. This stated that the King of Prussia would be the permanent President of the confederation of states that formed the Empire. Therefore, the role of Emperor was tied to the Prussian crown.

The creation of the federal Empire made Wilhelm the head of state and president of the federated monarchies that made up the 27 constituent territories.

JANUARY

19

1915

Two German Zeppelin airships known as L3 and L4 dropped bombs on the Norfolk towns of Great Yarmouth and Kings Lynn in Britain's first experience of an air raid.

Concerned about the safety of the British Royal Family, to whom he was related, the German Kaiser Wilhelm II had granted permission for aerial attacks on military and industrial buildings in Humberside, far away from London. At around 11am on the morning of 19 January three airships departed Germany.

One of the airships, L6, was forced to turn back after an engine malfunction. This left L3 and L4 to continue their mission. Having performed reconnaissance over the North Sea prior to nightfall, they headed towards the English coast but were forced to change course from their intended targets in Humberside due to bad weather. They consequently crossed over Norfolk shortly after 8.30pm.

Using incendiary bombs and flares to help to navigate in the darkness, L3 turned towards the seaside town of Great Yarmouth while L4 headed along the coast towards Kings Lynn. L3 dropped ten 110lb bombs and seven incendiary devices on the densely packed housing of St Peter's Plain in Great Yarmouth, killing two people. Meanwhile, L4 dropped eleven bombs on Sheringham and King's Lynn killing another two.

The four people killed in the attacks were all civilians, which served as a stark message about the changing nature of warfare in the 20th Century. The youngest victim was fourteen year old Percy Goate. In an inquest report his mother reported seeing the bomb drop through a skylight and on to the pillow where he was sleeping.

A number of senior Nazis met at the Wannsee Conference where they discussed what was referred to as the Final Solution to the Jewish Question.

SS-*Obergruppenführer* Reinhard Heydrich called the meeting, in which he outlined the deportation of European Jews to extermination camps in Poland where they would be systematically murdered.

Six months earlier, on 31 July 1941, Hermann Göring had ordered Heydrich to submit plans 'for the implementation of the projected final solution of the Jewish question'. Heydrich was a trusted member of the Nazi elite, and had been referred to by Hitler as 'the man with the iron heart'. He had helped to organise Kristallnacht, establish Jewish ghettos in Nazi-controlled territories, and commanded the Einsatzgruppen prior to his planning of the Final Solution.

Heydrich intended the Wannsee Conference to take place on 9 December 1941, but it was postponed due to the USSR's counter-offensive in the Battle of Moscow and the entry of the USA into the war. Fifteen representatives from a variety of government ministries attended the delayed meeting on 20 January.

By this time hundreds of thousands of Jews had been killed in the east, and the planning and construction of extermination camps had already begun. The meeting therefore focused on coordination between the various government agencies who were to implement the deportations.

Minutes from the meeting survive as what is known as the Wannsee Protocol, although the language was edited so that mass extermination was never explicitly recorded.

JANUARY

21

1793

Former French King Louis XVI was executed by guillotine at the Place de la Revolution in Paris.

Louis' trial began on 11 December 1792, and he was found guilty of treason by 693 of the National Convention's 721 deputies on 15 January. However, a much narrower majority of 387 to 334 voted for the death sentence three days later. His death warrant was finalised on 20 January, and his execution was scheduled for the next day.

A number of factors had contributed to him being found guilty, of which the Flight to Varennes and the events of 10 August were the most significant.

On the morning of his execution Louis woke at 5am, after which he made his confession and attended mass. Accompanied by the Irish-born priest Father Henry Essex Edgeworth, his carriage left the Temple prison at around 9am. 80,000 armed men lined the route to the Place de la Revolution, where a crowd of around 100,000 people had assembled to see the execution.

Louis calmly took off his coat at the foot of the scaffold and, as he stood next to the guillotine, attempted to address the crowd. His speech was drowned out by the beating of the soldiers' drums. He was then seized, had his hands quickly tied, and was placed under the blade.

The blade fell at 10.22am, after which it is reported that a number of members of the public rushed forward to dip their handkerchiefs in Louis' blood. His body was later buried and covered with quicklime to stop people obtaining relics. His wife, Marie Antoinette, was executed eight months later.

JANUARY

22

1905

The Bloody Sunday massacre took place in the Russian capital St Petersburg.

By 1905 there was growing discontent amongst the Russian urban working class. Father Gapon, a Russian Orthodox priest, had established the Assembly of the Russian Factory and Mill Workers of the City of St Petersburg to promote workers' rights in 1903 but, after four Assembly members from the Putilov ironworks were sacked from their jobs in December 1904, workers across the city went on strike.

Father Gapon sought to capitalise on the situation by drafting a petition to the Tsar calling for improved working conditions in the factories, alongside various other reforms. The petition received 150,000 signatures and, on the morning of 22 January, Father Gapon led workers and members of the Assembly on a march to deliver the petition to the Winter Palace. They carried religious icons and pictures of the Tsar with them.

Father Gapon had already notified the authorities of the petition and the march. In response approximately 10,000 armed troops from the Tsar's Imperial Guard were placed around the palace.

Why the soldiers began firing on the peaceful march is unclear. Even the number of marchers killed or injured is uncertain with estimates ranging from the government's official figure of 96 dead to revolutionary claims of more than 4,000.

The Tsar was not in the palace at the time, and did not give an order for the troops to fire. Despite this he was widely blamed for the massacre. In response to the bloodshed, strikes and protests spread around the country. They eventually developed into the 1905 Revolution.

JANUARY

23

1556

The deadliest earthquake ever recorded hit the Chinese province of Shaanxi and surrounding areas.

The Shaanxi earthquake, while being the deadliest on record, was by no means the highest magnitude ever recorded. However, a 520 mile wide area was seriously affected and up to 60% of the population of some cities was wiped out.

The reasons for this level of destruction were the joint factors of location and timing. Firstly, Shaanxi was one of the cradles of Chinese civilisation and was therefore a relatively densely populated area. By striking in that area, a huge number of people were bound to be affected by the earthquake. Secondly, the people of the time predominantly set up home in fragile cave-like structures known as yaodongs that were dug out of the loess soil that covers much of the area.

Loess soil is a silty sediment that is built up through the action of the wind. Although it is highly effective as an insulator, it is also incredibly fragile. Described by agricultural and biosystems engineer John M. Laflen as the 'most highly erodible soil on earth' some settlements in Shaanxi were dug entirely from it.

The force of earthquake – and the landslides that followed – destroyed huge numbers of the traditional dwellings. Scientists have since judged that the earthquake had a magnitude of around 8.0 on the Richter scale, and have had no reason to question the traditional estimates of around 830,000 deaths.

Gaspar da Cruz, a Portuguese Dominican friar who in 1569 published one of the first European books on China since Marco Polo, suggested that the earthquake was God's punishment for sinful behaviour by the Chinese people.

JANUARY
24
41

Caligula became the first Roman Emperor to be assassinated.

Caligula had come to power four years earlier following the death of his great uncle and adoptive grandfather Emperor Tiberius. The early stages of his reign saw him lauded by the people as 'our baby' and 'our star'. He built support for his rule by granting bonuses to the Praetorian Guard and other soldiers, and by providing the people of Rome with lavish games and circuses.

It is reported that Caligula's behaviour slowly became more tyrannical to the point of megalomania following a severe illness in October. Only two sources exist from his rule – those of Philo of Alexandria and Seneca the Younger – but both demonstrate acts of enormous cruelty and, according to some interpretations, insanity.

According to the sources Caligula banished or executed numerous rivals, including members of his own family. He was accused of numerous sexual transgressions including incest with his sisters and of turning the palace into a brothel. Furthermore, in the year 40 he began to style himself as a living god and introduced religious policies that required people to worship him as such. Caligula's erratic behaviour is perhaps most famously demonstrated in an account by the later Roman historian Suetonius who claimed that the Empror had wanted to make his favourite horse, Incitatus, a consul.

Such actions led to three failed assassination attempts against him, but on 24 January three Praetorian Guards led by Cassius Chaerea cornered Caligula in a cryptoporticus (an underground corridor) beneath his palace on the Palatine Hill and stabbed him to death. He was succeeded by his uncle Claudius.

JANUARY

25

1890

At 3.51pm American journalist Nellie Bly arrived in New Jersey after completing a 72 day, 24,899-mile journey around the world.

Born in 1864, Elizabeth Jane Cochran adopted the pseudonym Nellie Bly after securing a position as a journalist at the *Pittsburgh Dispatch*. However, she quickly became frustrated at being forced to write bland stories for the so-called 'women's pages' and headed to New York. While working in the city she proved herself to be a formidable investigative journalist after posing as a mental patient in order to report on the brutal and neglectful conditions inside the local Women's Lunatic Asylum.

Jules Verne's novel *Around the World in Eighty Days* had been published in 1873, and Bly came up with the idea to undertake a circumnavigation of the globe in attempt to turn it in to fact. In 1888 she met with John A. Cockerill, the managing editor of the *New York World*, and suggested that she should circumnavigate the world. She battled with the newspaper's senior executives for over a year as they preferred to send a man instead. She responded by telling them to 'start the man and I'll start the same day for some other newspaper and beat him'.

Eventually the board gave in. With £200 in English gold and banknotes, and a single bag that was smaller than modern carry-on luggage, Bly departed from Hoboken Pier in New Jersey on board the Augusta Victoria steamship on 14 November 1889.

Bly sent short reports to the newspaper by cable throughout her journey, while the full account of her journey was later published as the book *Around the World in Seventy-Two Days*.

United States President Bill Clinton appeared at a White House press conference and stated that he 'did not have sexual relations with that woman'.

The woman was Monica Lewinsky, a 22-year-old White House employee, and the affair and subsequent investigation led to the President's impeachment on charges of perjury and obstruction of justice. A year later the Senate voted to acquit him on both articles.

In 1992 Clinton had defeated George H. W. Bush to become the 42nd President of the United States. Two years after he took up office, Arkansas state employee Paula Jones filed a sexual harassment case regarding an alleged incident that occurred in 1991 when Clinton was Governor of Arkansas.

The following year Monica Lewinsky secured an unpaid summer White House internship, but moved to a paid position in December. Her affair with Clinton had begun a month beforehand, in November. Lewinsky later stated that over the next 18 months they had nine sexual encounters.

By April 1996 Lewinsky had been moved to The Pentagon, where she confided in co-worker Linda Tripp about the affair. Tripp began recording their phone calls and in January 1998 handed the tapes to an Independent Counsel after Lewinsky submitted an affidavit denying any physical relationship with Clinton as part of the Paula Jones case.

Following the appearance of the tapes, Clinton stated in the news conference that he 'did not have sexual relations' with Lewinsky. Seven months elapsed before he was called before a grand jury, where he admitted they had had a relationship that was 'not appropriate'.

Soviet soldiers from the 322nd Rifle Division liberated the Auschwitz-Birkenau concentration camp.

By the end of 1944 the Soviet Union was making significant gains against the Nazis on the Eastern Front. As a result SS chief Heinrich Himmler ordered the end of gassings across the Reich, and the systematic destruction of written records that referenced them. Approximately 65,000 prisoners were evacuated deeper into the Reich between August 1944 and January 1945, but tens of thousands of prisoners still remained in Auschwitz. Therefore, on 17 January, at least another 58,000 inmates were sent on a death march under armed guard. Of those who departed only around 20,000 made it to the Bergen-Belsen concentration camp in Germany.

More than 7,000 prisoners had been left behind in the camp because they were deemed too weak or sick to complete the march. Meanwhile, the Nazis continued to destroy evidence of the crimes committed in the camps by blowing up or burning many of the buildings including the crematoria. Remaining SS troops were ordered to kill the remaining inmates. They murdered over 600 of them before the Soviet forces arrived.

The advancing Soviet troops met some resistance from remaining Nazi troops in the Polish city of Oświęcim, but by 3pm they had captured the Main Camp and Auschwitz II-Birkenau. Due to the quick progress of the Red Army some buildings, as well as thousands of inmates, survived. After the liberation, hospital facilities were established within the camp to provide medical treatment for the survivors. On 2 July 1947, the Polish parliament passed an act that turned the camp in to a museum.

JANUARY

28

1986

NASA Space Shuttle orbiter Challenger broke apart 73 seconds after it lifted off from the Kennedy Space Centre in Florida.

The Challenger mission had three key objectives. Firstly, it was to deploy a satellite that was part of a system to enable NASA and other US government agencies to communicate. Secondly, it was to deploy the SPARTAN-203 satellite to observe Haley's Comet. Finally, on board Challenger was the first teacher from the Teacher in Space Project. This program had been implemented by President Ronald Reagan and would see teachers delivering lessons from orbit.

The night before the launch the temperature had dropped below freezing. Ice had formed on the launch tower and on the Shuttle itself. This led Rockwell, the contractor that built the shuttle, to express concerns. Furthermore, the company that provided the O-rings that sealed joints on the Solid Rocket Boosters used at launch only had enough test data to guarantee them working properly down to temperatures of 53 °F (12 °C). On the morning of the launch temperatures were 29 °F (−1.7 °C), which was way below the tested safe temperature for the component.

At 11.39am Challenger lifted off, and seventy-three seconds later the Shuttle began to disintegrate following a huge fireball. All seven members of crew were killed, and the disaster led to NASA suspending all Space Shuttle missions for over two and a half years.

The crew compartment was finally found 370m beneath the ocean surface after six weeks of searching. The compartment had been severely damaged by the force of the impact as it entered the water. An investigation determined that the disaster happened due to two of the O-rings failing as a result of the low temperatures during the launch.

JANUARY
29
1856

Queen Victoria introduced the Victoria Cross.

The Victoria Cross, which is commonly referred to as the VC, is the highest military decoration in the British honours system and takes precedence over every other order and medal. Queen Victoria introduced the medal to reward 'most conspicuous bravery, or some daring or pre-eminent act of valour or self-sacrifice, or extreme devotion to duty in the presence of the enemy'.

The extensive reporting of the Crimean War by journalists such as William Howard Russell had highlighted a range of acts of bravery that deserved formal recognition, and contributed greatly to the introduction of the Victoria Cross. At the end of January 1856, shortly before Russia accepted preliminary peace terms to end the Crimean War, Prince Albert encouraged Queen Victoria to create a new military award that did not discriminate against birth or class.

The VC medals themselves are cast from metal taken from cannon captured from Russian forces at the Siege of Sevastopol. Metallurgical research has since identified that those cannon themselves were originally of Chinese origin, and had been captured by the Russians in 1855. The first presentation ceremony of the medals took place on 26 June 1857 and, as of October 2016, a total of 1,358 VCs have been awarded. However, beginning in 1947 almost all Commonwealth countries began to introduce their own separate honours for gallantry and bravery.

The VC is explicitly awarded for valour in the face of the enemy. The equivalent but newer George Cross is awarded for equivalent acts of valour by civilians or by members of the armed forces who would not normally be awarded a military honour for their actions.

King Charles I of England, Scotland and Ireland was executed outside the Banqueting House in London.

The English Civil War had begun shortly after Charles' failed attempt to arrest the Five Members but, by the end of 1648, the Royalists had been defeated and Charles was arrested.

The King's trial began on 1 January 1649. He was accused of 'a wicked design to erect and uphold in himself an unlimited and tyrannical power to rule according to his will, and to overthrow the rights and liberties of the people of England.' He was also held personally responsible for all the death and destruction caused by the Civil War, which had resulted in an estimated 6% of the entire population losing their lives.

Charles, as a believer in divine right, refused to recognise the authority of the court. Despite this, he was found guilty of committing high treason and was sentenced to death by beheading. The sentence was passed on 27 January and the death warrant signed by 59 commissioners. Charles was executed on 30 January, having requested to wear two shirts as protection from the cold so that the crowd wouldn't think he was shaking from fear. Six days later, Parliament abolished the monarchy.

On 30 January 1661, the year after the restoration of the monarchy and exactly twelve years after Charles' execution, the body of Oliver Cromwell was exhumed from his grave in Westminster Abbey. Cromwell, who had been one of the regicides who signed Charles' death warrant and went on to become Lord Protector during the Interregnum, was then posthumously executed and his head placed on a spike.

JANUARY

31

1990

Fast food chain McDonald's opened its first restaurant in the Soviet Union on Moscow's Pushkin Square.

By 1990 the Iron Curtain was in tatters. The Berlin Wall, which had acted as a symbol of the East-West divide, had fallen in November the previous year, and the communist governments of other eastern European countries had fallen.

McDonald's had already opened restaurants in Belgrade, the capital of the former Yugoslavia, and the Hungarian capital Budapest in 1988. However, the expansion into the Soviet Union was evidence of the enormous changes taking place within the USSR itself. Glasnost and perestroika had already brought about seismic shifts in society and the economy, and the Soviet government even owned a 51% stake in the new McDonald's venture.

Interestingly, however, McDonald's in the USSR was developed by the Canadian branch of the company. This kept it independent of the chain's American headquarters. To ensure the supply chain also remained separate, dedicated farms and factories were developed to provide the ingredients. By the end of 1989 a reported 50 million Canadian dollars had been invested in the infrastructure.

At the time, the average monthly wage for a Russian worker was 150 roubles. When McDonald's opened, a standard hamburger cost 1.50 roubles which was equivalent to the price of ten loaves of bread. Despite the high prices, some news outlets estimated that 30,000 people passed through the doors on the first day. Even Boris Yeltsin, the future President of Russia, visited what remained the largest McDonald's restaurant in the world until a new restaurant on the London 2012 Olympic Park opened 22 years later.

FEBRUARY

FEBRUARY

1

1968

American photojournalist Eddie Adams took a photograph of South Vietnamese National Police Chief General Nguyen Ngoc Loan executing Viet Cong officer Nguyen Văn Lém in Saigon.

The photograph's publication in the *New York Times* rallied US citizens to the anti-war movement and earned Adams a Pulitzer Prize for Spot News Photography in 1969.

The Tet Offensive had begun on 30 January, and saw over 80,000 communist troops carry out a series of surprise attacks against South Vietnamese forces and their allies. It is reported that two days later, in the early morning of 1 February, Lém led a troop that attacked a South Vietnamese base and killed South Vietnamese National Police officers and their families.

Lém was captured later that day near a mass grave containing 34 civilian bodies and was taken to General Loan in Saigon. While still handcuffed, Loan shot Lém with his Smith & Wesson revolver. He was standing directly in front of photographer Eddie Adams and an NBC News television cameraman.

The photograph was printed in the *New York Times* and appeared, in an attempt to achieve balance, alongside a now-forgotten image of a child killed by the Viet Cong. The immediacy of Adams image made an enormous impact in America where it became strongly associated with the anti-war movement.

Adams spoke out many times in defence of General Loan, declaring that the photograph does not present the whole story. He later visited Loan many times, and apologised in person for the effect the photo had on his life. On hearing of Loan's death in 1998, Adams called him 'a hero'.

FEBRUARY

2

1852

The world's first modern public toilets opened in London.

Sited next to the Society of Arts at 95 Fleet Street, the toilets were exclusively for men. However, a public toilet for use by ladies was opened just over a week later on 11 February at 51 Bedford Street – a mile away.

Although public toilets had existed for millennia, these were often simple and unhygienic facilities. This situation changed in the 19th Century with the advent of the water closet. These flushable toilets were popularised following the installation of George Jennings' 'Monkey Closets' at the Great Exhibition in 1851, where users were charged one penny. This payment led to the euphemistic phrase 'to spend a penny'.

Despite the relatively low cost to the user, the Great Exhibition toilets generated a net profit of £1,790 in just 23 weeks. In modern money that would be well over £100,000. Aware of the potential to generate a new income stream, organisations such as the Society of Arts chose to develop public toilets to cash in on the new invention.

Despite their elegant mahogany and brass design, and an extensive promotional campaign that featured the distribution of 50,000 handbills alongside an advertisement in *The Times* newspaper, the toilets proved unpopular. It's reported that only 58 people visited them in the first month of opening, leading to the toilets closing down soon afterwards.

It is interesting to note that one of the members of the committee behind the Society of Arts' public toilet development was Sir Henry Cole. He is better known as the inventor of the commercial Christmas card and a man who had a key role in the introduction of the Penny Post.

Rock and roll pioneers Buddy Holly, Ritchie Valens, and The Big Bopper were killed in a plane crash near Clear Lake, Iowa.

On 23 January 1959, Buddy Holly launched the headline Winter Dance Party Tour of twenty-four cities in the American Midwest with support from Ritchie Valens, The Big Bopper and Dion and the Belmonts. Touring was a very profitable activity for musicians and Holly, who had recently married María Elena Santiago and was expecting their first child, was keen to pack in as many performances as possible.

The tour required the musicians to cover gruelling distances in a bus that soon developed a fault with its heating system. The situation was so bad that Holly's drummer Carl Bunch was hospitalised with frostbitten feet. The bus was replaced, but with less than half the dates covered the musicians were already frustrated and tired.

After playing a concert at the Surf Ballroom in Clear Lake, Iowa, on 2 February, Holly opted to charter a plane to get him to the next venue. The aircraft was a single-engined, V-tailed Beechcraft 35 Bonanza but was not called *American Pie* as some people claim. It was only identified by the serial number N3794N.

In addition to Holly and the pilot, 21 year-old Roger Peterson, Ritchie Valens and The Big Bopper flew in the plane following some negotiation and a coin toss. They took off at 12:55am on 3 February, but managed to fly only 6 miles before crashing amidst deteriorating weather.

The disaster became known as 'The Day The Music Died' as a result of Don McLean's song 'American Pie' that was released twelve years later.

FEBRUARY

4

1945

The Yalta Conference began, attended by the 'Big Three'.

The conference saw Allied leaders United States President Franklin D. Roosevelt, British Prime Minister Winston Churchill and Soviet Premier Joseph Stalin meet to discuss the government of post-war Europe.

The three leaders had previously met at the Tehran Conference in 1943 where they set out a unified military strategy for fighting the war. At Yalta the focus was exclusively on the end of the war and its aftermath. It was clear that the conflict in Europe was in its final stages, so they agreed to demand Germany's unconditional surrender after which the country, and Berlin, would be split into four zones of occupation. Germany was to undergo a process of demilitarization and denazification, and Nazi war criminals were to be hunted down and brought to justice.

The three leaders also considered the fate of Eastern European countries that had been under Nazi occupation. Poland was the focus of much of the discussion, but they intended for the agreement they reached to apply to every country that was liberated. The Protocol of Proceedings stated that the Allies would assist these countries to form 'interim governmental authorities broadly representative of all democratic elements in the population…and the earliest possible establishment through free elections of governments responsive to the will of the people.'

The terms of the agreement, when they were made public, were met with harsh criticism in Britain and the United States. Some of these came to be justified when, at the end of the war, the Soviet Union installed communist governments throughout Eastern Europe in contravention of the agreement for free elections.

FEBRUARY

5

1924

The BBC 'pips' were broadcast for the first time.

The BBC had successfully broadcast the chimes of Big Ben for the first time at New Year 1924. This led the Astronomer Royal, Sir Frank Watson Dyson, to suggest that reliable time signals could be broadcast more regularly. Having convinced BBC boss John Reith of the idea, the pendula of two mechanical clocks at the Royal Greenwich Observatory were fitted with electrical contacts that sent a signal to the BBC every second.

It was agreed that five short pips would signal the five seconds leading up to the hour, with a slightly longer pip marking the start of the new hour. Although now largely inaccurate as a result of the inherent delay in the encoding, transmission, and decoding of digital radio broadcasts, the pips are still a part of many BBC radio programmes.

The equipment that generated the pips moved from Greenwich in 1939, but the pips are still known officially as the Greenwich Time Signal. The name was even kept after the Greenwich Time Service stopped transmitting the pips in 1990. Since then, the BBC has generated the pips using an atomic clock in the basement of Broadcasting House.

Since they used as a time signal, the BBC doesn't allow programmes to broadcast the six pip sequence for any other reason. Until recently the BBC also discouraged its broadcasters from 'crashing the pips' which involved playing any other sound at the same time. Although the rule against crashing the pips is now less rigorously enforced, some BBC Radio 4 listeners continue to wait with baited breath in case a presenter accidentally talks over them.

FEBRUARY

6

1958

British European Airways flight 609 crashed at Munich-Riem Airport killing 23 members of the Manchester United football team, supporters and journalists.

The Manchester United team, nicknamed the 'Busby Babes' after team manager Matt Busby, were flying back to England from Yugoslavia following a 3–3 draw in a quarter-final match of the European Cup against Red Star Belgrade. Manchester United had not been beaten for eleven matches, and were attempting to become the third club to win three successive English league titles.

The aeroplane, an Elizabethan-class Airspeed Ambassador, wasn't capable of flying non-stop from Belgrade to Manchester so had landed in Munich to refuel. The flight was already an hour behind schedule due to some confusion over player Johnny Berry's passport and visa as he was leaving Belgrade. This delay was exacerbated by two abandoned take-offs from Munich as a result of an intermittent fault in the left engine.

Despite the engine problem, Captain James Thain opted to attempt a third take-off. By this time it had begun to snow. Thain accelerated slowly along the long runway to avoid stressing the faulty engine but, as the plane reached the speed required for take-off, the wheels hit slush that had built up on the runway.

The slush stopped the plane reaching take-off speed, but there was not enough runway left to safely abort the take-off. Consequently flight 609 skidded off the end of the runway before crashing through the airport fence, speeding across a road, and losing its port wing after catching on a house. Twenty of the forty-four people on board died instantly.

FEBRUARY 7 1964

The Beatles appeared on national television in the United States for the first time.

1963 had seen the release of The Beatles' first two albums – *Please Please Me* and *With The Beatles* – as well as them achieving five number one singles including 'She Loves You' and 'I Want to Hold Your Hand'. The latter was released in the UK on 29 November but was kept from the number one spot for two weeks. This was due to a resurgence in the popularity of 'She Loves You' following the media storm that kick-started Beatlemania.

A few weeks later, on 26 December, 'I Want To Hold Your Hand' became the first Capitol Records Beatles release in the USA. It sold a quarter of a million copies in the first three days and worked its way up Billboard Hot 100 to the number one spot on 1 February.

The Beatles' arrival in America six days after securing their first US number one couldn't have been any better timed, even though their scheduled American visit and television appearance on the popular Ed Sullivan Show had been booked long before the single was even released.

The band landed at New York's Kennedy Airport to be greeted by 3,000 screaming fans. This was unprecedented, even for a band that had already become accustomed to hordes of followers at home in Britain and in Europe. Within two days, their appearance on the Ed Sullivan Show had put them in front of around 40% of the entire population of the country – an estimated 73 million people.

By the time the The Beatles performed their first American concert to 20,000 fans at the Coliseum in Washington D.C. on 11 February, Beatlemania had taken a firm grip on America. They returned to the UK as conquering heroes.

FEBRUARY

8

1587

Mary Stuart, more commonly known as Mary, Queen of Scots, was executed in the Great Hall of Fotheringhay Castle in Northamptonshire.

Mary was a rallying point for Catholic and Spanish plots that sought to overthrow Queen Elizabeth I of England and install her as the new queen. This was because of her strong claim to the English throne through her paternal grandmother Margaret Tudor, Henry VIII's sister. This led Elizabeth to place her under house arrest in 1568.

Mary herself didn't hide her belief that she should be queen. She and her fellow Catholics viewed Elizabeth as illegitimate due to her being born to Anne Boleyn whom Henry VIII had married after his divorce from Catherine of Aragon.

Mary's imprisonment continued until a case could be made against her. Having been held for 19 years in a variety of castles and manor houses around the British Isles, she was accused of plotting to kill Elizabeth in 1586. Mary was finally charged with treason, despite not being an English citizen, after the spymaster Sir Francis Walsingham intercepted coded letters in which she expressed approval of the Babington Plot to assassinate Elizabeth.

Mary's trial took place in October 1586, and she was convicted on the 25th. However, Elizabeth was reluctant to sign her cousin's death warrant and hesitated for over three months before finally doing so. On 8 February 1587, Mary made her way from her chambers to the scaffold that had been erected in Fotheringhay Castle's Great Hall. It took the executioner three strokes of his axe to behead her.

FEBRUARY

9

1969

The first test flight of the Boeing 747 'Jumbo Jet' took place.

The 1960s saw an enormous increase in the use of air transportation, but existing planes such as the Boeing 707 only had a small passenger capacity. The first person to approach Boeing with the idea of developing a larger passenger aircraft was Juan Trippe, the president of Pan Am, although the company had already produced initial large airframe designs for a failed bid to build a cargo plane for the United States Air Force.

By 1966 the design for the 747 was still far from complete but, in April, Pan Am committed to buying twenty-five aircraft. Boeing agreed to deliver the first one by the end of 1969. This put enormous pressure on the company as a suitable engine still hadn't been created and the company didn't own a facility large enough to assemble the completed aircraft.

These issues were eventually overcome to allow the first test flight to take place on 9 February 1969. It was piloted by Jack Waddell who was accompanied by co-pilot Brien Wygle and flight engineer Jess Wallick. The plane, named the *City of Everett*, left the Paine Field runway near Everett in Washington State – about 30 miles north of Seattle – and successfully performed a number of tests before landing at 12.50pm.

Over 1,000 more test flights were conducted before the plane was certified by the Federal Aviation Authority on 30 December. The first passenger flight using the 747 took place on 22 January 1970, on Pan Am's New York to London route. The aircraft went on to hold the record for the largest passenger capacity for 37 years before it was surpassed by the Airbus A380 in 2005.

The British King, Edward VII, launched HMS _Dreadnought._ This revolutionary new type of battleship made all other ships obsolete.

At the time of her launch, she was the fastest and most heavily-armed ship in the world, and the name _Dreadnought_ began to be used to describe a whole class of similar ships.

Ever since the British government adopted the Two-Power Standard as part of the 1889 Naval Defence Act, the Royal Navy had been required to have at least the same number of battleships as the next two largest navies in the world combined. By 1906 Wilhelm II of Germany had begun aggressive military expansion, including the construction of battleships, to pursue the development of a German Empire under his 'World Policy' or _Weltpolitik._ German naval expansion put pressure on Britain to increase the size of its own navy. Although possessing the singularly most powerful ship in the world should, theoretically, have made Britain the undisputed champion of the seas, the launch of the _Dreadnought_ was problematic.

The new battleship caused problems for Britain's Two-Power Standard because the country now only possessed one more _Dreadnought_-class ship than every other country in the world. With all other ships obsolete in the wake of the new design, it was too easy for other countries to catch up.

Germany quickly began developing an equivalent ship and launched the first of its Nassau vessels in 1908. This in turn forced Britain to keep ahead by building more and more, in line with the demands of the Two-Power Standard. This naval arms race, and the tension that followed, was a major contributing factor to the outbreak of the First World War in 1914.

FEBRUARY
11
1979

Mohammad Reza Shah Pahlavi, the last Shah of Iran, was overthrown as a result of the Iranian Revolution.

Iran gained immense wealth under the Shah thanks to an abundant supply of oil. The Shah had come to power in 1941 and tried to secure support by using oil money to modernise the country. These reforms, known as the 'White Revolution' were interpreted by some as pandering to Western ideals that went against Iran's traditions while the vast majority of the population continued to live in poverty.

The Shah established the brutal SAVAK secret police to maintain control, but a growing number of Iranians were increasingly turning against him. They found a leader in the Muslim scholar Ayatollah Khomeini who, despite being forced into exile in 1964, continued to be a vocal critic of the Shah's government. He played down his intention of establishing an Islamic government, focusing instead on his desire to overthrow the Shah.

On 8 September 1978 over 500 people were killed by soldiers on what became known as 'Black Friday'. The Shah's attempts to restore calm had no effect on the public, who continued to call for his removal.

Recognising that his overthrow was becoming inevitable, the Shah and his wife left Iran on January 15 for the USA. Khomeini returned from exile two weeks later. Finally, on 11 February the Supreme Military Council ordered all troops back to their barracks and effectively handed control to Khomeini and his supporters.

The overthrow of Mohammad Reza Shah Pahlavi brought the 2,500 year old monarchy in Iran to an end and ushered in a theocracy overseen by the Ayatollah Khomeini.

The curiously-named Battle of the Herrings was fought between French and English forces near the French village of Rouvray.

During the Hundred Years War, on 12 October 1428, the English began to besiege the city of Orléans. By the end of the following January they were in need of additional supplies so a convoy of 'some 300 carts and wagons' was sent in response. As the troops would soon be observing Lent when Christians abstain from eating meat, the supplied included barrels of herrings.

Outside the village of Rouvray the convoy met a large opposing force of 3,000-4,000 French and Scottish troops led by Charles de Bourbon, Count of Clermont. The English arranged their carts into a defensive wagon fort with sharpened stakes similar to those used at the Battle of Agincourt positioned around the perimeter.

Unable to use their cavalry against the English army's impromptu palisade, the French launched a gunpowder artillery bombardment. This appeared to go well at first, but the attackers were forced to abandon the assault in order to avoid killing their Scottish allies who began to advance prematurely. The English army seized the opportunity for a counter-attack and forced the Scots to retreat. This caused chaos amongst the ranks and led to an English victory.

At the same time Joan of Arc was attempting to persuade Robert de Baudricourt to help her visit the French Dauphin Charles VII at Chinon. She reportedly told him of the terrible defeat near Orléans, something that was only confirmed several days later. De Baudricourt believed that Joan must have had divine help to have known this, so agreed to assist her.

William and Mary became co-regents of the Kingdoms of England, Scotland and Ireland after agreeing to the Declaration of Right.

On 5 November the previous year William, the Head of State of the Dutch Republic, had landed at Torbay after being invited by a group of English Parliamentarians to invade England. His Dutch fleet and army went on to overthrow the Catholic King James II, the father of his wife Mary, in the so-called Glorious Revolution. James was allowed to flee the country and later took up exile in France.

The Declaration of Right, which was formally passed by Parliament on 16 December, joined other documents such as Magna Carta and the Petition of Right as a central part of the uncodified British constitution. The Declaration placed limits on the monarch's power and confirmed Parliament's own rights, ensuring that it was free to function without royal interference. Furthermore, it banned Catholics from the throne.

Parliament originally only wanted to offer the crown to Mary, with William as Prince Consort, but the couple were reluctant to accept without co-regency. Parliament relented and so, on 13 February, the couple were declared King and Queen. Their coronation took place on 11 April.

The Glorious Revolution was not seen as such by everyone. The Bill of Right was both politically and religiously divisive, laying the foundations for generations of conflict. Beginning with the Williamite–Jacobite War that confirmed British rule in Ireland, the Protestant Ascendancy established political, economic and social domination of the country for over two centuries.

FEBRUARY

14

1929

Seven men with connections to Chicago's North Side Gang were gunned down in the Saint Valentine's Day Massacre.

Although nobody was ever brought to trial for the murders, it is generally accepted that the attack was carried out on the orders of South Side Gang boss Al Capone. The North Side Gang under George 'Bugs' Moran had battled with Capone for control of smuggling and trafficking operations in Chicago throughout the 1920s. Capone was already earning an estimated $60 million a year from his illegal activities, but is alleged to have sought to consolidate his control of the city by eliminating Moran.

On the morning of 14 February, the North Side Gang assembled at their headquarters in a garage behind the offices of S.M.C. Cartage Company at 2122 North Clark Street. Although there is some disagreement over why they were there, most accounts claim that they were lured with the promise of obtaining stolen whiskey at a good price. At 10.30am look-outs for the gunmen confirmed that the gang was inside and, within minutes, a stolen police car containing two men dressed in police uniforms and two in civilian clothes pulled up.

The fake policemen ordered the gang to line up against a wall inside the garage, and then signalled for the two men in civilian clothes to open fire. They did so with 70 rounds from two Thompson sub-machine guns.

When the real police arrived they found one victim barely alive, but he refused to reveal who had carried out the attack. Moran himself was not in the garage, but the ferocity of the attack made Al Capone 'Public Enemy No. 1'.

The United Kingdom and Ireland abandoned their old currency of pounds, shillings and pence and introduced a decimalised system.

Decimalisation wasn't seriously considered by the British Parliament until the Halsbury Committee presented its report on decimal currency in 1963. The majority of the Commonwealth had either already adopted, or were in the process of adopting, decimal currency and so the time seemed right to reconsider Britain's own stance. On 1 March 1966 the Chancellor of the Exchequer, James Callaghan, announced the government's acceptance of the report's recommendations and established the Decimal Currency Board.

Although the government didn't pass the Decimal Currency Act until May 1969, production of the new coins had already begun at the new Royal Mint site in South Wales that had opened the previous year. The gradual introduction of the new coins began in 1968, with 5p and 10p coins the first to enter circulation. They were exactly the same size and value as the existing one- and two-shilling coins, so ran alongside the old currency as their 'decimal twins'. The following year the world's first seven-sided coin was introduced, when the 50p piece replaced the 10-shilling note.

The early introduction of three of the six new coins, together with an extensive publicity campaign, contributed greatly to the smoothness of Decimal Day when it finally came about in 1971. Shops were able to accept 'old money' for a few weeks afterwards in order to remove old coins from circulation. Members of the public who found 'old' coins months later could also freely exchange them at any bank.

Howard Carter unsealed the burial chamber of the Pharaoh Tutankhamun.

Carter and his sponsor, Lord Carnarvon, had opened the first chamber of the tomb on 26 November the previous year. This led to them cataloguing and removing more than 2,000 artefacts from the antechamber and its annex, during which time they found a doorway with its rope seal still intact.

It was two and a half months before Carter and his team were ready to open the next chamber. Having secured permission from the Department of Antiquities of Egypt to open the sealed door, Carter came face-to-face with the enormous gilt shrine containing the king. The shrine filled the chamber, although it later emerged it was only the outer layer of four nested shrines inside which lay the king's sarcophagus.

It took Carter and his team 12 months to disassemble the shrines within the tight confines of the tomb and prepare to lift the lid of the sarcophagus, by which time Lord Carnarvon had died. His death in April 1923 contributed to the legend of the 'Curse of Tutankhamun', but was more likely due to complications associated with accidentally infecting a mosquito bite while shaving.

Carter didn't reach Tutankhamun's mummy itself until October 1925. Work to remove the remaining artefacts continued until 10 November 1930, eight years after the discovery of the tomb. The artefacts are now housed in the Egyptian Museum in Cairo, while Tutankhamun's mummy is displayed inside a climate-controlled glass box inside the tomb to ensure that humidity from visitors does not damage his remains.

Brian Wilson, the co-founder of the Beach Boys, began the first recording session for the song 'Good Vibrations' at Gold Star Studios in Los Angeles.

The Beach Boys were in the middle of recording their eleventh studio album, *Pet Sounds*, when the instrumental parts for the first version of the song were recorded on 17 February. Although originally logged as part of the *Pet Sounds* sessions, recording of 'Good Vibrations' was put on hold while the album was completed. Following the release of *Pet Sounds* a reported further ninety hours of recordings were made that were gradually edited into the three minutes and thirty-five seconds that make up the final song.

Referred to by Wilson as a 'pocket symphony', the modular process used for 'Good Vibrations' involved the recording and re-recording of individual sections of the song using the Wall of Sound formula that had been developed by record producer Phil Spector. The sporadic sessions for instrumental sections lasted until August, after which the vocal parts were recorded. The final mix of the song could only be completed after a final Electro-Theremin overdub was added on 21 September.

Finally released on 10 October 1966, 'Good Vibrations' reached the top of the charts on both sides of the Atlantic. It had cost up to $75,000 to produce which made it the most expensive single ever recorded at the time.

'Good Vibrations' is featured on the Rock and Roll Hall of Fame's list of 500 Songs that Shaped Rock and Roll. It arguably established the recording studio itself as an instrument, and secured the Beach Boys their first million-selling single.

FEBRUARY

18

1930

Nellie Jay, also known as Elm Farm Ollie, became the first cow to fly in an aeroplane.

Elm Farm Ollie was a Guernsey dairy cow who had been born and raised at Sunnymede Farms in Bismarck, Missouri. Despite weighing over 1,000 pounds (1450kg) she was chosen to fly to the International Air Exposition in St Louis due to her unusually high milk production and calm temperament.

The 72-mile journey was flown in a Ford Trimotor aircraft powered by three 220-hp engines. It was piloted, according to a contemporary newspaper clipping, by Claude M. Sterling. He was an instructor at St Louis' Parks Air College, the first federally certified flying school in America.

Due to the flight time and Ollie's high production, she required milking during the journey. She gave a total of 24 quarts (23 litres) of milk which was then packed into paper cartons and dropped by parachute to the crowds at the air show. Wisconsin native Elsworth W. Bunce was the man who milked her, making him the first person to milk a cow in flight. Among the alleged recipients of the mid-flight milk was aircraft pioneer and St Louis resident Charles Lindbergh who had made the first non-stop transatlantic flight from New York to Paris less than three years previously, and who was a guest at the air show.

The cow's flight was presented to the crowds and the press as part of a scientific study of the effects of flying on livestock and to demonstrate aircraft stability. In reality it was more of a publicity stunt for the air show, but it made a celebrity of Ollie who was given the nickname 'Sky Queen'.

FEBRUARY

19

1985

The BBC's flagship soap opera *EastEnders* was broadcast for the first time.

EastEnders was created by Julia Smith and Tony Holland, a producer and script editing team who had previously worked together on long-running police drama *Z-Cars*. In March 1983 they were asked by David Reid, the BBC's Head of Series & Serials, to come up with a bi-weekly evening television drama that could run for 52 weeks a year.

Smith and Holland were both from London, and opted to set the soap in the city's East End. They based the original twenty-four characters on their own families and people they had met in London's 'real' East End, and contacted casting agencies in search of actors to fill the roles. Their repeated phone calls in which they asked for 'real East Enders' provided Smith with the idea for the show's name.

The show required a huge set to be built at Elstree Studios in Hertfordshire. Meanwhile, composer Simon May created the now-iconic theme tune. This was to play over an aerial view of London that was pieced together from 800 separate photographs taken from an aeroplane flying 1000 feet over London.

EastEnders was first broadcast on 19 February 1985 as part of new BBC One controller Michael Grade's 'relaunch' of the channel. The first episode secured an audience of 17 million, which increased to 23 million by the end of the year. Now airing four episodes a week, the series has been broadcast continuously ever since and remains one of the most popular television shows in the United Kingdom.

Jimi Hendrix played his first ever live concert and was fired from the band after the first set.

Hendrix bought his first acoustic guitar for $5 in 1958, when he was 15 years old. Having formed a short-lived band called the Velvetones, he realised that this guitar was too quiet to be heard amidst the other instruments. He therefore managed to persuade his father Al to buy him an electric guitar – a white Supro Ozark – in early 1959.

Hendrix took time to fully master the instrument, but his passion and enthusiasm was quickly noticed by others. On 20 February, in the basement of the Temple De Hirsch synagogue in his home town of Seattle, he played his first gig.

The band, whose name has sadly been lost, were auditioning Hendrix to join them but after an exuberant first-set performance opted not to invite him back on stage for the second set. His girlfriend of the time, Carmen Goudy, recalled that the bandleader said his playing was too wild, and that it distracted people from dancing.

Rather than give in to the more pedestrian requirements of Seattle's dance bands, however, Jimi Hendrix continued to play in the same style. This set a pattern for the legendary guitarist's early years as he secured jobs in the backing bands for respected artists such as Little Richard and Tina Turner, but was often asked to leave due to his over-exuberant playing and performances.

It was exactly that ostentatiousness that made him stand out when he moved to London in 1966 and found success with the Jimi Hendrix Experience.

The Communist Manifesto was anonymously published in London although the text by Karl Marx, supported by Friedrich Engels, was in German.

Marx was born in Prussia in 1818, but was living in Brussels when the Communist League's Second Congress commissioned him and Engels to write the League's manifesto in December 1847. It wasn't until the League's Central Committee sent him an ultimatum to submit the completed manuscript by 1 February that he did any significant work on it. The pamphlet was modelled on Engels' 1847 *Draft of the Communist Confession of Faith* but Engels had little input to the manifesto itself.

Officially called *The Manifesto of the Communist Party*, the original pamphlet was just 23 pages long but went on to become a highly influential political document alongside Marx's more substantial *Das Kapital*. Ending with the now-iconic words, 'Workers of the world, unite!' publication of the *Manifesto* coincided with the outbreak of the 1848 revolution in France the next day. The revolution spread across Europe, but the *Manifesto* had little connection to this: only in Cologne did the Communist League play any major role.

The *Manifesto* gradually drifted into obscurity until its resurgence in the 1870s after Marx formed the First International. An updated edition was printed in 1872 and translated into six languages. The standard English version was first published in 1888 with a translation by Samuel Moore, but Marx himself had died penniless four years previously. His ideas lived on and directly led to 1917's Bolshevik revolution in Russia, the world's first socialist state to be founded according to Marxist ideology.

FEBRUARY 22 1943

The first three members of the White Rose resistance group were executed by guillotine in Germany.

Centred around Hans Scholl and his sister Sophie, the small group of university friends who formed the White Rose printed and distributed their first anti-Nazi leaflet in June 1942. They produced six leaflets in total, which were distributed around Germany by hand or by plain-packaged post. The Gestapo itself estimated that 10,000 copies had been produced of the fifth leaflet entitled 'A Call to All Germans!'

As the group became more confident of their activities, some members used stencils to paint the slogans 'Freedom' and 'Down with Hitler' around Munich over the course of three nights in early February. A few days later, on 18 February 1943, Hans and Sophie distributed over a thousand copies of their sixth leaflet in the hallways of the University of Munich. Having realised that a few copies were still nestled in the bottom of the suitcase they had brought them in, they chose to climb the stairs and fling them from the top of the atrium.

The Scholls were spotted by university janitor and Nazi Party member Jakub Schmid who immediately called the Gestapo. The siblings were taken away for interrogation before being sent to trial on 22 February. A third member of the group, Christoph Probst, was also tried after his handwriting was matched to a draft of a seventh leaflet found in Hans' possession.

The three defendants were found guilty of treason and were guillotined later that day in the grounds of Stadelheim Prison. Hans is known to have shouted 'Es lebe die Freiheit! - Long live freedom!' before being killed.

FEBRUARY

23

1455

Tradition dictates that Johannes Gutenberg published his printed Bible, which was the first book to be produced with moveable type in the West.

Gutenberg was not the first person in the world to use moveable type, and nor was the Bible his first foray into printing with it. He didn't even produce many copies, with estimates ranging from 160 to 185 completed Bibles of which only twenty-three complete copies survive. However, the process with which Gutenberg printed his Bible revolutionised the production of books and is viewed by many as crucial to the developments that followed in the Renaissance and the Reformation.

Moveable type uses individual components that can be ordered to produce a printed document. The earliest examples date back to China's Northern Song Dynasty at the turn of the last millennium, but the enormous number of characters in scripts based on the Chinese writing system made the system unwieldy. Gutenberg therefore benefited from the much smaller number of characters in the Latin alphabet, but also invented a reliable way to cast large quantities of individual metal letters using a device called the hand mould. Furthermore, he developed an oil-based ink that was optimised for metal-type printing onto paper.

Consisting of 1,286 pages, a complete copy of the Gutenberg Bible is now estimated to be worth up to $35 million dollars. The value of the printing press itself is immeasurable as Gutenberg's creation was responsible for an intellectual revolution. Although there is no definitive evidence for this publication date, numerous independent secondary sources state 23 February.

King Louis Philippe of France abdicated the throne amidst the revolutions that were beginning to sweep across the continent.

Having come to power following the July Revolution in 1830, Louis Philippe was known as the 'Citizen King' and the 'Bourgeois Monarch'. However, his rule soon turned sour as conditions deteriorated for many French people.

Louis Philippe came from the more liberal Orléans branch of the House of Bourbon and he had even been a member of the Jacobin Club in the early years of the French Revolution. Having fled the country during the Reign of Terror, he returned to France during the Bourbon Restoration. Following the abdication of Charles X in 1830 he was proclaimed King of the French by the popularly elected Chamber of Deputies.

Louis Philippe's reign began positively, but over time he faced mounting opposition as he favoured land owners over bourgeois industrialists, and reduced the electoral franchise to only about 1 percent of the population. This led to the appearance of the largely middle class Reform Movement who, by the summer of 1847, had begun to hold 'banquets' at which they began to form an organised opposition. A banquet to mark the birthday of George Washington on 22 February 1848 was prohibited by the government and provided the spark for civil unrest.

The following day the Prime Minister, François Pierre Guillaume Guizot, resigned. On hearing this, a crowd marched on the Ministry of Foreign Affairs where 52 people died in street violence. The next day Louis Philippe abdicated and fled across the Channel to Britain where he died two years later. Meanwhile, back in France, the opposition proclaimed the Second Republic.

FEBRUARY

25

1956

Soviet leader Nikita Khrushchev delivered his 'secret speech' in a closed session at the end of the 20th Party Congress of the Communist Party of the Soviet Union.

Officially called 'On the Cult of Personality and Its Consequences', Khrushchev's speech was a vehement denunciation of Stalin's abuses of power and his creation of a personality cult. It therefore laid the foundation for his wide-reaching de-Stalinisation campaign.

The speech signalled a dramatic reversal of Soviet policy, which Khrushchev said had come about due to Stalin's misinterpretation or misrepresentation of Marxist-Leninist doctrine. The 'secret speech' allowed Khrushchev to distance himself from the worst crimes of the Stalin's rule, even though he himself had been responsible for thousands of deaths. Additionally, and of great significance, Khrushchev also advocated a policy of 'peaceful coexistence' with the West rather than continue Stalin's policy of preparing for an inevitable war.

Although the full details of the speech were only supposed to reach the public gradually, rumours of its contents spread quickly. Israeli intelligence officers obtained a full copy of the speech and passed it to the United States government who leaked it to the press at the start of June. Although Khrushchev had already begun to implement de-Stalinisation by this point, the printing of the speech in the *New York Times* on 5 June dictated demands for a faster pace of change in Eastern Europe.

Large-scale change was, however, still slow. Although Poland's government granted some concessions in October, the situation in Hungary ended very differently.

FEBRUARY

26

1815

Napoleon Bonaparte escaped exile on the Mediterranean island of Elba and sailed to the French mainland.

On 11 April 1814 Napoleon had agreed to the Treaty of Fontainebleau, in which he abdicated the throne following his defeat in the War of the Sixth Coalition. The Treaty ended his rule of France but allowed him to keep his title as Emperor. He was granted sovereignty of the island of Elba and, following a failed suicide attempt, arrived on the island on 30 May.

Throughout the nine months and twenty-one days that he remained on Elba, Napoleon observed with interest the unfolding situation in France under the restored Bourbon king. Meanwhile he implemented a series of social and economic reforms to improve the situation on the island.

It was Napoleon's confidence in the likelihood of a popular revolt in his favour that led to him leaving the island. Furthermore the Great Powers were distracted by internal disagreements at the Congress of Vienna. The ships from the British Navy that were supposed to ensure Napoleon was unable to escape his exile were not in the area when, on 26 February, he left the island and headed for the French mainland on board the brig *Inconstant* accompanied by almost a thousand troops.

Napoleon's arrival in France was greeted with enthusiasm. After landing at the coastal town of Golfe-Juan on 1 March, he quickly secured support from a small army with whom he marched to Paris. His arrival on 20 March led Louis XVIII to flee the city and heralded the start of a period of Napoleonic government that became known as the Hundred Days.

The Reichstag building in Berlin was set on fire in an arson attack.

Adolf Hitler had been appointed Chancellor of Germany on 30 January, but had demanded new elections for the Reichstag. These were scheduled to take place across Germany on 5 March. Hitler hoped that they would increase the Nazis' share of the seats and therefore allow him to pass the Enabling Act to take control of political decisions for himself.

Shortly after 9pm on the evening of 27 February, Goebbels was informed that the Reichstag was on fire. Although the blaze was extinguished before midnight, the inside of the building was destroyed. Communists were blamed for starting the fire, and Dutch communist Marinus van der Lubbe was found and arrested.

The following day Hitler persuaded President Hindenburg to pass the emergency Decree of the Reich President for the Protection of People and State. This suspended many civil liberties and allowed the Nazis to arrest their opponents. Thousands of communists, liberals and Social Democrats were rounded up by the SA and placed in so-called 'protective custody'. Van Der Lubbe was tried, convicted, and executed.

Although there is debate over the exact circumstances surrounding the fire, historian Sir Ian Kershaw says there is a general consensus among the vast majority of scholars that van der Lubbe did set the fire.

There is no argument, however, that the fire was exploited by the Nazis who used it as the first step in the creation of a single-party state.

FEBRUARY

28

1525

Cuauhtémoc, the last Aztec Emperor, was executed on the orders of the Spanish conquistador Hernán Cortés.

Little is known of Cuauhtémoc's early life. By the time he was elected leader of Tenochtitlan in 1520 the Aztec city-state had already been invaded by the Spanish and had experienced the successive deaths of Moctezuma II and his brother Cuitlahuac. The new ruler attempted to defend the city against the continued Spanish attacks, but was captured on 13 August 1521 while trying to escape.

Cuauhtémoc surrendered to Cortés and was spared. Contemporary sources claim that the conquistador initially treated his captive with respect but, having failed to find large quantities of gold in the city, later tortured Cuauhtémoc by covering his feet in oil and placing them over a fire.

Despite his ordeal Cuauhtémoc allegedly refused to give away the location of his treasures, although a small amount of gold was later found in the house of a noble. Having survived his torture, Cuauhtémoc was allowed to keep the title of tlatoani but was stripped of his sovereign powers.

In 1525, when Cortés undertook an expedition to Honduras, he took Cuauhtémoc with him. Some commentators suggest that this is because he was concerned the former emperor might lead a revolt in his absence. While they were away Cortés was informed of a rumour that Cuauhtémoc was conspiring to kill him. He ordered him to be hanged on 28 February alongside other nobles.

Cuauhtémoc, which means 'One who swoops down like an eagle' continues to be a highly regarded in modern-day Mexico as the only Aztec emperor to have survived the Spanish conquest.

FEBRUARY

29

1940

American actress Hattie McDaniel became the first African-American to win an Oscar at the Academy Awards.

Hattie McDaniel was born in Wichita, Kansas to two ex-slaves and, by the early 1930s, had begun to establish herself as a film actress. Although McDaniel was facing criticisms from the NAACP for perpetuating the stereotype of black women as servants by almost exclusively played maids or cooks, she auditioned for and won the role of Mammy, an outspoken house slave, in the 1939 motion picture *Gone with the Wind*.

The Southern United States' Jim Crow laws meant that McDaniel was banned from attending the film's première at Loew's Grand Theater in Atlanta, Georgia. Although she was able to attend the subsequent Hollywood première two weeks later, the Twelfth Academy Awards ceremony the following February further highlighted the extent of racial inequality in the United States. McDaniel and her escort were racially segregated from her co-stars, and were forced to sit at a separate table at the back of the Coconut Grove Restaurant of the Ambassador Hotel in Los Angeles where the ceremony was held.

Gone with the Wind won a total of ten Academy Awards that night, but it was arguably McDaniel's award for Best Supporting Actress that was most significant. However, while McDaniel's victory at the Academy Awards was a breakthrough for African-Americans, *Gone with the Wind* itself was sharply criticised for its positive portrayal of the Old South. Despite this it is heralded as one of the greatest films of all time and, when adjusted for inflation, is the most successful film in history.

MARCH

The Salem witch trials began in Massachusetts.

Salem's witch hysteria began in January 1692 when both the daughter and niece of the Reverend Samuel Parris each began to suffer violent fits. The local doctor couldn't find a physical cause for their illness so blamed the supernatural. Other young girls in the community soon began to display similar symptoms, and three local women were accused of bewitching them.

Sarah Good, Sarah Osborne and Tituba were brought before local magistrates in Salem Village, Massachusetts. Significantly, the three women were all in some way social outcasts – Tituba was a slave; Sarah Good was a homeless beggar and Sarah Osborne was a poor elderly woman who rarely attended church.

Although both Good and Osborne denied their guilt to magistrates Jonathan Corwin and John Hathorne, Tituba confessed to being 'the Devil's servant'. The reason for her confession is unclear, but it is presumed that she sought to act as an informer in a bid to save herself.

Over the next few weeks dozens more people were accused of witchcraft including the four-year old Dorothy Good, Sarah's Good's daughter, who was imprisoned for nine months before being released on bond for £50.

Of the three women first accused of witchcraft in Salem, only Sarah Good was executed. Sarah Osborne died in jail before her trial finished while Tituba was eventually freed from jail after an anonymous person paid her fees. In total twenty people were executed, and a further seven died in jail, before the paranoia came to an end.

MARCH

2

1965

The United States, alongside the Republic of Vietnam Air Force, began Operation Rolling Thunder.

Operation Rolling Thunder lasted for three and a half years and saw hundreds of thousands of tons of bombs dropped on North Vietnam. It had been approved by President Lyndon B. Johnson on 13 February with the intention of pressuring the communist North Vietnamese government to end their support for the National Liberation Front, otherwise known as the Viet Cong. By destroying North Vietnamese infrastructure the USA hoped they would stop supplies going to the south, whilst the population would become demoralised. Simultaneously it was hoped that the attacks would boost the confidence of the non-communist South Vietnamese government.

Assisted by the USSR and China, North Vietnam was able to develop a highly effective anti-aircraft system that went on to bring down almost 900 American planes involved in the operation. Simultaneously, the Viet Cong began to attack American airbases in South Vietnam. It was to protect these bases that Johnson began authorising more ground troops to be sent to Vietnam.

Estimates place the cost of the damage inflicted by Operation Rolling Thunder on North Vietnam at around $300 million. However, the lost American aircraft alone cost $900 million. It was also clear that Rolling Thunder had not succeeded in stopping supplies entering South Vietnam as the devastating Tet Offensive was able to be carried out in 1968. Similarly, North Vietnam used the damage inflicted by the campaign to fuel an anti-American propaganda campaign that mobilised hundreds of thousands of civilians to repair the damage.

The Treaty of Brest-Litovsk was signed between Russia and the Central Powers.

By the winter of 1917 the Russian economy was in tatters as a result of the strain of maintaining the war effort. Tsar Nicholas II had abdicated in February, and the subsequent Provisional Government was overthrown in the Bolshevik Revolution later that year after they continued to fight alongside the Entente Powers.

The new Russian Bolshevik government vehemently opposed the war and received some support from Germany in their efforts to seize power. For example they allowed passage for Vladimir Lenin to return from exile in Switzerland to lead the revolution against the Provisional Government.

After coming to power Lenin appointed Leon Trotsky as Commissar of Foreign Affairs, but peace negotiations with the Central Powers were fraught with difficulties. The situation became so bad that, in mid-February, Trotsky declared that he would agree to 'neither war nor peace'. This meant that Russia would stop fighting, but not sign a peace treaty. The announcement incensed the Germans who responded by restarting their advance into Russia in Operation Faustschlag. Concerned by the speed of the German attack, Lenin threatened to resign if Russia didn't accept the new peace terms delivered on 23 February.

The Treaty was a humiliation for Russia. The country lost approximately a third of the entire Russian population alongside around one million square miles of land including fertile farmland, natural resources, and industrial areas. The Treaty was cancelled as part of the Armistice with Germany on 11 November 1918.

MARCH

4

1789

The United States constitution went into effect when the first US Congress met.

The Congress met in New York City, but the 18th Century's slow forms of transport meant that many of the members didn't arrive in time for the scheduled start date. The gruelling journey from the more distant states had to be completed on horseback, by stagecoach, or by sailing ship. Consequently the House of Representatives didn't reach quorum until 1 April, while the Senate was delayed until 6 April.

It was only then, once Congress had the necessary number of members to be quorate, that a joint session to count the Electoral College votes could begin. Their first action was to certify that George Washington had been elected President with John Adams as Vice President.

In line with the Constitution, Adams became President of the Senate while Frederick Muhlenberg of Pennsylvania was elected Speaker of the House. He was later to become the first to sign the Bill of Rights, which became the first ten amendments to the Constitution.

Representative James Madison had presented the Bill of Rights on 8 June and, after three months of discussion, twelve articles were approved by Congress on 25 September. Ten of these – articles Three to Twelve – were ratified two years later and became the Bill of Rights on 15 December 1791.

4 March continued to be a significant date for Congress for nearly two centuries. It was only after the 20th Amendment to the Constitution was ratified in 1933 that 3 January became the first day for Congresses to meet.

Winston Churchill described the post-war division of Europe as an 'Iron Curtain' in his 'Sinews of Peace' address at Westminster College in Fulton, Missouri.

Often interpreted as a key event in the origin of the Cold War, Churchill's speech played a significant role in changing western perceptions of their former Soviet ally.

Churchill, as the British Prime Minister, had led Britain to victory in the Second World War but suffered a landslide defeat to Clement Attlee's Labour Party in the General Election of July 1945. Despite being in opposition he continued to be highly respected abroad and visited the United States in 1946. During this trip he was invited to deliver a speech to an audience of 40,000 people at Westminster College in the 7,000-person town of Fulton.

Churchill was introduced at Fulton by President Harry Truman, and opened his speech by complimenting the United States as standing 'at the pinnacle of world power'. As the speech progressed, he became increasingly critical of the Soviet Union's policies in Eastern Europe.

Churchill was not the first to use the term 'Iron Curtain' as a metaphor for a strong divide and versions of it had been in use for many centuries. Nor was the 'Sinews of Peace' speech the first time that he himself had used the term. However, his use of the term in a speech with such a large audience thrust it into wider circulation and associated it directly with the post-war situation.

Stalin accused Churchill of warmongering, and defended the USSR's relationship with Eastern Europe as a necessary barrier to future attacks.

MARCH
6
1869

Russian chemist Dmitri Mendeleev presented his periodic table to the Russian Chemical Society.

Mendeleev was both a teacher and an academic chemist, and in the early 1860s published a prize-winning textbook that placed him at the forefront of chemical education. He was, however, frustrated by the apparent disorder of the chemical elements so set about developing a way to classify them.

Other scientists had been trying to find ways to arrange the elements since at least the middle of the 18th Century. In 1864, just a few years before Mendeleev presented his periodic table, the British chemist John Newlands published his 'Law of Octaves' which classified the known elements into eight groups in order of their relative atomic masses. However, Newlands' work was ridiculed at the time. His work was only formally recognised in 1887.

Mendeleev, meanwhile, was unaware of Newlands' work because the Society of Chemists had refused to publish his findings. The Russian chemist therefore continued to work on his own system. Tradition dictates that he wrote the characteristics of the known elements on cards and played a game of 'chemical solitaire' with them. He apparently fell asleep during one of these card games and had a dream in which he saw the cards 'fall into place'. Mendeleev realised that the features of the elements repeated in a predictable pattern, based on their atomic weight.

While Mendeleev's approach led to there being some gaps or spaces in 'periods' where he believed an element should exist, he was able to calculate the missing element's atomic mass and properties. His predications later turned out to be correct when missing elements such as gallium were discovered.

MARCH

7

1936

The German Army under control of Adolf Hitler violated international agreements by remilitarising the Rhineland.

The Rhineland area of Germany, which lay on the border with France, had been banned under the terms of the Treaty of Versailles from containing armed forces within a 50km-wide strip. Germany was also unable to maintain any fortifications within the area.

This agreement had later been confirmed by Foreign Minister Gustav Stresemann in the Locarno Treaties of 1925. However, by 1936 Hitler had come to power and had begun to break the terms of Versailles by increasing the number of German weapons beyond the agreed limits and reintroducing conscription.

The Western powers had failed to respond to these moves with anything more than diplomatic grumbling, so Hitler felt emboldened to further test the limits of the Versailles settlement. After France and Russia signed the 1935 Franco-Soviet Pact, Hitler chose to send three battalions, or approximately 22,000 German troops, into the Rhineland. They entered on the morning of Saturday 7 March in what he claimed was a defensive move against 'encirclement'.

Hitler's own generals were expecting retaliation from France, and had even been ordered to stage an immediate withdrawal if the French army made a move. Despite Hitler's concerns, however, France refused to move against Germany without the support of Britain. Having been severely weakened by the impact of the Great Depression and distracted by the unfolding Abyssinia Crisis, Britain sympathised to an extent with the German desire to defend its own border and refused to intervene. Hitler therefore successfully remilitarised the area.

The Volkswagen Type 2 – more commonly known as the 'transporter', the 'bus' or the 'camper' – went into production at the company's Wolfsburg factory in Germany.

Volkswagen was founded in 1937 under the Nazi regime of Adolf Hitler, and was operated by the German Labour Front. Austrian-born engineer Ferdinand Porsche was called in to design a mass-produced 'people's car' that would be affordable to most Germans. However large-scale production of what we now call the Beetle didn't begin until after the Second World War when the factory was placed under the control of British Army officer Major Ivan Hirst. Although Hirst was a civilian member of the Military Government, he wore his officer's uniform in the factory as he found that it made the workers more responsive to his orders.

Volkswagen began to develop the Type 2 after Ben Pon, a Dutch businessman who imported Volkswagen cars into the Netherlands, produced a sketch of a proposed van. The final design was approved on 29 May 1949 but, due to the factory already running at capacity to turn out the increasingly popular Type 1 Beetle car, production didn't start until March the next year.

The Type 2 finally debuted on 12 November and by the end of its first year over nine and a half thousand vehicles had rolled off the production line. Having got over the initial concerns of its Nazi roots, the hippie movement in the United States adopted the Type 2 and made it an icon of the counterculture movement in the 1960s.

The Type 2 continued to be produced until 31 December 2013, when the last one rolled out of the Volkswagen factory in São Bernardo do Campo, Brazil.

The US Supreme Court ruled that captive Africans who had seized control of the *Amistad* ship had been taken into slavery illegally and were therefore free under American law.

Early in 1839 a number of Africans, including Joseph Cinqué from Sierra Leone, had been kidnapped by Portuguese slavers and transported to Cuba. This was in clear violation of international laws that prohibited the African slave trade.

Once smuggled into Cuba, where slavery remained legal, the Africans were sold as slaves and transported along the coast on the Spanish-owned *Amistad*. It was during this journey that Cinqué led the slaves in a revolt against the crew that resulted in the deaths of the ship's captain and cook.

The Africans demanded that the remaining crew return them to Africa, but instead they sailed north for sixty days. Having been spotted by American authorities the ship was taken into US custody off the eastern tip of Long Island, New York. A long legal battle then ensued, with Cuba demanding the return of the 'slaves', Spain demanding them go on trial for piracy and murder, and abolitionists pushing for their return to Africa.

A key argument in the case was that, since the Africans had been illegally captured, they were not slaves. The long case eventually went before the Supreme Court who ruled that they had been unlawfully held and thus rebelled in a natural right to self-defense. The court set them free.

The *United States vs. The Amistad* case was a landmark legal battle in the struggle against slavery and provided the abolitionist movement with huge publicity.

MARCH

10

1876

Scottish-born inventor Alexander Graham Bell made the first successful telephone call when he contacted his assistant, Thomas Watson.

Bell moved with his family to Canada when he was 23 years old. Here he continued his previous work on hearing and speech. His father was a renowned phonetician, and his mother had gradually become deaf through his teenage years. Both his parents had a strong impact on their son's work. By 1871, however, Bell had moved away to Boston where he trained teachers of the deaf.

It was while in Boston that Bell's experiments with sound waves and electricity led to his development of a telegraph-like system to transmit the vibrations associated with speech. His 'harmonic telegraph' was patented on the same day as fellow inventor Elisha Gray filed a similar caveat with the US Patent Office. Although Bell was awarded patent 174,465 on 7 March for his invention, there continues to be considerable debate over whether Bell stole the telephone from Gray.

It wasn't until three days later, while using a liquid transmitter similar to Gray's design, that Bell succeeded in getting his idea to work. He recorded in his journal that he shouted the phrase, 'Mr. Watson, come here – I want to see you!' Watson soon appeared, saying that he heard the words clearly.

Despite legal challenges the courts always upheld Bell's claim to the invention. Bell never used the liquid transmitter in public demonstrations, focusing instead on his own electromagnetic design. Fellow inventor Thomas Alva Edison later made a significant improvement with his invention of the carbon microphone.

MARCH

11

1918

The first confirmed case of what was to become known as Spanish Flu was identified at Camp Funston in Fort Riley, a large military facility in Kansas.

The exact geographical origin of the disease has never been identified, but the first confirmed case was company cook Private Albert Gitchell in Kansas who reported to the camp's infirmary when he woke in the morning. By midday 107 soldiers had been admitted with the same symptoms.

The outbreak of the disease came while American soldiers were being shipped to Europe to fight in the First World War. The conditions in the trenches of the Western Front accelerated the spread of the virus, and contributed greatly to it becoming a pandemic. Poor hygiene and nutrition provided a fertile breeding ground for the flu, which soon made its way into the civilian populations of Europe as well.

Within 18 months the disease had become a pandemic that infected up to a third of the entire world's population. With between 10-20% of all infected persons dying, modern estimates suggest that the flu took anywhere between 20 to 100 million lives.

Due to wartime censorship, governments limited reports on the virulence of the flu and played down the death toll. However, newspapers in neutral Spain faced no such limitations, resulting in people believing Spain was suffering disproportionately high cases which led to it gaining the name Spanish Flu.

Even if figures from the lowest estimates are used, the pandemic killed more people than had died on all sides in the First World War itself.

MARCH

12

1930

Mohandas Gandhi began the 240 mile (390 km) Salt March to the coastal village of Dandi.

The Salt March took place just two months after the Indian National Congress promulgated the Declaration of the Independence of India, which supported the idea of civil disobedience to achieve complete self-rule.

Gandhi chose to focus his protest on the 1882 Salt Act which placed a government monopoly on the collection and manufacture of salt. Gandhi claimed that, 'next to air and water, salt is perhaps the greatest necessity of life.' He wrote to the Viceroy, Lord Irwin, ahead of his protest in an attempt to negotiate but the Viceroy refused to meet him.

Gandhi and 79 supporters departed his base at Sabarmati Ashram on 12 March, and by the end of the twenty-four day march had built a procession that reportedly stretched for two miles. He intended to produce salt from seawater to avoid paying tax and thus undermine Britain's salt monopoly.

After he broke the Salt Laws by picking up a piece of natural salt at Dandi on 6 April, millions of people around the country did the same. Meanwhile, international media coverage of the march brought the issue of Indian independence to a worldwide audience.

The British authorities responded by arresting 60,000 people by the end of April. Gandhi himself was jailed on 5 May. Despite this reaction, Gandhi called off the civil disobedience campaign in January 1931. This led to him attending the Round Table Conference in London where he began to discuss India's demands for independence as an equal negotiating partner.

MARCH
13
1881

Tsar Alexander II of Russia was assassinated in a St Petersburg street by a member of the People's Will revolutionary movement.

Despite introducing a number of reforms such as the emancipation of the serfs in 1861 and the abolition of capital punishment, Alexander's government remained autocratic. After a failed assassination attempt in 1866 he began to brutally repress those who sought political change.

By the 1870s the government was coming under increasing pressure from liberals and radicals to introduce further changes. Land and Liberty, a group of reformers who sought land reform, soon gave rise to the People's Will which favoured terrorism as a way to achieve their aims. The Tsar became the focus for a number of attacks from 1879 onwards, and finally succumbed to their tactics in 1881.

Alexander was travelling close to the Catherine Canal when a bomb was thrown at his closed carriage by a member of the People's Will. The blast killed one of the accompanying Cossacks and injured many others, but the Tsar was unharmed. Emerging shaken from his armoured carriage, however, another assassin threw a second bomb which landed at Alexander's feet.

Suffering from severe bleeding, the Tsar was taken to the Winter Palace where he died from his wounds. Somewhat ironically, Alexander had just that morning signed the Loris-Melikov constitution which would have established an elected parliament known as a Duma. However, this was rejected by his son and heir, Alexander III who instead further suppressed civil liberties through the Okhrana. Alexander II's death therefore arguably slowed down, rather than sped up, the move to a parliamentary democracy.

MARCH

14

1950

The FBI first published its list of Ten Most Wanted Fugitives.

The origin of the list lay in a conversation between the Director of the FBI, J. Edgar Hoover, and the Editor-in-Chief of the *International News Service*. This conversation led to a news story on 7 February 1949 that highlighted the 'toughest guys' the FBI wanted to capture. The story had such a huge impact on the public that Hoover opted to make the FBI's 'Ten Most Wanted Fugitives' a permanent program the following year.

In many ways the Ten Most Wanted list was a 20th Century version of the classic 'Wanted' posters that had been in use since the invention of the printing press. Even the use of newspapers to apprehend people on the run wasn't new. During the 18th Century, for example, 'wanted' adverts for runaway slaves were often listed by their owners.

What made the FBI's list unique was that it brought dangerous fugitives to nationwide attention. The development of the internet has made the list's reach global, though it is still an exclusively FBI program. Candidates for inclusion are submitted by the FBI's network of 56 Field Offices, which are reviewed by the Criminal Investigative Division at FBI Headquarters before final approval by the Director.

The first person to be listed was bank robber, murderer and prison escapee Thomas James Holden. He was arrested fifteen months later in Beaverton, Oregon after the Ten Most Wanted list was printed in the local newspaper.

Over 500 fugitives have appeared on the list, of which less than 2% have been women. The vast majority have been apprehended or located.

Roman dictator Julius Caesar was stabbed to death near the Theatre of Pompey in Rome.

Julius Caesar was a respected military general whose return to Rome saw him quickly gain respect from many ordinary citizens due a sweeping series of political, social and economic reforms.

While Caesar's reforms won support from some, others became concerned as he received numerous honours that began to propel him to a position akin to a king. Caesar's apparent arrogance through accepting such honours, combined with his reluctance to stand out of respect when approached by members of the Senate, further fuelled a conspiracy against him.

On 15 March, amidst rumours of a conspiracy and despite warnings from his doctors and his wife, Caesar attended the Senate on the urging of Decimus. Having taken his seat, Caesar was then approached by Cimba who pulled back Caesar's robes. He was quickly surrounded by the other conspirators who, according to Eutropius, formed a crowd of up to 60 men.

Casca was the first to strike and caused a stab wound to Caesar's neck. He suffered a total of 23 stab wounds in the attack. The earliest known post-mortem report in history later stated that he died of blood loss.

Julius Caesar's death, coming shortly after he had been declared dictator for life by the Senate, was intended to stop him seizing more power and restore the Roman Republic. However, it instead resulted in a period of instability and civil wars that culminated in the ascendancy of his adopted son Octavian who became Caesar Augustus, the first Roman Emperor.

MARCH
16
1968

US soldiers from Company C of the Americal Division's 11th Infantry Brigade committed the My Lai Massacre.

The troops were taking part in a search and destroy mission by Task Force Barker. They were aiming to wipe out the 48th Viet Cong Local Force Battalion that was believed to be hiding in the area. It is widely believed that their commanding officer, Captain Ernest Medina, had told them that any person found there should be considered a member of the Viet Cong or a Viet Cong sympathiser should be killed. The victims were almost exclusively women, children and old men who were rounded up and brutally murdered.

The soldiers arrived by helicopter at around 7.30am and the first killings took place barely half an hour later. Commanded by Lieutenant William Calley, the troops killed between 347 and 504 unarmed civilians in hamlets around the South Vietnamese village of Son My.

The killings continued until 11am when Captain Medina ordered a ceasefire. Not a single shot had been fired back at the Americans and, although there were members of the company who had not taken part in the attacks, they did not intervene to stop them.

A helicopter crew piloted by Warrant Officer Hugh Thompson Jr. intervened to save some civilians from the massacre. Thompson also reported what he had seen to his superiors. However, the massacre was covered up by senior officers. It was only revealed to the public in November 1969 following an investigation by journalist Seymour Hersh.

A court martial only began in 1970 after the scale of the killings had been published in the press.

The first recorded Saint Patrick's Day parade took place in the city of New York.

Saint Patrick was a Romano-British Christian missionary who converted thousands of Irish Pagans before his death in 461. Although the legend that he rid Ireland of snakes is known to be fiction, since there has never been any evidence that Ireland ever contained snakes, he was responsible for converting the vast majority of the country and driving out Paganism. Records indicate that 17 March, the reputed date of Saint Patrick's death, had been marked with feasting by the end of the 10th Century although it was not officially recognised by the Catholic Church until the early 17th Century.

Within a century Irish immigrants to America had begun to mark the date in their own ways. Significantly, the early settlers were predominantly Protestant. This helps to explain why many Saint Patrick's Day celebrations across the world are secular rather than religious, since they are associated more with celebrating Irish culture than the Catholic Saint.

Irish soldiers serving in the British Army led the first recorded parade which, due to the high number of Irish immigrants in New York, quickly became an annual tradition. The first parade in Ireland didn't take place until 1903 in Waterford.

The secularisation of Saint Patrick's Day has drawn criticism from some Church leaders who have criticised its 'mindless alcohol-fuelled revelry'. In the past, pubs and bars in Ireland had actually been required to close on 17 March due to concerns over excessive drinking, although that law was repealed in the 1970s.

Jacques de Molay, the last Grand Master of the Knights Templar, was executed on the orders of King Philip IV.

The Knights Templar had been the final Christian defenders of Acre in 1291. Although little is known of Jacques de Molay's early life he was almost certainly among the troops that defended the city. He was elected Grand Master the following year, but struggled to build support among Europe's leaders for a new Crusade to reconquer the Holy Land.

By early 1307 Molay had travelled from the Templar base in Cyprus to France, where he had been invited to attend a meeting with Pope Clement V. However, this coincided with a series of accusations of sacrilege levelled against the Templar Knights regarding their initiation ceremony. On 13 October, the day after he served as a pallbearer at the funeral of King Philip's sister-in-law, Catherine of Courtenay, Molay and a number of other Templar knights were arrested on the orders of the King.

The knights were tortured into confessing to various sacrilegious acts, but then began a protracted period of confession and retraction that lasted for a number of years. Finally on 18 March 1314 Molay and three other senior Templars were sentenced to indefinite imprisonment. However Molay and fellow Templar Geoffroi de Charney then professed their innocence, causing King Philip to declare them relapsed heretics and condemn them to death. They were burnt at the stake later that day.

The Knights Templar was formally abolished by Pope Clement V, but Molay's execution secured his place as one of the Order's most famous members.

MARCH 19 1962

American singer-songwriter Bob Dylan released his eponymous debut album.

Dylan had arrived in New York from Minnesota the previous year, but had quickly worked his way into the coffee houses and folk clubs of Greenwich Village. It was here that he became known to the established folk singer Carolyn Hester who invited him to join her as a harmonica player. While rehearsing in her apartment in September, Dylan met Columbia Records' talent scout John H. Hammond who stated he decided to sign Dylan 'on the spot' although in reality the contract wasn't finalised until the end of October.

The album was recorded in six hours of sessions from 20 to 22 November. A popular legend claims that the album cost $402 to produce, but this figure was only stated as a joke by John Hammond – the true cost is unknown. Although there were a couple of false starts, five of the final recordings were the first take as Dylan refused requests to do a second.

Only two tracks on Dylan's debut album were his own compositions and it failed to hit the Billboard 100. The album sold less than 5,000 copies in its first year and earnt Dylan the nickname 'Hammond's Folly' from record executives.

Despite this set-back, Dylan returned to the studio shortly after the release of his first album to begin work on his second. *The Freewheelin' Bob Dylan*, which consisted almost entirely of original songs and opened with the now-classic *Blowin' in the Wind*, was released on 27 May 1963. It was this second album that established Dylan as one of the greatest songwriters of his generation. He was awarded the Nobel Prize for literature on 13 October 2016.

MARCH 20 1890

Kaiser Wilhelm II of Germany formally accepted Otto von Bismarck's resignation.

As Minister President and Foreign Minister of Prussia, Bismarck had overseen the unification of Germany in 1871. He then continued as Chancellor of Germany for almost two decades. Throughout this time Germany dominated European politics and controlled the balance of power to ensure peace.

The death of Kaiser Wilhelm I, which was quickly and unexpectedly followed by his son Frederick III, led to the young and relatively inexperienced Wilhelm II taking the throne. Rather than allow his Chancellor to govern as he had done for the previous few decades, Wilhelm preferred to have a greater say in the running of the country. This led to confrontations between the two men in the tussle for political control.

The situation came to a head in early 1890 when the two men disagreed over social policy. While Bismarck was keen to introduce permanent anti-socialist laws, Wilhelm preferred to be more moderate. The stark difference in their positions became most obvious when Bismarck said he sought a violent confrontation in order to suppress the socialists. Wilhelm later took offence at Bismarck negotiating a new political alliance without his knowledge.

With their relationship in tatters, Wilhelm insisted that the 75 year old Bismarck should resign. He submitted his resignation on 18 March, two days before formally leaving office. His departure ushered in the new age of *Weltpolitik*. He was succeeded as Chancellor by Leo von Caprivi, and dedicated the rest of his life to writing his memoirs.

MARCH
21
1556

Thomas Cranmer, the Archbishop of Canterbury, was executed heresy.

Cranmer's early career had seen him present the case for Henry VIII's divorce from Catherine of Aragon. Although his argument did not result in the Pope agreeing to annul the marriage, Cranmer was appointed Archbishop of Canterbury by the King in March 1533 after which he quickly moved to declare Henry's marriage to Catherine void. Within a few years he also annulled Henry's marriages to Anne Boleyn and Catherine Howard and had begun to work with Thomas Cromwell on the production of an English Bible.

Cranmer's actions led to him developing a large and powerful opposition which grew under the reign of Edward VI. His support for the Protestant Lady Jane Grey as Edward's successor, rather than his Catholic older sister Mary, ultimately led to him being put on trial for treason in 1553. As a leader of the English Reformation he had not only promoted Protestantism but had also established the first structures of the Church of England. Despite having signed a number of recantations or retractions of his Protestant faith, on the day of his execution he in turn recanted these recantations before being burned at the stake.

Cranmer's execution in 1556 for heresy was intended to act as way to discredit Protestantism. However, his eleventh-hour rejection of his earlier recantations against the Reformist movement meant that his death ultimately undermined the Marian Counter-Reformation.

He died at the stake having placed his right hand into the fire first. This was the hand with which he had signed his recantation and he burnt it as punishment for being 'unworthy'.

Dutch legal scholar Hugo Grotius, also known as Hugo de Groot, escaped imprisonment in Loevestein Castle concealed inside a book chest.

Grotius is known as one of the founding fathers of international law for such masterpieces as 'On the Law of War and Peace' and 'The Freedom of the Seas' that applied natural law to international politics. Even as a teenager his intellectual ability had been noted by King Henry IV of France who referred to him as the 'miracle of Holland'.

At the time, the United Provinces were experiencing an internal conflict between the tolerant Protestantism of the Remonstrants and the Counter-Remonstrants who advocated orthodox Calvinism. In 1618 the Counter-Remonstrant Prince Maurice, the executive and military leader of the United Provinces, launched a coup d'état. Shortly afterwards he ordered the arrest of the leaders of the Remonstrants, which included Grotius. He was given a life sentence for treason.

Grotius was permitted to have books sent to him in prison, and these were transported in a large chest. Over time his guards became less vigilant regarding the chest's contents which led his wife and maid-servant to propose a plan to smuggle him out by hiding him inside it. The plan worked and, having escaped his imprisonment, Grotius fled to France apparently disguised as a mason. It was while exiled in Paris that he wrote his most famous works.

Grotius became Sweden's ambassador to France in 1634 but died eleven years later after being shipwrecked on return from a visit to the Swedish monarch.

MARCH
23
1540

Waltham Abbey in Essex became the last abbey to be dissolved by Henry VIII.

Henry had visited the Waltham Abbey a number of times and is known to have stayed there with Queen Anne Boleyn in 1532. However, despite surviving for a number of years the abbey eventually succumbed to the Dissolution of the Monasteries. This caused an economic disaster in the town as it had grown prosperous due to pilgrims visiting the abbey.

The Dissolution of the Monasteries saw all the religious houses that existed in England at the start of Henry VIII's reign disbanded and their property taken by the crown. Although only some of these were actual 'monasteries' England's 850 religious houses together owned between a quarter to a third of all the land in England. Furthermore, many of them were rumoured to tolerate decidedly un-monastic behaviour.

Having severed his ties with the Catholic Church in the 1534 Act of Supremacy, Henry was free to deal with religious houses without needing approval from the Pope. Within two years his ministers began to shut down religious houses on financial grounds, and by 1540 all the abbeys except for Waltham had been closed. Abbot Robert Fuller surrendered the abbey and its property on 23 March 1540, and within just a few years all the buildings except for the parish nave had been demolished or had collapsed due to neglect.

The Dissolution of the Monasteries was completed in less than four years and brought Henry significant income. It also acted to suppress political opposition from those who might have sided with the Pope.

German composer Johann Sebastian Bach dedicated what were to become known as the Brandenburg Concertos to Margrave Christian Ludwig of Brandenburg-Schwedt.

Bach was born into a family of musicians and, from 1708, began to quickly earn a reputation as a talented organist and composer. It was while employed as the Kapellmeister, or director of music, for Leopold, Prince of Anhalt-Köthen that he sent the bound manuscript of six concertos to Margrave Christian Ludwig, the younger brother of King Frederick I of Prussia. Bach had performed for the Prince during a visit to Berlin two years earlier in 1719, after which he had commissioned Bach to write him some music.

It's unclear why Bach waited until 1721 to send the manuscript to the Margrave, especially as it's generally accepted that the six pieces were drawn from compositions possibly dating back as far as 1708. What is clear, however, is that Bach never received any acknowledgement or pay for the pieces from the Margrave. The concertos may have never even been performed because Christian Ludwig didn't have good enough musicians to play the complex pieces.

The manuscript therefore languished in the Margrave's library until his death in 1734 when it once again disappeared. It was finally rediscovered over a century later, in 1849. The pieces became known as the 'Brandenburg Concertos' after the term was coined by Philipp Spitta in his later 19th Century biography of the composer.

The six works now rank among the world's most famous pieces of orchestral music, and are widely considered to be some of the best compositions of the Baroque period.

The Treaty of Rome, which laid the foundations for the European Economic Community, was signed by Belgium, France, Italy, Luxembourg, the Netherlands and West Germany.

The EEC, sometimes referred to as the Common Market, was formally established on 1 January 1958. It survived, with some changes under the Maastricht Treaty, until 2009 when it was absorbed into the European Union.

The aim of the EEC was to establish economic integration between its members, such as a common market and customs union. However in reality the EEC operated beyond purely economic issues since it included organisations such as the European Atomic Energy Community that sought to generate and distribute nuclear energy to its member states.

The EEC was preceded by the European Coal and Steel Community, which came into force in 1952. The ECSC sought to amalgamate European coal and steel production in order to reconstruct Europe after the devastation of the Second World War. The hope was that this would reduce the threat of a future conflict by establishing mutual economic reliance. Within just three years the idea of a customs union was being discussed, and the 1956 Intergovernmental Conference on the Common Market and Euratom established the parameters for the Treaty of Rome.

Over time the EEC expanded its membership. Denmark, Ireland and the United Kingdom joined in 1973 while the 1980s saw the addition of Greece, Spain and Portugal. With the creation of the European Union in 1993 and its absorption of the EEC in 2009 the union expanded to contains 28 states.

MARCH
26
1945

The Battle of Iwo Jima ended at 9am after US Marines officially secured the island from the Japanese Imperial Army during the War in the Pacific.

The US invasion of Iwo Jima, known as 'Operation Detachment', led to five weeks of fierce fighting between around 21,000 Japanese troops and 110,000 Americans. The United States suffered 26,000 casualties of which nearly 7,000 died. Meanwhile the Japanese forces were virtually wiped out.

The objective of Operation Detachment was to capture Iwo Jima and its three airfields in order to provide a base for US aircraft involved in attacks on the Japanese mainland. The island had been subjected to nine months of aerial bombings and naval bombardments prior to the US invasion, but the Japanese had dug an extensive network of tunnels beneath the volcanic island that provided shelter for much of the defence force.

The first Marines landed on the island on 19 February and, despite facing little initial opposition, suffered significant casualties as they struggled to make their way inland. The strong Japanese defences meant that despite their superior numbers the Americans were sometimes only able to progress a few hundred metres a day.

The key location of Mount Suribachi was eventually captured and the iconic photograph of five Marines raising the United States flag was taken – albeit when a second, larger, flag was raised to replace the first. On 16 March the island was declared secure, but sporadic fighting continued until the night of 25 and 26 March when a final Japanese assault by 300 soldiers was defeated in a vicious 90-minute firefight.

Dr Richard Beeching, the Chairman of the British Transport Commission, published his report entitled *The Reshaping of British Railways.*

By the end of the Second World War road transport had grown exponentially and many of the nation's railway lines were in a poor state of repair. In 1948 the railways were nationalised and became British Rail, but economic recovery and the end of petrol rationing spurred a 10% annual increase in road vehicle mileage through to the 1960s. This had a devastating impact on the railways, which saw income slowly fall below operating costs. By 1961 British Rail was operating at a loss of £300,000 per day.

Beeching was called upon by Conservative Prime Minister Harold Macmillan to make the railways profitable. His detailed analysis of rail traffic identified stations and lines that ran at a constant loss by raising very little income while their fixed operating costs remained high. He pointed out that stations and railway lines had broadly the same fixed costs whether they saw 1,000 passengers a week or 6,000.

Beeching wrote two reports that outlined his plans for an extensive reduction and restructuring of the British railway network. The first of these, *The Reshaping of British Railways*, recommended that 6,000 out of the existing 18,000 miles of British railway line should be closed entirely, while others should only serve freight. Meanwhile 2,363 stations were to close.

Not all the recommendations were implemented, but the subsequent Beeching Cuts resulted in the closure of 2,128 stations, thousands of miles of track, and the loss of up to 70,000 jobs.

The Paris Commune was proclaimed and met for the first time.

The city of Paris had been besieged by the Prussian army since September 1870. Following the surrender of the moderate republican government the following January many Parisians, of whom thousands had joined the 'National Guard' militia to defend the city, revolted. They refused to hand over the 400 cannons positioned in Paris to government forces and, on 18 March, killed Generals Clément-Thomas and Lecomte of the regular army who had been sent to take the cannons by force.

The government, regular forces and police subsequently evacuated the city for Versailles. The vacuum of power was filled by units of the National Guard. By the next evening the red flag of the Commune was flying over the Hôtel de Ville. Elections were called and, on 26 March, ninety-two representatives were elected to form the Commune council. However, as a result of some nominees securing victories for multiple seats, and some candidates who had been nominated without their approval refusing to take up their seat, only 60 representatives actually joined the Council.

The results were declared on 27 March and the Council held its first meeting the following day. Within a week, however, the first skirmishes between the Commune's National Guard and the regular army from Versailles had begun.

The refusal of the Communards to accept the authority of the French government led to the Commune being brutally suppressed by the regular French army in May during 'The Bloody Week'. By 28 May the Commune had been defeated. Estimates say that between 10 and 50,000 Communards were killed or executed.

MARCH

29

1973

The last American troops withdrew from South Vietnam.

As the number of US troops sent to fight in Vietnam increased throughout the 1960s, opposition to the war within America grew. The spring of 1969 saw the new President Richard Nixon, who had been elected the previous November, to begin implementing the Nixon Doctrine. More commonly known as the policy of Vietnamization, Nixon intended to 'expand, equip, and train South Vietnam's forces and assign to them an ever-increasing combat role, at the same time steadily reducing the number of US combat troops.'

Public pressure for American troops to completely evacuate Vietnam increased after news of the My Lai Massacre emerged on 12 November. Troop withdrawals therefore continued, although the United States began attacks on Cambodia and Laos in an attempt to flush out Viet Cong and disrupt their supply lines. This coincided with the killing by National Guardsmen of four student protesters at Kent State University which turned yet more members of the American public against the war.

Throughout this period Nixon's National Security Advisor, Henry Kissinger, took part in secret talks with the leadership of North Vietnam. Despite a number of setbacks, the Paris Peace Accords were signed between the US, North Vietnam, South Vietnam and the Viet Cong on 27 January.

The last American troops withdrew on 29 March. This ended eight years of direct American military involvement in Vietnam. The last American civilians didn't leave South Vietnam until they were evacuated in Operation Frequent Wind during the North Vietnamese takeover of Saigon two years later.

MARCH
30
1939

Batman made his first appearance when *Detective Comics* #27 went on sale.

The first issue of *Detective Comics* had appeared in March 1937 and featured an anthology of hard-boiled detective stories. It was the third series to be released by National Allied Publications, which had already experienced enormous success with Superman. By early 1939 the publisher was looking to include more superheroes in its comics to meet the public's demand.

Batman was created by Bob Kane and Bill Finger, and first appeared in a story called 'The Case of the Chemical Syndicate' along with Commissioner Gordon. In the story, the Bat-Man (with a hyphenated name) solves the death of a chemical manufacturer. At the end he is revealed to readers to be the alter-ego of billionaire philanthropist Bruce Wayne.

The popularity of the character in subsequent issues of *Detective Comics* led to him being given his own title in 1940. Within a year the comic was selling 800,000 copies every issue.

Although the cover date of the first issue was May 1939, it was normal for magazines to go on sale before their cover date. One reason is that an advance date fooled customers into thinking that a particular issue was still 'current' and so secured higher sales. Another reason was that cover dates acted as an indicator to retailers of when to remove that issue from sale.

Detective Comics #27 is now widely considered to be one of the most valuable comics in the world. It originally retailed for 10 cents but the most expensive copy sold at auction for $1,075,000 in February 2010.

MARCH

31

1905

Kaiser Wilhelm II of Germany landed in the Moroccan city of Tangier and expressed his support for the Sultan's independence from foreign powers.

The Kaiser's speech in Tangier was a direct challenge to the French Foreign Minister, Théophile Delcassé, who had previously secured wide European support for control of Morocco. Despite initial reservations both Spain and Britain – the latter through the signing of the Entente Cordiale – accepted French control of the country.

The Kaiser's speech in Tangier promoted an 'open-door' policy regarding Morocco and sought an international conference to discuss the matter. The French, who believed that their control of the country was now a foregone conclusion, opposed this suggestion but eventually agreed due to the threat of war. The diplomatic crisis that followed is now referred to as the First Moroccan Crisis. This contributed to the tensions that led to the outbreak of the First World War ten years later.

The Algeciras Conference took place between January and April 1906 and was a diplomatic disaster for Germany. Of the thirteen nations present, only Austria-Hungary supported Germany's position. Even Italy, who was a member of the Triple Alliance alongside Germany, sided with the French.

Although an agreement was eventually reached, Kaiser Wilhelm emerged bitterly humiliated. His attempt to drive a wedge between France and Britain had failed, and had resulted in turning the Entente Cordiale into a loose military alliance. The Second Moroccan Crisis in 1911 subsequently created further tensions between Europe's power blocs.

APRIL

Adolf Hitler was found guilty of treason for his role in the Beer Hall Putsch and sentenced to five years in jail.

The Beer Hall Putsch, also known as the Munich Putsch, had begun on 8 November 1923 when Hitler led an attempted coup against the Weimar Government by trying to seize power in the Bavarian city of Munich.

Despite a reasonably successful first evening, the coup quickly stalled the following day. The police and army engaged the much smaller Nazi Party in open street fighting. Hitler was wounded but escaped the scene.

The Nazi leader hid in a friend's house, and his arrest for treason two days later could have ended his political career. However, he chose to defend himself during his public trial and took the opportunity to use it as a propaganda platform. Hitler openly admitted trying to overthrow the government but claimed that he was not guilty of treason since 'there is no such thing as high treason against the traitors of 1918.'

The trial secured Hitler enormous media attention and catapulted both him and the Nazi Party to national prominence. His comfortable *Festungshaft* (which translates as fortress confinement) in Landsberg Prison lasted for only eight months before he was released for good behaviour. Hitler's detention provided him with the opportunity to write *Mein Kampf*, his blueprint for power, and to rethink the tactics he would use to take that power in Germany.

Despite being banned from public speaking, Hitler was able to rebuild the Nazi Party following his release along less revolutionary lines that eventually saw him appointed Chancellor in January 1933.

APRIL
2
1982

The Falklands War began when Argentina launched an amphibious invasion of the Falkland Islands.

The Falkland Islands have long been the subject of a sovereignty dispute between Britain and Argentina. In 1982 Argentina's military government, led by General Galtieri, sought to use the country's claim to the islands to boost patriotic feelings at home and draw attention away from criticisms of economic mismanagement and human rights abuses.

Despite increased tensions in the South Pacific following the raising of the Argentinian flag on the island of South Georgia two weeks earlier, Britain did not expect a military invasion of the Falkland Islands. The small garrison of British Marines were overwhelmed by the Argentine invasion on 2 April and the islands' governor Rex Hunt surrendered. As the last Telex conversation from the Falklands to London stated at 4.30pm that day, 'you can't argue with thousands of troops plus enormous navy support when you are only 1800 strong.'

The next day the United Nations passed Resolution 502 which condemned the invasion and demanded an immediate withdrawal of all Argentine forces. On 5 April the British Government, led by Prime Minister Margaret Thatcher, ordered a naval task force that numbered more than 100 ships to retake the islands.

Bitter fighting and the deaths of over 900 people on both sides led to the Argentinian surrender that undermined the military government. The Argentine occupation of the islands formally ended on 14 June. Argentina's 1983 general election returned the country to civilian rule, while in Britain the Conservatives secured a landslide election victory.

APRIL

3

1882

The American outlaw Jesse James was shot dead by fellow gang-member Robert Ford.

James had been a famous Confederate guerrilla fighter during the Civil War. In the years following the Union's victory he had moved into criminality and soon become America's most wanted outlaw thanks to a series of high-profile bank robberies and other holdups.

As a train robber, James and his gang rarely robbed passengers. This may have led to their popular association with the legend of Robin Hood who was famous for stealing from the rich to give to the poor. However, there is no evidence that the James gang actually shared their loot with anyone but themselves.

Despite their early success, by 1881 the gang was falling apart. Many members had fled or been killed or arrested, and so James was forced to ally with new gang members. In January 1882 one of his new associates, Robert Ford, met with Missouri Governor Thomas T. Crittenden and agreed to kill James in return for a full pardon for his own crimes and a $10,000 reward.

On the morning of 3 April, shortly before leaving their safe house to rob the Platte City bank, James noticed a dusty picture on the mantelpiece. As he stood on a chair and turned to clean it Robert Ford shot him in the back of the head from virtually point-blank range.

Ford later presented himself to the police. Justice moved quickly. On the same day Ford was charged with murder, pled guilty, was sentenced to death by hanging, and was then granted a full pardon by Governor Crittenden as agreed.

APRIL

4

1968

Civil Rights leader Martin Luther King Jr. was assassinated in Memphis, Tennessee at the age of 39.

The previous day King had appeared at the Mason Temple in Memphis where he delivered what was to become his final public speech. Known as the 'I've Been To The Mountaintop' address, he urged peaceful protest to ensure the focus remained on racial injustice. Towards the end of the speech he also made reference to the threats against his life.

King was standing on the balcony outside his room at the Lorrain Motel in Memphis when he was hit by a single bullet that shattered his jaw and several vertebrae. Despite being rushed to St Joseph's Hospital where doctors worked to keep him alive, he was pronounced dead at 7.05pm.

Two months after the assassination an escaped convict called James Earl Ray was arrested at Heathrow Airport in London and extradited back to America for trial. Ray confessed to the assassination and was sentenced to 99 years imprisonment, but withdrew his confession a few days later. His attempts to withdraw his guilty plea have fuelled allegations of a conspiracy that used James Earl Ray as a scapegoat.

King's death was met with riots across America that lasted for two days, reflecting anger that King's non-violent approach had been met with violence. Fortunately all was calm at his funeral on 9 April in which a recording of his last sermon at Ebenezer Baptist Church was played at his own request.

King didn't want people to remember him for his awards and honours, but for trying to 'feed the hungry', 'clothe the naked', 'be right on the Vietnam war question', and 'love and serve humanity'.

APRIL

5

1621

The *Mayflower* returned to England from the settlement at Plymouth, having carried the Pilgrim fathers to America.

The *Mayflower* was an English-built merchant ship that was a similar style to the Dutch cargo fluyts that dominated 17th Century shipping. The ship had regularly made short journeys to France to trade English woollens for French wine and other goods, but is known to have travelled as for as Norway and may even have gone as far as Greenland prior to transporting the Pilgrims. By 1620 the *Mayflower* was already reaching the end of its working life.

The story of the *Mayflower* usually focuses on its journey to New England, with the ship itself being a central character in the story of European settlers in North America. In reality, the ship itself was nothing special. To the ship's crew the voyage to the New World was just a delivery contract between the Pilgrims and the ship's master, Christopher Jones. With the Pilgrims safely ashore in America, Jones and his crew were free to return to England.

However, the bitter winter and outbreak of disease among the Pilgrims meant that construction of a settlement on land was not completed until March 1621. Furthermore, with many of the ship's crew struck down by disease, Jones was forced to stay until those of his crew who survived were fit enough for the return journey at the start of April.

After the ship's return Jones used the *Mayflower* for some other trading runs to France, but he died just a year later. By 1624 the ship had also reached the end of its life. Legend says that it was sold and broken up for scrap, with the beams used to construct a barn in the county of Buckinghamshire.

APRIL

6

1896

The first modern Olympic Games opened in Athens.

Known as the father of the modern Olympics, Frenchman Pierre de Coubertin had organised a congress at the Sorbonne in Paris in 1894 to discuss his plans for an international sporting competition. The congress supported his plans, approved Athens as the host city, and established the International Olympic Committee.

The games opened as planned two years later. American athlete James Connolly won the first final for his 13.71m triple jump, leading the USA's 14 competitors to win a total of 11 events between them. The most successful individual competitor was the German Carl Schuhmann who won the team events in the horizontal bar and parallel bars events, the horse vault event and, despite being considerably smaller than his opponents, the wrestling competition.

Schuhmann didn't receive any gold medals, however. Winners at the 1896 Olympics were instead presented with a silver medal, an olive branch, and a diploma. It wasn't until 1904 that the tradition of awarding gold, silver and bronze medals to first, second and third place began.

The 1896 Summer Olympics laid down many traditions including the first competitive marathon race. A Greek water carrier called Spyridon Louis won the race in a time of 2 hours 58 minutes and 50 seconds. The same route, finishing at the stadium used in the 1896 games, was used when the Olympics returned to Greece in 2004. The winner finished almost 45 minutes faster than in the 1896 competition.

By the time of the 2004 games the rope climbing competition, which had seen competitors climbing a 14m rope in 1896, had been removed.

APRIL
7
1498

A group of Franciscan monks met their Dominican rivals, led by Savonarola, in the Piazza della Signoria in Florence to take part in the first trial by fire in 400 years.

The Dominican friar Girolamo Savonarola, who has been called a 'moral dictator' by historian Richard Cavendish, had built a powerful following in Florence with his passionate sermons against vices and luxuries that tempted people to sin. The previous year he had been excommunicated for defying Pope Alexander VI's order to stop preaching sermons in which the Pope himself was criticised for corruption and greed.

Savonarola chose to ignore the Pope's order and continued to preach and to celebrate mass. Combined with his support for the French invasion of northern Italy, which he claimed was God's punishment for the Florentines' sinful past, Savonarola began to face an increasingly large and vocal opposition.

By early 1498 Savonarola had begun suggesting that he had performed miracles, and this prompted monks from the rival Franciscan order to propose a trial by fire to prove Savonarola's holiness. The belief was that God would intervene to protect the rightful side from the flames as they walked over them. However, when the two sides met on 7 April they squabbled for so long that a rainstorm eventually led to the cancellation of the event.

With Savonarola unable to prove his claim, the crowd turned against him. The next day the Convent of San Marco where Savonarola lived was stormed by an angry mob and he was arrested. Within six weeks he and two fellow friars had been executed for heresy by hanging while fires burned beneath them to destroy the bodies.

**A series of agreements between Britain and France known as
the Entente Cordiale were signed.**

The agreement marked the end of years of intermittent conflict
between Britain and France and set the stage for the series of
agreements known as the Triple Entente that bound Britain, France
and Russia together at the start of the First World War.

Throughout the late 19th Century the German Chancellor Otto
von Bismarck had been constantly toying with the European balance
of power to keep France from forming alliances with other European
nations. Meanwhile, Britain had actively maintained its own 'splendid
isolation' in which it focused on ruling its sprawling Empire. The
Entente Cordiale therefore marked a significant change in European
politics.

However, it was not a military alliance. Despite being closely
associated with the First World War due to the later emergence of the
Triple Entente involving Russia, the Entente Cordiale was a foreign
policy agreement between France and Britain relating to three very
specific imperial issues over which the two nations had quarrelled.
The name is French for 'warm understanding', and the Entente
Cordiale settled the imperial disputes in places such as Egypt and
Morocco.

The centenary of the agreement was celebrated with great
fanfare in 2004. Posters at the Gare du Nord railway station in Paris
and the Waterloo railway station in London were emblazoned with
the words 'Entente Cordiale'. The irony that Waterloo was named
after the battle where a British-led coalition destroyed Napoleon's
army was not lost on either side.

APRIL

9

1865

Confederate States Army General Robert E. Lee surrendered to Union Lieutenant General Ulysses S. Grant.

Prior to the surrender, Lee's army had been forced to abandon the Confederate capital of Richmond, Virginia, and was retreating with the hope of joining with other Confederate forces in North Carolina. The Union army managed to cut them off with cavalry and infantry. With his army surrounded and his men weak and exhausted, Lee had no option but to surrender.

Lee and Grant sent a series of messages to each other that led to them meeting in the village of Appomattox Courthouse. Here they both signed the surrender documents in the parlour of a house owned by Wilmer McLean. The terms were as generous as Lee could have hoped for, since Grant wanted to avoid any possible excuse for a subsequent uprising.

Among the key terms granted to the Confederates were that all officers and men were pardoned and allowed to return home with their private property including their horses. Furthermore all Confederate officers were allowed to keep their side arms and would be fed with Union rations.

With the surrender signed, Grant is reputed to have stepped outside and declared, 'The war is over. The Rebels are our countrymen again'. Lee's surrender encouraged other Confederate forces across the south to do the same and marked the beginning of the end of the American Civil War.

By the time the war reached its final conclusion it had lasted for four years. Approximately 630,000 people had died, and there were over one million casualties on both sides.

APRIL

10

1858

Big Ben, the bell inside the clock tower at the Palace of Westminster in Britain, was cast.

Big Ben and the clock tower are two of the most evocative symbols of London. The bell has chimed the hours almost non-stop since it first rang in July 1859, over a year after the bell itself was cast at the Whitechapel Bell Foundry.

Weighing 13 ½ tons, the bell is actually damaged. Within two months of being installed it cracked under the weight and force of the hammer striking against it, and repairs took nearly three years to complete. This consisted of the removal of a square of metal near the crack and turning the bell an eighth of a turn on its axis so that the hammer would strike a different part. The bell continues to operate now with the repair in place. As a result it sounds slightly different to what was originally intended.

As for the bell's nickname, sources disagree on the origin. While some believe that it was named after a contemporary heavyweight boxer Benjamin Caunt, the most commonly accepted explanation comes from a Parliamentary debate. It's said that a large and imposing politician, Sir Benjamin Hall, made a long and passionate speech about the bell. He was known as 'Big Ben' and, on sitting back down, someone else in the chamber apparently shouted out 'Why not call it Big Ben and have done with it?'

There is a common misconception that the name Big Ben applies to the clock at Westminster, but in reality it is only the name of the bell. The tower is officially known as the Elizabeth Tower, which in turn was renamed from the uninspiring 'Clock Tower' in 2002 to celebrate Queen Elizabeth II's Diamond Jubilee.

The trial of Nazi SS Lieutenant Colonel Adolf Eichmann began in Israel.

Eichmann was known as the architect of the Final Solution, the man who coordinated the transportation of Jews from across Europe to Death Camps in the East.

Eichmann had fled Europe at the end of the Second World War in an attempt to escape being tried for war crimes. Using false documents under the assumed name Ricardo Klement he eventually arrived in Argentina where he and his family lived for a number of years. Eichmann worked in a series of menial jobs before securing a position in a Mercedes-Benz factory.

As one of the world's most wanted Nazi war criminals, the Israeli secret police – the Mossad – spent years tirelessly searching for him. Having been given the tip-off that he may be in Buenos Aires, they eventually captured him on 11 May 1960 and forcibly took him to Jerusalem for trial.

Eichmann sat inside a purpose-built bullet-proof glass booth for the duration of the trial. The hearing lasted for sixteen weeks and exposed for the first time the full extent of the atrocities that occurred in the Holocaust. Eichmann's main line of defence was that he was not personally involved with the killings, and was just following orders.

On 15 December 1961 the three judges hearing the case unanimously found Eichmann guilty of the 15 charges against him and sentenced him to death. Eichmann was executed by hanging six months later, his was body cremated, and his ashes were scattered at sea.

APRIL

12

1945

Harry Truman became the 33rd President of the United States when his predecessor, Franklin D Roosevelt, suddenly died while having his portrait painted.

Truman was Roosevelt's Vice-President, but had only held the position since January. Meanwhile, Roosevelt had been President for four terms and had overseen both America's recovery from the Great Depression and its involvement in the Second World War.

Truman faced an enormous challenge simply by being the person to follow Roosevelt as President, let alone the ongoing struggles of the Second World War. He told reporters that he 'felt like the moon, the stars, and all the planets had fallen on me'. Even Roosevelt's wife, Eleanor, recognised the scale of the task facing the new President. When he asked if there was anything he could do for her she is said to have replied, 'Is there anything we can do for you? For you are the one in trouble now.'

Eleanor Roosevelt's words were not an overstatement as the task facing the new President was enormous. World War Two was still raging in both Europe and the Pacific. His predecessor had not told him about the worsening relationship with the USSR, nor about the Manhattan Project's development of the atomic bomb that was just a few months away from completion.

Truman took the decision to continue with the bomb's development and in August that year left a lasting mark on international politics by ordering the bombings of the Japanese cities of Hiroshima and Nagasaki.

It is for his role in the origins of the Cold War that Truman is now probably most well remembered.

APRIL

13

1970

The spacecraft Apollo 13 was rocked by an explosion from one of its oxygen tanks.

The explosion on board Apollo 13 occurred after a routine procedure to stop gases settling in their tanks. An investigation by NASA later found that a spark from an exposed wire in the oxygen tank caused a fire, leading to an expansion of gases that eventually blew apart the tank. The explosion ripped off the side of the Service Module, vented oxygen into space, and left the crew stricken in a damaged craft.

The resulting emergency led to the calm announcement by the crew of, 'Houston we've had a problem'. However, most people misquote the phrase as 'Houston we have a problem' after the award-winning 1995 film *Apollo 13* changed the tense. The movie also placed the words in the mouth of Commander Jim Lovell despite it being Command Module Pilot Jack Swigert who first reported the issue.

Apollo 13 was intended to be the third manned mission to the moon but, following the explosion, focus quickly changed to bringing the crew safely home. Improvisation was vital as the crew were forced to turn their landing unit into a lifeboat to ferry them back to Earth before transferring back to the Command Module for re-entry.

The crew were faced with numerous problems including limited power that led to a loss of cabin heat and potable water. They also needed to make repairs to the carbon dioxide removal system using a series of improvised parts. Fortunately the spacecraft's heat shield had not been damaged in the explosion, and the crew splashed down safely in the South Pacific Ocean on 17 April.

APRIL

14

1561

The people of Nuremberg in Germany witnessed a 'dreadful apparition' in the sky.

The spectacle in the skies above Nuremberg was recorded by the artist Hans Glaser who lived in the city and so presumably witnessed the event himself. He published a woodcut and text in a local 'broadsheet', a kind of tabloid newspaper that revelled in reporting strange or violent stories. The woodcut shows cylindrical objects, multiple-coloured discs and globes, crosses, and even tubes that look like cannon barrels all moving across the sky.

Modern UFO enthusiasts have used the Nuremberg celestial phenomenon as evidence of extra-terrestrial life, although scientists have also put forward their own explanations of why hundreds of people saw what was described as an aerial battle raging in front of the sun.

There's no way of knowing how accurate Glaser's woodcut is, nor what caused the shapes in the sky. However, recent science has suggested that atmospheric phenomena are responsible. UFO-skeptic Frank Johnson has written a convincing argument suggesting that the people of Nuremberg witnessed a parhelion, otherwise known as a sundog, which is caused by light refracting through clouds of ice crystals. His argument suggests that this was combined with other atmospheric tricks of the light such as a low viewing angle of the sun due to the early time of day at which the phenomenon took place. Other commentators have suggested that a city-wide outbreak of ergotism, in which fungus growing on grain can cause hallucinations, may have been responsible. Whatever the actual cause, the celestial phenomenon terrified the people of Nuremberg who interpreted it as a warning from God.

APRIL

15

1755

Samuel Johnson published 'A Dictionary of the English Language' in London.

Historians broadly agree that the first true dictionary was created by Sir Thomas Elyot who published a book called a Dictionary in 1538 while working for Henry VIII. Johnson's later work far superseded this by being the most comprehensive and detailed collection of the English language to date. Johnson's dictionary was the 'go to' reference for the English language until the publication of the first Oxford English Dictionary in 1888 – 173 years after Johnson published his.

Johnson's finished dictionary contained 42,773 words, each of which featured a number of notes on their specific usage. Perhaps most astounding is the fact that Johnson wrote the entire dictionary himself, taking 9 years to do so, and earning the modern equivalent of £210,000 British pounds for his efforts. His biographer, Walter Jackson Bate, described the work as 'one of the greatest single achievements of scholarship'.

Despite the impact of Johnson's dictionary, it created a number of problems that have been inherited by the modern English language. Most significantly, Johnson's spellings have become the standard format despite there being a number of inconsistencies in his use of particular letter orders and sounds.

Johnson himself was well aware of the shortcomings of his work and the fact that he would face such criticisms. In a letter to an Italian lexicographer in 1784 he stated that 'dictionaries are like watches: the worst is better than none, and the best cannot be expected to go quite true.'

APRIL
16
1922

Former First World War enemies Germany and Russia signed the Treaty of Rapallo.

When Germany drew up the harsh Treaty of Brest-Litovsk in 1918, Russia had been forced to sign away large swathes of land. The Treaty of Rapallo meant the two countries ended all territorial and financial arguments stemming from Brest-Litovsk and agreed to 'co-operate in a spirit of mutual goodwill in meeting the economic needs of both countries'.

Both Germany and Russia had been excluded from the League of Nations, and this acted as a catalyst for the pact. The Treaty of Rapallo was therefore particularly important for Russia as it was the first international recognition of the Bolsheviks as the official government. However, it was the secret military clauses that were most valuable to both sides. German factories that produced military goods were able to move to Russia and were able to bypass the Treaty of Versailles' limits on German weaponry. Furthermore the two armies conducted joint training exercises deep inside Russia. These enabled the German army to continue to use technology banned by Versailles such as tanks and warplanes.

The Russians benefitted from this agreement as well. They were able to see Western European military technology, and work with German engineers who shared expertise that was to be the bedrock of Stalin's Five Year Plans.

The Rapallo Treaty alarmed the Western Powers, but the danger was short-lived. By the middle of the 1920s Germany under Stresemann had begun to improve relations as a result of the Locarno Treaties. This meant that the close relationship with Russia was less vital.

APRIL
17
1492

The Catholic Monarchs of Spain, Queen Isabella and King Ferdinand, agreed to support Christopher Columbus' voyage in which he crossed the Atlantic and discovered the Americas.

The Capitulations of Santa Fe granted a number of official titles to Columbus as well as ten per cent of any treasure he was able to secure on his voyage. The Capitulations specifically mentioned the possibility of pearls, precious stones, gold, silver, spices, and – just in case he found anything else – 'other objects of whatever kind, name and sort'.

Columbus did not plan to reach the Americas on his voyage. He was instead trying to find an alternative route to the valuable spice markets of Asia by sailing west across the open Atlantic, rather than having to navigate around Africa. A popular modern belief that people at the time feared he would drop off the edge of a flat earth is false, since the majority of people had accepted that the Earth is a sphere since the time of the Ancient Greeks.

Columbus' fleet of three ships set off from the Canary Islands on 6 September 1492. After a five week voyage across the Atlantic the crews landed in what are now the Bahamas. Columbus was made Governor of the Indies by the Catholic Monarchs, although they removed him from this position after accusations of cruelty. The Spanish rulers said that this cancelled the terms of the Capitulations of Santa Fe, meaning that they also refused to give him the 10% of all profits that had originally been agreed.

Most scholars state that, despite a wealth of evidence against him, by the time Columbus died in 1506 he still refused to acknowledge that he had not discovered the Western route to Asia.

APRIL

18

1775

Paul Revere rode from Charleston to Lexington with his message that 'the Regulars are coming out!'

Revere's 'midnight ride' went on to signal the start of the American Revolutionary War and has since passed into legend. Whether Revere referred to the approaching army as 'regulars' or 'Redcoats' is unclear, but his cry had the intended consequence of signalling the march of troops towards the Massachusetts village of Concord. His message was spread throughout the area before he arrived in Lexington where he met with John Adams and Samuel Adams.

Revere certainly didn't signal that the 'British' were coming. At the time the American settlers would still have seen themselves as British, albeit living in a distant colony and ruled by a faraway king. It is also highly unlikely that Revere loudly shouted his warning as he passed peoples' houses. His mission was secret, and the countryside was known to contain army patrols and royalist sympathisers.

Seventy-seven militiamen had assembled in the town of Lexington by the time British troops arrived the next morning. Their leader, Captain John Parker, knew that his men were outnumbered and so gave an order that is now engraved on a stone at the site: 'Stand your ground; don't fire unless fired upon, but if they mean to have a war, let it begin here.'

The leaders of both sides ordered their men not to fire, but a single shot from an unknown source rang out. The Battle of Lexington lasted for just a few minutes, killing eight militiamen and wounding a further ten. Moving on to the town of Concord, however, the British met significantly more opposition. This signalled the start of the American Revolution.

APRIL

19

1770

The British explorer Captain James Cook first caught sight of Australia.

This date of the sighting, recorded in the log of HMS *Endeavour*, is inaccurate. The cause of this problem was that Cook and his crew had been at sea for nearly 2 years. In that time they had sailed west from Britain across the Atlantic to South America and then onwards across the southern Pacific. By the time they arrived on the southeast coast of Australia, they had – in terms of the calendar – skipped a day. According to some sources, therefore, Cook arrived in Australia on 20 April.

Irrespective of whether we use the ship's log or the modern calendar to record the date, the arrival of *Endeavour* was significant for being the first European voyage to reach the east coast of Australia. The ship had previously surveyed and mapped the coast of New Zealand which led Cook to determine that he had not yet located *Terra Australis*, a landmass that had first been assumed to exist by Aristotle.

After sighting land it was another ten days before the crew actually stepped ashore. The first sighting had been of Point Hicks, but it wasn't until the ship had travelled some distance along the coast to what is now known as Botany Bay that Cook and his crew felt they had found a suitable mooring.

Botany Bay is now a major transportation hub, since it is home to Sydney's cargo seaport and two runways of Sydney airport. For many years, however, the name Botany Bay conjured up different images of transportation since Botany Bay had been the first proposed site for a British penal colony.

Workers began painting skylight windows at the Houston Astrodome to limit glare from the sun.

The Astrodome was a covered stadium that was the first of its kind. It was built in order to avoid the need to cancel sports fixture as a result of the hot, humid, and therefore often rainy Texas summers. It was given its 'Astro' name to reflect the fact that Houston was home to the control centre of the US space program.

The stadium had cost nearly $32 million to build, and the painting of the skylights added another $20,000 dollars to the cost. The paint job had been made necessary due to glare from the windows affecting the vision of baseball outfielders. Painting the windows significantly improved the situation for the players, but in turn led to other problems inside the stadium.

Primarily, the forty per cent reduction in sunlight making its way inside the structure meant that the specially-bred Bermuda grass used for the field died. This was despite the originally believing that painting the windows might improve the growth of the grass, since it had been formulated to grow indoors.

Left with no grass, the stadium owners were forced to resort to a second paint job in which they painted the dirt floor green. The next year they installed artificial grass instead. This grass was called originally called ChemGrass but, following the successful use of it in the 1966 baseball season at the Astrodome, the manufacturer rebranded it.

AstroTurf was born: an artificial grass that got its name from an indoor sports stadium, which had in turn got its name from the space program.

The ancient city of Rome was founded.

The Italian foundation myth of the city of Rome relates to Romulus and Remus, the twin brothers who were suckled by a she-wolf. According to the legend, as adults the twins decided to establish a new city but disagreed on the location. After a quarrel about the location and the height of their competing city walls, Remus was killed by his brother in a fit of rage. Romulus consequently named the city after himself.

While this foundation myth became closely associated with the story of Rome, scholars have looked for firm evidence of its foundation and almost all accept that this can be dated to 21 April 753 BCE. The precise date seems implausible at first glance, but there's a clear reason that it is used.

The ancient Roman scholar, Marcus Terentius Varro, is the person who pinpointed the founding of Rome to this exact date. He did this by creating a reverse timeline of Roman history using a combination of a list of Roman consuls and a little bit of historical license to allow for periods of dictatorial rule.

Varro's timeline is therefore known to be slightly inaccurate, but nobody has ever provided sufficiently trustworthy evidence to propose a different calendar. As a result his system is accepted as the standard chronology.

Despite the known inaccuracies in Varro's work, the discovery of ancient walls on Palatine Hill support the legend that Romulus ploughed a furrow to mark his new city. The boundary markers have been dated to the 8th Century BCE, and this broadly supports Varro's chronology.

APRIL

22

1915

Poison gas was first used effectively in the First World War at the Second Battle of Ypres.

A form of tear gas had previously been used by the Germans fighting the Russians at the Battle of Bolimów in Poland at the end of January, but it had proved wholly unsuccessful. The freezing temperatures meant that a lot of the gas failed to vaporise, and that which was successfully released was blown back towards the German trenches due to a change in the direction of the wind.

At Ypres, near the small Belgian hamlet of Gravenstafel, the situation was dramatically different. 5,700 gas canisters weighing over 40kg each were released by hand over a 4 mile (6.5km) stretch of the front line. Every canister contained highly poisonous chlorine gas. Despite the improved organising, the rudimentary system of release still depended on the wind to blow the gas towards the enemy. Some Germans were killed or injured in the process of releasing the gas but the attack was terribly effective as the gas successfully vaporised and sank into the enemy trenches.

Over five thousand French Algerian, Moroccan and territorial troops died within ten minutes of the gas being released. A further five thousand were temporarily blinded, with nearly half of them becoming prisoners of war.

The Germans didn't expect the gas to be as effective as it was, and so didn't fully exploit their initial advantage. However, by the end of the battle on 25 May, the Germans had certainly scored a tactical victory. They had compressed the size of the Ypres salient and had demonstrated the effectiveness of chemical warfare. The Allies soon developed their own poison gas, making chemical warfare part of the offensive strategy for the rest of the war.

The Coca-Cola Company introduced 'the new taste of Coca-Cola', when they replaced the original Coca-Cola formula with a new version.

Marking the first major formula change in 99 years, 'new Coke' is widely heralded as one of the biggest marketing failures in history. However, the short-term problems arising from its introduction were far outweighed by the sales boost achieved when the company reintroduced the old formula as 'Coca-Cola Classic'.

By 1983 Pepsi Cola was outselling Coke in American supermarkets. The new drink formula was introduced as a response to Pepsi's increasing market share. Coca-Cola executives ordered the start of 'Project Kansas' a secret research and development project focused on reformulating the drink to challenge the sweeter taste of Pepsi.

Taste tests of the new formula were overwhelmingly positive. Even after the new taste was introduced to the market place, public surveys suggested that the majority of drinkers liked the new taste. Despite this positive feedback, however, a small but vocal minority spoke out against it.

As criticism of the change emerged in the press it became clear to Coca-Cola executives that the issue was not a problem with the introduction of the new formula but the fact that it completely replaced the old one. When the company reintroduced the old formula three months later, there was a surge in sales of 'Coca-Cola Classic'. In the words of marketing Vice-President Sergio Zyman, 'New Coke was a success because it revitalised the brand and reattached the public to Coke.'

Sir Ernest Shackleton and five companions set off in *James Caird*, a recovered lifeboat, to sail from Elephant Island to South Georgia in the southern Atlantic Ocean.

The crew had been forced to make their way to Elephant Island after *Endurance* sank due to pack ice in the Weddell Sea off the coast of Antarctica the previous October. Having made their way off the ice in *Endeavour*'s lifeboats at the start of April, Shackleton decided to kit out the strongest lifeboat, *James Caird*, for a perilous 720-nautical-mile voyage across the Southern Ocean to South Georgia. Their mission was to organize a rescue party for the shipwrecked crew of *Endurance*.

Despite all the odds stacked against them, the crew of the tiny boat reached South Georgia in 16 days. A smaller team of three, led by Shackleton, then undertook what was to be the first confirmed land crossing of South Georgia. This 17-mile, 36 hour journey resulted in them reaching the whaling station at Stromness on 19 April where they summoned help.

Historian Carol Alexander has since said that the perilous voyage of *James Caird* is one 'one of the greatest boat journeys ever accomplished.'

The final word on the achievement of the crew must go to Shackleton himself. In 'South: the story of Shackleton's last expedition 1914-1917' he said:

'We had suffered, starved and triumphed, grovelled down yet grasped at glory, grown bigger in the bigness of the whole...We had reached the naked soul of man.'

APRIL

25

1792

The world's first use of the French guillotine as a method of execution.

Nicolas Jacques Pelletier, a French highwayman who was found guilty of killing a man during one of his robberies, was the first but by no means last victim of the French decapitation machine.

Pelletier's status as a common criminal was significant. Prior to the French Revolution, beheading as a form of execution had been reserved for the nobility. Commoners were usually subjected to longer and considerably more painful deaths through hanging, or worse. Drawing on arguments put forward in the Enlightenment in order to end the privilege of the nobility, the National Assembly therefore made decapitation the only legal form of execution.

It was recognised that manual beheading was, however, still a gruesome form of execution. On 10 October 1789 physician Joseph Guillotin argued that every execution should be swift and mechanical. The National Assembly agreed and acknowledged that capital punishment should simply end life, not purposefully cause pain as well.

Another physician, Antoine Louis, was appointed to lead a committee to develop a quick and efficient decapitation machine. Although Guillotin was a member of this committee, it is therefore Antoine Louis who is credited with the device's invention, even though it carries the Guillotin's name.

As for the highwayman Pelletier, his execution went smoothly, much to the disappointment of the crowd who expected better 'entertainment'. Although excited to see the new machine in action they were disappointed at its speed and efficiency.

APRIL

26

1937

The Basque town of Guernica experienced what is seen by many as the first large-scale modern air raid against a civilian population.

By the spring of 1937, Guernica was just 30km away from the front line fighting of the Spanish Civil War and lay within the focal area for the Nationalist army's advance on the city of Bilbao. Guernica town was also a Republican communication centre, and was the location of a weapons factory.

Documents released in the 1970s show that the attack on Guernica was part of a larger Nationalist strategy in the north, in which roads and bridges would be destroyed in order to upset Republican troop movements.

Historian César Vidal Manzanares notes that, despite its part in the wider Nationalist plan, the level of destruction wrought on the town was disproportionate to Guernica's strategic value. Five waves of bombers initially attacked Guernica over a period of 90 minutes. Further waves came in the early evening, along with a number of fighter planes that strafed the roads leading out of the devastated town, increasing the civilian death toll as people tried to escape the burning ruins.

The number of civilian casualties resulting from the attack has never been fully determined, although figures in excess of a thousand that were cited until the 1980s are now known to have been exaggerated.

Historians now generally accept that between 170 and 300 civilians were killed in the bombing, although it's likely that many more died from their injuries.

APRIL

27

1509

Pope Julius II excommunicated the entire population of Venice.

Venice had gradually taken land from the Papal States throughout the fifteenth and early sixteenth centuries. Having been elected pontiff in 1503, Julius II was determined to reclaim this territory.

The Papacy joined together with France, Spain, and the Holy Roman Empire to form the League of Cambrai in December 1508. This signalled their readiness to mount military action to seize control of the Romagne region from Venice. Shortly before invading, the Pope issued the interdict against the Republic that excommunicated every single one of Venice's citizens.

The interdict deprived the Venetians of their spiritual salvation, and was therefore a formidable weapon. When Venetian forces were defeated at the Battle of Agnadello the following month the Republic entered what was referred by one contemporary as a 'foul mood'.

Peace negotiations between Venice and members of the League of Cambrai were concluded on 24 February the next year, at which point the interdict was lifted. France and the Holy Roman Empire, however, were keen to maintain their advance. Having underestimated his former allies the Pope sought to stop the French advance that began to threaten the Papal States.

Julius II consequently formed a new alliance between the Papal States, Spain and Venice. He then placed France under papal interdict. By the time he died in 1513, Julius II had therefore both fought and formed alliances with France, Spain, Venice and the Holy Roman Empire.

APRIL

28

1923

The original Wembley Stadium in London opened with the FA Cup Final between Bolton Wanderers and West Ham United.

Wembley Stadium had originally been built for the British Empire Exhibition that was to take place in 1924, but it was finished ahead of schedule. Despite concerns that there wouldn't be enough spectators to fill the enormous stadium, the FA chose to play the match there anyway. They also arranged for King George V to present the trophy to the winning team.

An orderly queue of people made their way inside after the gates were opened at 11.30am. Just over two hours later the steady flow had increased to the point where stadium authorities decided they needed to close the gates. The pressure of the increasing number of people outside the stadium soon forced the gates open, leading to spectators flooding the pitch. Official figures placed attendance at 126,000 people – 1,000 more than the stadium's capacity – but estimates suggest that the crowd was probably twice that size.

It was only after mounted police arrived that the situation began to calm down. The police managed to clear the pitch enough for the match to begin just 45 minutes behind schedule.

Although many other police horses were involved, it was a light grey horse called Billie who became the symbol of the day. Billie was ridden by PC George Scorey and appeared white on the black and white newsreel footage. This led to the match becoming known as the 'White Horse Final'. The bridge outside the new Wembley Stadium was subsequently named White Horse Bridge.

In terms of the football match itself, Bolton Wanderers beat West Ham 2-0.

APRIL

29

1975

America began Operation Frequent Wind to evacuate over 1,000 American civilians and a further 6,000 'at-risk' Vietnamese from Saigon using helicopters.

North Vietnamese troops were closing in on the South Vietnamese capital by March 1975. The United States had already evacuated 45,000 people by 29 April but further fixed-wing evacuations impossible due to the approaching army. US Ambassador Graham Martin therefore ordered the commencement of Operation Frequent Wind. American Forces Radio made their pre-arranged signal 'The temperature in Saigon is 105 degrees and rising', and followed it by playing Bing Crosby singing 'White Christmas'. The evacuation began at around 2pm.

The main muster point was the Defense Attaché Office, from where thousands of people were successfully airlifted in a relatively orderly manner. At the US Embassy thousands more people had gathered. This was considerably more people than it would be possible to evacuate even with helicopters landing every 10 minutes.

With hundreds of eligible Vietnamese civilians still at the Embassy, at 3.27am President Ford ordered Ambassador Martin to stop evacuating anyone other than American personnel. The Marines guarding the compound were ordered to move further inside, and shortly afterwards the crowds broke through the gates. The last of the Marines were flown out at 7.53am, leaving approximately 400 evacuees still inside the Embassy when it fell to the communists.

The largest ever helicopter evacuation had lasted for 19 hours and involved 81 helicopters shuttling the evacuees to US Navy ships moored in the South China Sea.

APRIL

30

1803

The Louisiana Purchase Treaty was concluded between the United States and France.

In the Treaty, France agreed to sell 828,000 square miles of North American territory that stretched from the Mississippi River to the Rocky Mountains. The sale doubled the size of the existing United States. Although the land transfer went on to include a vast area that now forms part of fifteen separate states, the United States' original interest was only in buying the area around the port of New Orleans.

The city of New Orleans offered important access to both the Mississippi River and the Gulf of Mexico. It was therefore vital to American trade and the provision of supplies to the new Western territories that were being settled at the time. When France regained control of the city from Spain in the early 1800s it raised fears that the new settlements would struggle to trade.

These fears were realised when, on 18 October 1802, Americans were banned from using warehouses in New Orleans. President Jefferson had already ordered diplomats to begin talks in Paris with the aim of buying the city from France but, on 11 April 1803, the French negotiators offered to sell the entire Louisiana Territory to the Americans for $15 million.

The offer came about because France had failed to suppress an uprising in present-day Haiti by slaves and free blacks, and was facing an impending war with Britain. The government found that it simply couldn't afford to send troops to occupy and control the Mississippi valley. Deciding to cut their losses, the French government therefore agreed to sell the entire territory at less than 3 cents per acre.

MAY

The Mr Potato Head first went on sale.

The idea for making a 'funny face man' by attaching moulded plastic to a vegetable was first proposed by George Lerner, an inventor and designer from Brooklyn, in the 1940s.

In 1951 Lerner successfully sold his idea of push-pin plastic face pieces to a breakfast cereal manufacturer who planned to include the accessories in their cereal packets. When the Hassenfeld brother who had founded the Hasbro toy company met with Lerner later that year they agreed to buy the concept back off the cereal company for $7,000. The cereal company had originally bought the idea from Lerner for $5,000. Hasbro then set about finding a way to produce and market Mr Potato Head as a toy.

The day before Mr Potato Head released by Hasbro he featured in the first ever television advert for a toy that was aimed directly at children. This revolutionary marketing worked and led to over a million Mr Potato Head kits being sold in the first year alone.

Unlike the modern Mr Potato Head, the original version only included plastic body parts and accessories. Customers were expected to supply their own potato for the body itself. This led some members of the public to criticize the toy for encouraging food waste in the aftermath of wartime rationing.

Twelve years passed before a plastic potato body was included with Mr Potato Head and this only happened because of government safety regulations. The plastic parts had to be less sharp, meaning that a real potato was too difficult to puncture. Mr Potato Head has since gone through many design changes, and it wasn't until the 1980s that he took on the shape we now recognise.

MAY

2

1952

The world's first passenger jet aircraft carried 36 passengers from London to Johannesburg.

The De Havilland DH 106 Comet operated by the British Overseas Airways Corporation reduced the overall journey time by a third. Despite this time difference it still needed to stop in Rome, Beirut, Khartoum, Entebbe, and Livingstone in order to refuel. The crew was also replaced in Beirut and Khartoum due to the length of the flight.

One of the passengers was journalist Aubrey O. Cookman, Jr. who wrote for the American-produced *Popular Mechanics* magazine. In an article written shortly after the flight, he noted that his fellow passengers included a dentist, a chemist, a policewoman, a composer, and a number of engineers and businessmen.

Despite the significant differences to the conventional propeller aircraft journey, and the fact that this was the first passenger jet aircraft, the ticket cost exactly the same amount of money. The cost was £175 single or £315 return, and travel insurance premiums remained the same. Fortunately for the passengers and crew, the flight went successfully

The De Havilland Comet's reputation suffered irreparable damage as a result of three devastating accidents just a year after its first commercial flight. This led many airlines to switch to new models such as the Boeing 707 and the Douglas DC-8.

A heavily modified version of the Comet was introduced by the Royal Air Force for military service in 1969. Known as the Nimrod, it was retired in 2011 having seen action in the Falklands War, the First Gulf War, Afghanistan and Iraq.

MAY

3

1830

The world's first steam-powered passenger service began operating on the Canterbury and Whitstable Railway.

It's important to add some clarification to the Crab and Winkle line's claim to fame. Firstly, it wasn't the world's first passenger railway as the Stockton and Darlington railway in the north of England holds that accolade. However the Stockton and Darlington only used steam locomotives for goods transportation. Horses were used to pull passenger carriages along the tracks.

What made the Canterbury and Whistable Railway unique was the use of the steam locomotive *Invicta*. Built by George and Robert Stevenson in Newcastle, and transported to Whitstable by sea, 'Invicta' was the first steam locomotive to haul passengers on a public railway line.

Even *Invicta* wasn't used for the entire journey. The steam locomotive only transported passengers over a short, flat, section of the line. Due to steep inclines and the very low power of *Invicta* that was rated at just 9hp, stationary steam engines hauled carriages attached to long cables for the majority of the six mile journey.

The railway line was also significant for the 757 metre long Tyler Hill Tunnel. This was studied by Isambard Kingdom Brunel while he designed his landmark tunnel through Box Hill for the Great Western Railway.

Due to Whitstable being a seaside town, the line became affectionately known as the Crab and Winkle line, and continued to operate a passenger service for just over a hundred years before becoming goods-only. It closed in 1952 and now serves as a footpath and cycleway between Canterbury and Whitstable.

MAY

4

1932

Al Capone began life as a convict in Atlanta Federal Penitentiary.

Capone had risen to dominate Chicago's organised crime scene since becoming gang boss in January 1925 when he was just twenty-six years old. Although his primary business was bootlegging and distributing alcohol, Capone expanded the gang's activities to include prostitution and protection rackets.

His downfall began when the Supreme Court ruled that illegally earned income needed to be declared for tax purposes. Capone ordered his accountant to make the declaration and, in 1930, an income of $100,000 dollars was declared for the year 1928-29. This provided the evidence that Capone had failed to pay taxes and was able to be prosecuted.

Capone was found guilty on 17 October 1931 of Federal Income Tax Evasion and was sentenced to eleven years imprisonment by Judge James Herbert Wilkerson. Arriving at Atlanta Federal Penitentiary as prisoner number 40886, Capone was diagnosed with syphilis and gonorrhoea. It is presumed that he picked up both of these diseases while working as a bouncer at a brothel in his early twenties. Alongside the effects of cocaine withdrawal, the onset of neurosyphilis led to Capone becoming increasingly reliant on his cellmate, Red Rudinsky, to protect him from other inmates.

Having secured unlimited access to the prison Warden, rumours of 'special treatment' soon began to emerge. To ensure that Capone was unable to manipulate the system any further, he therefore became one of the first inmates to be sent to Alcatraz in August 1934.

MAY

5

1260

Kublai Khan was declared Emperor of the Mongolian Empire.

A grandson of Genghis Khan, Kublai reigned for 34 years. He established the Yuan dynasty that was the first non-Han dynasty to control the whole of China. This is significant, because the Mongols were traditionally a nomadic tribe who ruled by the sword rather than diplomacy.

The area governed by Kublai Khan was enormous. It swept from the Pacific Ocean in the east to the Black Sea in the west, and from Afghanistan in the south to Siberia in the north. Historian John Man, who wrote a well-regarded biography of Kublai, estimates that this area was approximately one fifth of the entire world's populated area.

Having had little experience of political government, Kublai Khan was only able to rule his vast Empire by employing a range of civil servants and foreign administrators. Arguably the most famous of these was the Venetian explorer, Marco Polo, who apparently met and worked for him for a number of years.

Although he was not the first European to visit China, Marco Polo was the first to document life in the Empire in any great detail. He is also the western origin for many accounts of life in China under Kublai Khan. His writings broadly praised Kublai as the model sovereign, but there is debate over whether Polo even visited China. Some suggest that his account was based on tales collected from other travellers he met.

Despite being heralded as a Chinese Emperor, it was Kublai's failure to fully integrate the Mongols into Chinese society that led to the decline of his Yuan dynasty a century later.

MAY

6

1937

The German passenger airship LZ 129 _Hindenburg_ experienced a mid-air explosion at Lakehurst, New Jersey and was engulfed in flames in just 32 seconds.

At the time, the _Hindenburg_ was the fastest and most luxurious way to cross the Atlantic. It had already completed 63 flights from its base in Germany to a range of destinations that went as far as Rio de Janeiro. The airship had also been used as a propaganda tool to support Hitler's remilitarisation of the Rhineland in 1936, and flew over the Berlin Olympics later that year.

The _Hindenburg_ began its maiden transatlantic flight exactly one year before the disaster, on 6 May 1936. By the end of the year it had crossed the Atlantic 34 times, transporting 3,500 passengers and 30,000kg of mail. It was, therefore, a proven and reliable form of transport although high ticket prices placed it out of the reach of most ordinary Germans.

When the _Hindenburg_ arrived at Lakehurst on 6 May 1937, Captain Max Pruss delayed landing due to poor weather conditions. Three hours later he returned to Lakehurst and carried out a swift landing to take advantage of an improvement in the weather. The landing ropes were dropped at 7.21pm, and shortly afterwards the _Hindenburg_ was engulfed by flames.

The most widely accepted explanation for the fire is that the airship was statically charged as a result of flying through the storm. The landing ropes consequently 'earthed' the airship, resulting in a spark that ignited the airship. However, the biggest single reason for the huge fire is simple: the _Hindenburg_ contained 7 million cubic feet of explosive hydrogen gas.

MAY
7
1794

Maximilien Robespierre formally announced the creation of the Cult of the Supreme Being in a meeting of the National Convention.

The Cult of the Supreme Bring had been devised almost exclusively by Robespierre. Its creation followed a period of dramatic de-Christianisation that had seen the French Church stripped of its authority. The Republic had fought hard to remove the influence of the Church from politics, and had even changed the calendar to strip it of all religious connotations.

What made the Cult of the Supreme Being unique as the state religion was that it recognised that God had created the universe, but that he did not interfere or intervene in its operation. Therefore it taught that humans were responsible for their own actions and destinies.

In the words of Robespierre the existence of God and the immortality of the human soul were 'constant reminders' of the virtuous way people should live their lives in the Republic, which echoed some of the Enlightenment thought that had driven the early years of the French Revolution.

On 20 Prairial (8 June 1794), Robespierre ordered a national celebration known as the Festival of the Supreme Being. The most significant celebrations were held in Paris, where a huge man-made papier-mâché mountain was built on the Champs de Mars.

The Festival of the Supreme Being is seen by many as marking the pinnacle of Robespierre's influence on French political life. Within just eight weeks the Thermidorian Reaction had removed him from power and executed him.

MAY

8

1945

A British public holiday was declared to celebrate the end of the Second World War in Europe, known as Victory in Europe Day.

The German army originally only wished to surrender to the Western Allies, and therefore continue to fight against the Soviets. American General Dwight D. Eisenhower refused to accept such terms and insisted on a complete unconditional surrender. Nazi leader Karl Dönitz, who had become *Reichspräsident* after Adolf Hitler committed suicide at the end of April, realised the futility of continuing the war and agreed.

Although the complete unconditional surrender was signed on 7 May in the city of Reims in France, the Soviet Union's representative in the city did not have the authority to accept it. Therefore a second Instrument of Surrender was signed the next day in Berlin by Georgy Zhukov, the Soviet officer who had led the Red Army through Eastern Europe. Because the Berlin surrender was signed after midnight Moscow time, the former Soviet Union celebrates Victory Day on 9 May.

VE Day was declared a public holiday in Britain and was marked with jubilant scenes across the world, much as the end of the First World War had been met with cheers and dancing.

By coincidence 8 May also marks the date when Edward George Honey, an Australian soldier and journalist, first suggested that the end of war should be marked by a period of silence rather than celebration. He made his suggestion in a 1919 letter to the London Evening Standard, making him the first person to suggest the Remembrance Day silence. He asked for 'five little minutes only. Five silent minutes of national remembrance. A very sacred intercession.'

MAY
9
1887

Buffalo Bill Cody's _Wild West Show_ opened in London at the American Exhibition in West Brompton.

This was the first time Buffalo Bill had travelled to Britain, and also marked the first time that many Europeans had seen the fabled 'Cowboys and Indians'.

Over 100 performers travelled from New York aboard the steamship _State of Nebraska_, including members of a range of indigenous tribes who staged a very scripted and stage-friendly version of life on the Great Plains. Alongside the performers were a further 200 animals including horses, buffalo, elk, donkeys and deer and an original Deadwood stagecoach that was used in a scene depicting an attack by hostile tribes.

Alongside such choreographed scenes, the show also included demonstrations of so-called 'cowboy skills' such as the lassoing of galloping animals and sharp-shooting. The famous exhibition shooter Annie Oakley and her husband, Frank E. Butler, both travelled to London with Buffalo Bill and featured heavily in the show. A highlight was the point at which Annie shot a cigar from her husband's mouth.

One of the reasons for the show's success was the early support of Queen Victoria. The Queen, who was celebrating her Golden Jubilee the same year, was present at a command performance two days after the show opened and also went to visit the show again 6 weeks later.

The royal seal of approval was a publicity coup for the show, which went on to play to over two and a half million people before it closed 6 months later.

**Deputy Führer of the German Nazi Party, Rudolf Hess, flew
from Germany to Scotland on a mission to strike a peace deal
with the British government.**

In preparation for his mission Hess had learned how to fly a 2-
seater Messerschmitt Bf 110 under the guidance of Wilhelm Stör, the
chief test pilot at Messerschmitt. Hess took off in his specially
adapted plane off from the airfield at Augsburg-Haunstetten.
Travelling solo, and navigating by spotting landmarks on the ground,
he reached the north-east coast of England at around 9pm.

Continuing in the air for another two hours, Hess parachuted
out of his plane a total of six hours after departing Germany. He
landed twelve miles away from his intended destination of Dungavel
House, the home of the aviator Douglas Douglas-Hamilton, the
Duke of Hamilton, with whom he hoped to open peace negotiations.

Hess' arrival in Britain was not met with the enthusiasm he had
hoped. He was discovered by a ploughman working in a nearby field
and soon found himself in custody.

Other than a couple of close confidantes nobody – not even
Hitler himself – knew what Hess had planned. On finding out about
Hess' actions, Hitler is said to have taken the mission as a personal
betrayal. He signed a secret order that Hess be shot on sight if he
ever returned.

Hess was held in Britain until the end of the war, after which he
was found guilty of crimes against peace at the Nuremberg War
Trials. He was sentenced to life imprisonment at Spandau Prison in
Berlin. When he died in 1987 he had been the prison's only inmate
for 21 years.

MAY

11

1997

The IBM computer Deep Blue beat Garry Kasparov 3½-2½ over six matches to become the first computer to defeat a reigning world chess champion under tournament conditions.

Deep Blue began life as a graduate research project at Carnegie Mellon University in Pittsburgh, Pennsylvania. Developed over eight years by a team of eight computer scientists, it operated through brute force computing power. Ranked as the 259th most powerful computer in the world, Deep Blue was able to evaluate 200 million separate chess positions per second.

The Deep Blue team used records of Kasparov's previous games to program the computer with his known strategies. The programmers were also allowed to adapt the computer's algorithm between rounds to take account of the last game. Kasparov, meanwhile, was playing blind since this model of Deep Blue hadn't played any previous tournament games.

Kasparov was unnerved by the behaviour of Deep Blue in the first match. Although the computer lost the match, Kasparov believed that it had shown 'superior intelligence' when it sacrificed a playing piece. IBM later claimed that the sacrifice was a result of a bug in the software that resulted in the computer playing a fall-back move.

The illogical move in the first game unsettled Kasparov and put him at a psychological disadvantage for the remaining games of the tournament. He refused to accept the defeat and accused IBM of human intervention. The company strenuously denied the accusation but consistently refused his requests for a rematch.

The Soviet Union ended its blockade of West Berlin.

Instigated on 24 June the previous year, the Soviet blockade prevented all rail, road, and water transport between Berlin and the West of the Germany.

Germany had been divided into four parts at the end of the Second World War. Britain, France, the USA and the USSR each administered one area. Buried deep inside the Soviet-controlled zone, the city of Berlin was also divided into four sectors that were controlled by the four powers. It was to the area controlled by the West that the USSR blocked access.

Faced with the possibility of all-out war if they forced their way through the blockade on the ground, the United States opted to make use of the three air corridors that provided unrestricted access to small airfields in Berlin. The USSR knew it risked war if it shot down any aircraft, and was therefore powerless to stop them. Launched four days after the blockade, the Berlin Airlift went on to see over 200,000 individual flights transport up to 8,500 tons of supplies each day.

The pilots and ground crews quickly settled into an efficient rhythm of loading, transporting and unloading. An unusually short winter also helped to keep the airlift running. By the spring of 1949 it was clear that the Western powers had achieved the impossible by supplying West Berlin by air alone.

On 15 April the USSR expressed a willingness to end the blockade and, after a period of negotiation, it was lifted at one minute past midnight on 12 May 1949. Although the blockade was over the Cold War had just begun.

MAY
13
1787

The eleven ships of the 'First Fleet' set sail under Captain Arthur Phillip from Portsmouth, England, to establish a penal colony in Australia.

The ships carried officers, crew, marines and their families in addition to over 1,000 convicts who had been sentenced to transportation.

It took 252 days for the six convict ships, three store ships, and two Royal Navy escort ships to complete the journey. The route involved the fleet sailing first from Portsmouth to Tenerife, and then to Rio de Janeiro.

In Rio the crews restocked their ships' provisions of food and fresh water, and took livestock on board to allow them to establish the new settlement. They then sailed via Cape Town to Australia. This route ensured optimal usage of the prevailing winds to speed up the journey.

Despite the lengthy voyage and numerous dangers on the journey, the entire fleet of eleven ships arrived safely in Botany Bay. Captain Phillip went ashore to investigate Captain Cook's proposed site for the penal colony. He instead chose to find a different location because the soil was poor quality and there was limited access to fresh water. After six days of exploration he moved the fleet a few kilometres north to Sydney Cove. The British flag was raised to mark the site of the new settlement.

Forty-eight people had died during the journey, but over 1,400 members of the First Fleet survived. They established the first European outpost in Australia on 26 January 1788, the date which still marks Australia Day.

English physician and scientist Edward Jenner purposefully infected 8-year James Phipps with cowpox in order to test the process of vaccination.

Rather than committing an act of gross medical negligence Jenner was scientifically testing, and proving, that infection with the mild disease of cowpox gave immunity to the more dangerous smallpox disease.

By modern estimates smallpox was killing up to 400,000 people a year across Europe by the end of the 18th Century. It is also known to have devastated the leaders of the royal families of Austria, Spain, Russia, Sweden and France. Attempts to reduce the impact of the disease were already well established.

The process of smallpox inoculation, also known as variolation, involved purposely infecting a person with the smallpox disease using fluid from pustules on an already-affected patient. Although this was less risky than contracting the disease naturally, it was still a dangerous process. Therefore the ability to prevent smallpox using a safer alternative was highly desirable.

Jenner's process was a medical revolution, although contrary to popular belief he was not the first person to link cowpox infection to smallpox immunity. For example Dr John Fewsty had presented a paper called 'Cowpox and its ability to prevent smallpox' to the Medical Society of London in 1765, 31 years before Jenner's experiment. However, Fewsty never published his paper, and did not carry out any experiments to prove the connection.

Jenner conducted, recorded, and published a methodical scientific process it is he that is credited with the discovery of vaccination.

MAY

15

1928

The first animated cartoon to feature Mickey and Minnie Mouse was shown to a theatre audience.

The cartoon that was shown that day was not *Steamboat Willie*, which is the cartoon most people know as Mickey Mouse's debut. Mickey's first animated appearance was in a silent short called *Plane Crazy*, but the cartoon failed to secure a distributor until a soundtrack was added a year later. It was finally released on 29 March 1929, 11 months after its first silent showing. This made it the fourth Mickey Mouse cartoon to be released to the public.

The Mickey shown in *Plane Crazy* is nothing like the mouse we know today. Whereas the modern Mickey is caring and compassionate, in *Plane Crazy* he was rather mischievous and cruel. In his first appearance he was aggressive towards Minnie, and took dangerous risks when flying the aeroplane that is central to the storyline.

Mickey was also visually different as he didn't wear his famous gloves or shoes. These developments came much later, and demonstrate how rough the original ideas for Mickey Mouse really were.

Although it was an underwhelming first appearance for Mickey, *Plane Crazy* was an important release for the Disney studio. Animated almost exclusively by Walt Disney's trusted friend Ub Iwerks, the cartoon featured a range of highly developed techniques including the very first animated 'point of view' sequence and a range of sophisticated perspectives. Although it has since been overshadowed by the enormous success of *Steamboat Willie*, *Plane Crazy* is still a vitally important part of animation history.

16

1966

The 'May 16th Notification' effectively started the Cultural Revolution in China.

The notification suggested that the Communist Party had been infiltrated by enemies of communism, and that only Mao Zedong's leadership could remove the traitors.

Senior party officials were not exempt from the purges and violence of the Cultural Revolution, although the greatest suffering occurred within the greater population at the hands of fanatical Red Guards. These were groups of Communist Party members, many of whom were still at school.

The Red Guards were determined to rid China of the so-called 'Four Olds' – old customs, old culture, old habits, and old ideas. Spurred on by Mao's desire for a 'great disorder', the Red Guards shut down and sometimes looted religious buildings, burned books, destroyed historical sites, and even desecrated the grave of Confucius.

If the Red Guards needed a guide it came in the form of the Little Red Book, a collection of quotes from Mao of which 350 million copies had been printed by December 1967. However, the Red Guards often interpreted the words to suggest the most extreme actions that included public humiliation, torture, and even murder.

By the time the Cultural Revolution ended in 1976 an estimated minimum of 400,000 people had died through torture, execution, or suicide. However, the number is likely to be much higher. In 1981, the Communist Party itself declared that the Cultural Revolution had 'brought serious disaster and turmoil to the Communist Party and the Chinese people'.

An ancient analogue computer known as the Antikythera mechanism was first identified by Greek archaeologist Valerios Stais.

Although Stais didn't discover the mechanism, he was the first to notice inscriptions and a gear wheel embedded in a lump of corroded bronze and wood brought up from an ancient Greek wreck. The wreck itself had been discovered in 1900 by a team of sponge divers, and archaeologists had focused on other more obvious artefacts found at the site such as bronze and marble statues that helped to date the find. What is known as the world's oldest computer had therefore been in plain view for two years before anyone realised what it was.

Nobody in 1900 would have expected to find anything like the mechanism, and even modern scientists are still working to uncover its secrets. What is known is that the clockwork computer uses a system of bronze gears to calculate astronomical phenomena such as eclipses, and the cycle of forthcoming Olympic Games.

The level of complexity identified in the early 1900s led many people who studied the mechanism to declare that it could not be from the time of the other ancient finds from the wreck. Interest in the mechanism therefore waned again, and serious research didn't begin until the 1970s.

It is generally accepted that astronomical clocks of similar complexity didn't fully emerge until the 14th Century. If the mechanism is accepted as being a contemporary of the wreck, this explains the words Cardiff University professor Michael Edmunds describing it as 'just extraordinary, the only thing of its kind'.

MAY

18

1291

The Crusader-controlled city of Acre was seized by the Muslim forces of the Mamluk Sultan Al-Ashraf Khalil.

Acre had been under Christian control since it was besieged in 1191 during the Third Crusade, and had quickly become the capital of the Kingdom of Jerusalem. With the rise of the Mamluk Sultanate in nearby Egypt in 1250, Crusader holdings became targets for conquest.

The spark for the attack on Acre was the suspected killing of a Muslim for an affair with the wife of a Christian. This coincided with the arrival of over 1,600 poorly disciplined Italian reinforcements for the city, who allegedly pillaged nearby towns for supplies and killed a number of Muslims in the process.

These killings were cited by the Mamluks as reason to cancel a ten-year truce they had signed with the Crusaders. Having amassed an army of many thousands, Sultan Khalil began the siege on 5 April and within less than a month his forces had reached the city walls and begun to mine out the base of the walls and defensive towers.

The walls began to collapse on 8 May and a few days later the full infantry attack on the city began. By nightfall on 18 May the Christians had been defeated, their leaders having either fled by boat or been killed in the fighting.

The Siege of Acre, sometimes known in Christendom as the Fall of Acre, marked the last attempt to exert Crusader influence in the Holy Land. Although the Crusaders continued to hold a fortress in the city of Tartus in modern north-western Syria, Papal attempts to mount further attempts to regain the Holy Land gathered little support.

MAY

19

1536

Anne Boleyn, Henry VIII's second wife and mother of the future Elizabeth I, was beheaded in the Tower of London.

Anne was arrested on 2 May 1536 and taken to the Tower of London having been charged with adultery, treason, and incest. Her trial began on 15 May.

Some historians believe that Anne's involvement in court politics led the influential Thomas Cromwell to engineer her downfall. Meanwhile, other historians point to the problem of her not having bourn the king a male heir. A series of miscarriages in the months prior to her arrest suggested she wouldn't do so in the future. The lack of a son from his first wife, Catherine of Aragon, had originally driven Henry to find a new wife. Anne therefore found herself in a precarious situation. She gave birth to a stillborn son in January 1536 and soon afterwards Henry took Jane Seymour, one of Anne's ladies-in-waiting, as a mistress.

Although found unanimously guilty by a jury of 27 peers, the evidence against Anne was questionable. Only the Flemish musician Mark Smeaton admitted to having an affair with her, and this confession is reputed to have been extracted under torture.

Because she was the Queen the Treason Act of 1351 meant that her infidelity was treasonous. The punishment for a woman was burning alive, but Henry commuted it to beheading and had an expert French swordsman brought over to carry out the execution with a single stroke.

Anne maintained her innocence to the end. She was buried in an unmarked grave, but the site was identified in 1876 and is now marked with a marble slab.

MAY

20

1873

Levi Strauss and Jacob Davis secured the patent for riveted blue jeans.

Strauss was a German-born businessman who sold fabric on the West Coast of the USA, and Davis was a Latvian-Jewish immigrant tailor working in Nevada. Their relationship began as supplier and customer since Davis used to buy fabric from Strauss's warehouse to manufacture garments.

Davis came up with the idea of reinforcing the stress points of garments with rivets after the wife of a woodcutter asked if he could make a pair of durable trousers for her husband. The rivets strengthened the jeans, reducing the likelihood of tearing and making them perfect for manual labour.

Realising that his idea had enormous potential, Davis wanted to patent it. He approached Strauss with a business proposal whereby Strauss would finance the paperwork and the two men would share the patent. Strauss agreed and patent 139,121 was granted on 20 May 1873. In return Davis became the production manager for Levi Strauss & Co.

Marketed as 'waist overalls' at the time, the term 'jeans' didn't become commonly associated with the finished product until the 1920s. However, the product proved to be an enormous success and led the company to open their first dedicated factory less than a decade later.

Just a few months after securing the patent for copper riveted jeans Davis came up with another idea that continues to be an identifying feature of Levi jeans – the double orange thread design on the back pocket.

MAY
21
1927

Charles Lindbergh became the first person to make a solo non-stop flight across the Atlantic. Exactly five years later, Emilia Earhart became the first woman to fly solo across the Atlantic.

Lindbergh flew 3,600 miles from New York to Paris in *The Spirit of St Louis*. The journey earned him not only enormous fame but also the $25,000 Orteig Prize that had been offered by a French-born New York hotelier to the first person to make a non-stop flight between New York and Paris.

Earhart's flight from Harbour Grace, Newfoundland took her as far as Northern Ireland. She was forced to abandon her intended destination of Paris due to technical difficulties and landed in a pasture at Culmore, north of Derry. Earhart was met by farmhand Dan McCallion who asked if she had flown far. She reportedly replied, 'From America.'

Earhart later stated that she made the flight to prove that women were just as good as men in 'jobs requiring intelligence, coordination, speed, coolness, and willpower'. She already held the record as the first woman to fly across the Atlantic, but she did that as a passenger in 1928.

The very first non-stop transatlantic flight had occurred in 1919. Two British aviators, John Alcock and Arthur Whiten Brown, flew a modified Vickers Vimy bomber aircraft from Newfoundland to Ireland in just under 16 hours. Their achievement won them the £10,000 *Daily Mail* aviation prize for the first non-stop flight across the Atlantic. Their prize was presented to them by the then Secretary of State for Air, and future British Prime Minister, Winston Churchill.

MAY

22

1455

The Wars of the Roses began at the First Battle of St Albans which was fought between Richard, Duke of York, and King Henry VI.

The Wars of the Roses were fought between the Houses of Lancaster and York, both of whom had claims to the English throne. Although the Lancastrians had ruled England since 1399, Henry VI had come to the throne in 1422 when he was just 9 months old. England had therefore been ruled by regents for 15 years, during which time the monarchy was weakened.

The situation didn't improve after Henry took full control of the country in 1437, since he experienced periods of mental illness and instability that affected his behaviour and decisions. Having experienced a long period of mental instability from August 1453 the 'kingmaker' Richard Neville, Earl of Warwick, made Richard, Duke of York, protector of the realm.

When Henry recovered 18 months later, Richard was excluded from the royal court. In response he led an army to London, but encountered the King's forces 22 miles north of the city in St Albans. After many hours of failed negotiations between the two sides Richard ordered his troops to attack. The battle was fought in the streets, lanes and gardens of St Albans and lasted for less than an hour before the Lancastrians were outflanked by the Yorkists who stormed the market square and killed a number of key Lancastrian nobles.

Henry was taken prisoner and was escorted back to London where Richard was declared Protector of England just a few months later. The Wars of the Roses raged for another three decades.

MAY

23

1915

Italy entered the First World War on the side of the Triple Entente and declared war on Austria-Hungary.

Under the terms of the previously-formed Triple Alliance, Italy was Austria-Hungary's ally. However, Italy was well within its rights not to provide military assistance to Germany and Austria-Hungary at the outbreak of the war as the alliance was entirely defensive. Austria-Hungary had been the one to instigated hostilities against Serbia, and so Italy argued that the alliance was void.

The Italian government remained neutral for the first nine months of the war. Behind the scenes, however, Prime Minister Antonio Salandra and his minister of Foreign Affairs, Sidney Sonnino, were investigating which side would be the best to join.

In a secret agreement signed on 26 April in London, Italy agreed to leave the Triple Alliance, join the forces of the Triple Entente, and declare war on Austria-Hungary and Germany. The agreement stated that, assuming they won, Italy would receive large areas of territory from the Central Powers. This would include the predominantly Italian-populated areas of Austria-Hungary around the Adriatic Sea.

Italy duly entered the war and began hostilities against Austria-Hungary. They outnumbered their enemy almost 3-to-1, but constantly struggled to gain the upper hand against the Austro-Hungarians.

Despite their struggles, the Italians emerged on the victorious side and Premier Vittorio Emanuele Orlando represented Italy at the Paris Peace Conference. However, the offers of land were not as much as Italy had been led to expect and so he left the Conference in a boycott.

MAY

24

1956

The first Eurovision Song Contest took place in Lugano, Switzerland.

The Eurovision Song Contest has become one of the most watched non-sporting events in the world, but emerged from humble beginnings. The original idea for the contest came from Marcel Bezençon, the chairman of the European Broadcasting Union, at a meeting in Monaco in 1955. Founded in 1950, the EBU was looking for a way to bring the countries of Europe together after the devastation and division of the Second World War. However, of the 23 member countries at the time, only seven countries chose to participate in the first Eurovision competition and only three more opted to broadcast the show.

Demonstrating just how far communication technology has come since those early days, it's worth noting that the first Eurovision Song Contest took place over a year before Sputnik, the first artificial satellite, was put into orbit. The first competitions were therefore relayed across Europe using a terrestrial microwave network that linked the countries of Europe together like an invisible spider's web.

Although the contest is now as much about geopolitics as music, the geography of Eurovision is intriguing. Countries do not have to be within the continent of Europe to be eligible to enter, nor do they need to be members of the European Union. Eligibility is based on the European Broadcasting Area which, even more confusingly, covers an area extending into North Africa and the Middle East. This helps to explain the regular appearance of Israel, and also the appearance of Morocco in 1980 with an entry that finished second-to-last with just 7 points.

American President John F. Kennedy made the announcement to a joint session of Congress that he had set his sights on a manned moon landing before the end of the decade.

To many people, including some personnel at NASA, Kennedy's address seemed to be pure fantasy. The USA had only sent its first man into space twenty days earlier and, although Alan Shepard's spaceflight aboard Freedom 7 was a huge success, the USSR's Yuri Gagarin had become the first man in space three weeks before that. Taking on the USSR at a technological game that their opponent was already winning appeared reckless.

An underlying issue was that, as part of his election campaign, Kennedy had promised to outperform the Soviet Union in the fields of space exploration and missile defence. In his famed television debate with Richard Nixon, Kennedy had mocked the fact that Nixon had declared his pride that the USA was ahead of the USSR in terms of colour television technology while trailing in terms of rocket thrust.

Gagarin's successful spaceflight had proved to the world that the USSR was 'winning' the Space Race and put pressure on Kennedy to increase spending on the Apollo space program. Having received a memo from Vice-President Lyndon B. Johnson in which he reported that the USA was unlikely to ever outperform the USSR under the current spending arrangements, Kennedy launched the largest peacetime financial commitment ever made.

The $24 billion dollars of investment did work, however, and Apollo 11 achieved Kennedy's goal by landing on the moon on 20 July 1969.

Bram Stoker's Gothic horror novel _Dracula_ was first published.

Although not the first ever vampire novel, _Dracula_ was enormously influential in defining modern ideas of vampires, and for forever associating them with Romania.

Vlad III was the ruler of Wallachia, an area that covered a large part of Romania's current land mass. It was due to Vlad's apparent lust for blood that he was given the epithet 'the Impaler'. However, during his lifetime he also had another, more instantly recognisable name. Vlad III was known as Dracula and many people therefore reported that Stoker based his character on a real historical character, but the evidence does not support this.

Vlad III's father, Vlad II, was a member of the Order of the Dragon, a chivalric order charged with fighting the enemies of Christianity. In the case of the Wallachian ruler, this meant the Turks on his southern border. As a member of the Order of the Dragon, Vlad added the Romanian word for dragon – _dracul_ – to his name, and became known as Vlad Dracul. As son of the dragon, Vlad III was referred to as Vlad Dracul_a_. Importantly, however, the word _dracul_ has a dual meaning in the Romanian language as it also means 'devil'. This made Vlad III the son of the devil.

We know from his notes that Bram Stoker read the 19th Century British Consul William Wilkinson's book about life in Romania, 'Account of the Principalities of Wallachia and Moldavia'. The book made several references to the term Dracula, but Stoker's only interest in the word was that it was associated with people who portrayed devilish or cruel behaviour. It was because of the literal meaning of the word that Stoker took it to name his blood-sucking creation.

MAY

27

1199

King John of England was crowned at Westminster Abbey.

The previous king, John's brother Richard I who is perhaps better known as 'the Lionheart', had died after being shot in the shoulder by a crossbow bolt fired by Betrand de Gurdon during a siege of the castle of Châlus-Chabrol.

John's claim to the throne wasn't entirely clear-cut since Arthur, the son of John's older brother Geoffrey, was another possible heir. His claim was also supported by a large contingent of French nobles, and the French king Philip II himself, who hoped to fragment the Angevin Empire. This laid the foundations for John's ongoing struggles in mainland Europe, which gradually eroded his control over the lands of the Angevin Empire.

The fact that John succeeded in his bid to be crowned was significant. Medieval monarchs got their legal authority from their coronation, where they swore the coronation oath and were then anointed, girted, crowned, invested and enthroned. Although the coronation gave the King the legal authority to rule the country, it was still based on him abiding by the coronation oath. Rebellious barons argued that John failed to do this since, like his predecessors, he sometimes took executive decisions on the basis that the king was above the law. This set in motion calls for a 'law of the land' that was to result in the Magna Carta.

John ruled for seventeen years before contracting dysentery while in Kings Lynn, an illness from which he later died. John's reign had seen him lose control of the Angevin Empire, lose the crown jewels in the mud of East Anglia, and lose significant monarchical power under the terms of the Magna Carta.

MAY

28

1987

An eighteen year-old amateur pilot from Hamburg in West Germany illegally landed a private aircraft near Moscow's Red Square.

Mathias Rust had clocked up only 50 hours of flying time before commencing his journey that took in the Shetland and Faroe Islands, Iceland, Bergen and Helsinki before flying to Moscow.

Rust's flight was an enormous risk for the young pilot. Less than five years earlier a South Korean commercial plane had been shot down after it strayed into Soviet airspace. Rust himself was tracked by three separate surface-to-air missile units, and a total of four fighter planes were sent to monitor him, but none of them were given permission to attack.

Rust approached Moscow in the early evening, and after passing the 'Ring of Steel' anti-aircraft defences continued towards the city centre. Abandoning his idea of landing in the Kremlin, he touched down on a bridge next to St Basil's Cathedral and taxied into Red Square.

Within two hours he had been arrested. He was sentenced to four years in a labour camp for violating international flight rules and illegally entering the Soviet Union, but was released after serving 14 months in jail.

In a 2007 interview, Rust claimed that he hoped his flight would build an 'imaginary bridge' between east and west. What it actually did was cause massive damage to the reputation of the Soviet military for failing to stop him. This in turn led to the largest dismissal of Soviet military personnel since Stalin's purges, and allowed Gorbachev to push ahead with his reforms.

MAY 29 1453

The troops of the Ottoman Empire under Sultan Mehmed II successfully took control of Constantinople, the capital of the Byzantine Empire.

The Ottomans began their siege of the city on 6 April. However, they found that their enormous cannon was unable to break the walls and their ships were unable to cross the defensive chain that protected the Golden Horn. Attempts to dig tunnels and lay mines to blow up the walls also failed because the Byzantines intercepted the tunnels before they were completed.

Despite these setbacks for the Ottomans, the continuing siege slowly weakened the resolve of Constantinople's inhabitants. A Greek legend even says that as the Ottomans began to plan their final offensive on 26 May, the Holy Spirit left the Hagia Sophia under cover of a strange fog that had descended on the city.

Around midnight on the night of 28 and 29 May, the first Ottoman troops attacked the city. Three waves of increasingly experienced troops made only limited progress at first, but when Giustiniani, the commander of the Byzantine troops, was mortally wounded the city's defence quickly began to collapse. A Turkish flag was soon raised over the northern Kerkoporta Gate and the defence crumbled.

Three days of looting followed the capture of the city, although some Greeks managed to escape and move west. The knowledge and ancient documents they took with them helped to fuel the Renaissance. The capture of the city effectively brought the Roman Empire to an end and, for many historians, also marks the end of the medieval period.

Joan of Arc, also known as the Maid of Orleans, was burned at the stake in the French city of Rouen.

Joan was accused of being a witch and a heretic due to the voices she heard and visions she witnessed, but the crime that condemned her to death was that of wearing men's clothing. Joan had worn male military clothing and armour during campaigns against the English army in the Hundred Years War, and this was deemed by the church to be heretical.

During her trial Joan faced seventy charges relating to heresy and witchcraft. These gradually dwindled to twelve but, having been found guilty of these crimes and afraid of immediate execution if she continued to plead innocence, Joan admitted her guilt and also promised to stop wearing men's clothing.

A few days later Joan claimed that the voices had returned to tell her she had made a mistake. Additionally, although she had begun to wear female clothing again in prison, she said that someone had attempted to rape her in her cell and so began to again wear men's clothing to deter further attacks. Combined with the voices she heard, this act was interpreted as a relapse into heresy which made it a capital offence. She was consequently condemned to death by burning.

It is believed by many historians that Joan died of smoke inhalation before the flames fully consumed her. After her death, her remains were burned a further two times to reduce them to ashes which were then scattered in the River Seine. On 7 July 1456, after a retrial authorised by Pope Callixtus III, Joan was declared to have been innocent.

MAY

31

1669

Samuel Pepys wrote the final entry of his famous diary.

Pepys had begun writing his diary in January 1660. Since being published in 1825 it has become an important source for historians studying the period of the Restoration. It is also invaluable for its detailed eyewitness accounts of key events in London's history such as the Great Plague and the Great Fire of London.

Pepys' diary is particularly useful to historians because he meticulously recorded even the smallest and seemingly trivial pieces information in his diary. Pepys' is by far the most complete and detailed record of daily life during the period that exists, and Pepys' frankness – presumably because he never intended for the diary to be published – exposes elements of life that professional memoirs would normally try to ignore. His detailed observations on life have seen him referred to by many as the greatest diarist of all time.

Despite these positive aspects, Pepys' diary is not perfect. In particular it is not reflective of life for the majority of Londoners at the time since he was a member of the upper-middle class and became one of the most celebrated and important civil servants of his time.

Pepys stopped writing his diary due to a fear that constant writing by candlelight was damaging his eyesight. By this time he had written over a million words of shorthand that were bound into six volumes. They are now housed alongside the rest of his 3,000-volume library in Magdalen College, Cambridge, from where he had obtained his Bachelor of Arts degree. Despite his health concerns, Pepys went on to live for another 34 years without developing any eye problems.

JUNE

The Beatles released *Sgt. Pepper's Lonely Hearts Club Band*, their eighth studio album.

The Beatles had declared their retirement from touring on 29 August 1966, after having played to a crowd of 25,000 people at Candlestick Park in San Francisco. The decision to stop performing live gave them the freedom to focus on creating music in the studio that would have been impossible to recreate on tour.

The album made use of a huge range of instruments and studio effects. Together with their producer, George Martin, and audio engineer, Geoff Emerick, the band creatively applied audio compression, limiting, and reverb in entirely new ways. The studio engineers also devised ways to offset the limitations of the studio's four-track recording equipment, enabling a 40-piece orchestra to be recorded after the band had already finished their tracks.

Sgt. Pepper's was the first Beatles album to be released simultaneously worldwide, and it received almost universal praise. Just three days after its release, guitar legend Jimi Hendrix opened a live show in London by performing the title track – something that Paul McCartney regards as one of the greatest honours in his career.

The album won four Grammy Awards following its release and is widely regarded as one of the most influential albums ever recorded. It has since sold in excess of 30 million copies worldwide and regularly features in lists of the world's greatest albums.

As well as being famed for its musical impact, *Sgt. Pepper's* is also highly regarded for its iconic cover art. Designed by pop artists Peter Blake and Jann Haworth, the elaborate cover alone cost £3,000 to produce.

JUNE

2

1946

Italians voted in a referendum to abolish the monarchy and turn their country into a republic.

Italy had emerged from the Second World War as a country torn apart by conflict. The royal family was blamed by many people for allowing the growth and domination of Mussolini's fascist regime, and was therefore also seen as being responsible for Italy's involvement in the war and its subsequent defeat. Even the wartime king, Victor Emmanuel III, had recognised the precarious nature of his position when Mussolini's government collapsed in 1944, and so handed over the responsibilities of head of state to his son, Crown Prince Umberto.

Umberto II formally ascended to the Italian throne in May 1946 but, despite his relative popularity with the Italian population compared to his predecessor, the pro-monarchy campaign was unable to gain sufficient support. The referendum question was simple: Monarchy or Republic? More than 89% of eligible Italian citizens voted in the referendum, with 54.3% voting in favour of a republic.

The results of the referendum demonstrated a very clear split between a generally pro-republican north where two-thirds of the population voted to abolish the monarchy and establish a republic and a pro-monarchist south where two-thirds of the population wanted to keep it.

Umberto II was magnanimous and dignified in defeat. In his final speech to the Italian people he stated that he didn't bear them any ill will, and encouraged them to be loyal to the republic. The monarchy formally ended on 12 June 1946, and Umberto was exiled to Portugal. He died in 1983, having never set foot in Italy again.

The Chinese People's Liberation Army began firing on protesters taking part in the student-led Tiananmen Square protests.

The Tiananmen Square protests began after the death of a deposed liberal reformer within the ruling Communist Party in April. Protesters made their way to the streets to call for government accountability, freedom of the press, freedom of speech, and the restoration of workers' control over industry.

Having initially consisted mainly of university students, the protests soon gained support from the wider population and spread to over 400 cities nationwide. By the end of May, and with no end to the protests in sight, the Chinese Politburo began to consider approving the use of force to disperse the protesters. The final authorisation was given at 4.30pm on 3 June.

When the army began to advance on Tiananmen Square later that evening, thousands of civilians filled the streets to build barricades despite warnings from state-controlled television to stay inside. At around 10pm, while still approximately 10km from Tiananmen Square itself, the army first used live ammunition on the crowds.

The army continued its advance towards the square throughout the night, arriving shortly after midnight. Although some students hurled projectiles at the soldiers, the vast majority maintained a peaceful protest. The army continued its advance and eventually forced the students to retreat from the square.

Official figures reported 241 deaths but unofficial estimates, including one by the US Ambassador at the time, place the figure at more than twice that.

JUNE

4

1913

Suffragette Emily Wilding Davison was hit by King George V's racehorse at the Epsom Derby after she stepped onto the track.

Davison joined the Women's Social and Political Union in 1906, and soon began to take part in their militant and confrontational activities that were designed to win the right to vote for women. She developed a reputation as a particularly violent campaigner and was imprisoned nine times for various illegal activities. During her prison sentences she went on hunger strike, and so was subjected to force-feeding by the prison authorities.

The Epsom Derby is a highlight of the British horseracing calendar, and historians agree that Davison wanted to use the event to draw attention to the women's suffrage movement. Newsreel footage of the event taken from different angles shows her ducking under the barrier and running onto the track as the horses raced past her.

Davison appeared to try to grab the bridle of one of the last horses – which happened to be King George V's horse, Anmer – but was violently thrown to the ground by the force of the impact and was trampled by the horse's hooves. She died four days later from a fractured skull and other internal injuries.

The majority of commentators hold the view that Davison did not intend to martyr herself, but rather wished to attach a 'Votes For Women' scarf to the horse as a way to gain publicity for the movement. Various pieces of evidence support this view, including the return portion of a train ticket found in her purse. However, she did not share her plan with anyone so her true intentions will never be known.

JUNE

5

1967

Israel launched a series of pre-emptive strikes against the Egyptian air force that marked the start of the Six Day War.

The causes of Six Day War are highly contested, with historians apportioning responsibility for the war in different ways. There is no doubt, however, that tensions in the Middle East had been steadily increasing since the 1948 Arab-Israeli War. Egypt then expelled United Nations peacekeepers from the Sinai Peninsula in May 1967, increased the Egyptian military presence, and blocked Israeli access to the Gulf of Aqaba in the Red Sea. This led Israel to begin to prepare for war.

The Israeli airstrike at the beginning of the conflict destroyed around 90% of the Egyptian air force. Having also destroyed the Syrian air force, Israel's air superiority allowed it to achieve staggering victories on the ground that included the seizure of the Gaza Strip and the entire Sinai Peninsula up to the eastern bank of the Suez Canal within just three days.

When King Hussein of Jordan joined the war and began shelling Israeli strongholds, an Israeli counterattack soon forced the Jordanian army out of East Jerusalem and most of the West Bank. Similarly, Syrian shelling of northern Israel was met with an Israeli attack that took control of the Golan Heights.

By the time a final ceasefire was signed on 10 June, the Arabs had suffered approximately 18,000 casualties whereas Israel had only 700. Israel's territorial gains also put around a million Arabs under Israeli control which signalled the start of a new phase in Arab-Israeli relations.

JUNE

6

1944

The Allied forces of the Second World War launched Operation Neptune, more commonly known as the D-Day landings.

The amphibious landings in Normandy are still the largest seaborne invasion ever to be staged, and marked the start of the Allied invasion of Nazi-held Western Europe.

The invasion was focused on a 50-mile stretch of Normandy coastline that had been divided into five codenamed sections known as Utah, Omaha, Gold, Juno and Sword beaches. German Field Marshall Erwin Rommel, nicknamed the Desert Fox for his leadership of Italian and German forces in the North African campaign, commanded the Nazi defence along what was known as the Atlantic Wall.

Prior to the landings, an airborne force of 24,000 Allied troops had been dropped behind enemy lines to seize or destroy features such as bridges, crossroads and key gun batteries. Despite this, the work of the first seaborne divisions was still difficult as they fought to clear the beaches under heavy fire from the numerous smaller gun emplacements that overlooked them. Rommel had previously identified the Normandy beaches as a possible invasion point and so had installed a range of obstacles such as wooden stakes, metal tripods, mines, and anti-tank devices that slowed down the Allied landing.

The Allies failed to achieve all their objectives on the first day and suffered at least 10,000 casualties. However, they did successfully establish a foothold on the continent. They expanded these gains over the next few months, leading to the liberation of France and the defeat of the Nazis in the west.

JUNE

7

1628

The Petition of Right was approved by King Charles I.

The Petition of Right is a major British constitutional document that recognises four key principles of government: no taxation without the consent of Parliament, no imprisonment without cause, no quartering of soldiers on subjects, and no martial law in peacetime. It is still in force today.

A major reason for the Petition of Right was that Charles firmly believed in divine right – the idea that God had chosen him to rule. This encouraged him to rule by Royal Prerogative, meaning he tried to govern without consulting parliament.

Parliament began to believe that Charles was overreaching his authority, especially after he began gathering 'forced loans' from his subjects and imprisoning anyone who refused to pay. MPs were angered by Charles taking money from his subjects without Parliamentary approval, and by imprisonment without trial that undermined Magna Carta and *habeas corpus*.

What was most notable about the passage of the Petition of Right was that both the House of Commons and the House of Lords, which had traditionally supported the monarchy, had approved it. Despite this, Charles was initially unwilling to ratify it and even sent a message to the Commons 'forbidding them to meddle with affairs of state'.

When it became clear that Parliament would not back down, Charles finally relented and ratified the Petition on 7 June. However he continued to govern the country in much the same way as before, setting in place a major factor for the outbreak of the English Civil War that broke out less than fifteen years later.

JUNE

8

1972

One of the most iconic photographs of the Vietnam War was taken of Phan Thi Kim Phúc, a nine year old girl from the South Vietnamese village of Trang Bang.

In the photograph, Kim Phúc is shown running away from a napalm attack, having stripped off her clothes after being severely burned. The photograph, which went on to win a Pulitzer Prize, was taken by Nick Ut, a Vietnamese photographer for the Associated Press. He was one of number of press photographers who were with the group of fleeing civilians after the village had been bombed South Vietnamese planes.

Ut took Kim Phúc and other injured children to a hospital in Saigon before delivering the film to be developed. He maintained contact with her throughout her recovery despite being told that her burns were so severe she was unlikely to survive.

The photograph was initially rejected by Associated Press due to the full-frontal nudity. However, the image was deemed to capture such a powerful news story that these concerns were put aside. When the picture appeared on the front page of the *New York Times* four days later, it had such a dramatic impact that President Nixon discussed with his chief of staff whether the shot had been 'fixed'.

Kim Phúc stayed in hospital for fourteen months and underwent seventeen surgical procedures and skin transplants before she was able to return home. Against the expectations of the doctors she survived and, having sought political asylum in Canada during an aircraft refuelling stop on her honeymoon, she now lives in Ontario where she runs a charitable foundation that provides medical and psychological assistance to child victims of war.

The 'Final Act' of the Congress of Vienna was signed, nine days before Napoleon's final defeat at the Battle of Waterloo.

The Congress was chaired by Metternich, the Austrian principal minister, and led by the 'Four Great Powers' of Austria, Russia, Britain, and Prussia alongside France. In total over 200 states were represented in some way at the Congress, making it the largest diplomatic event of its time. However, the key terms were discussed and decided by the Great Powers in informal meetings.

The Congress met with the purpose of reviewing and reorganising Europe after the Napoleonic Wars. By doing this, the Great Powers hoped to achieve a lasting peace. Having first met after the defeat and surrender of Napoleonic France in 1814, the meetings continued in spite of the renewal of hostilities following the period known as the Hundred Days in which Napoleon returned from exile and took back control of France.

The Final Act of the Congress set in place a map of Europe that remained largely unchanged for the next forty years, and which laid the foundations for the First World War. Historians and politicians in the later 19th Century even criticised the attendees for focusing more on achieving a balance of power than on maintaining peace.

The Final Settlement largely ignored the emerging nationalist sentiments in parts of Europe, and this exclusion was particularly heavily criticised by later commentators. Although nationalist movements were a key factor in the disputes and conflicts that emerged later, it's important to remember that the Congress did succeed in its primary aim of securing wider European peace for the best part of a century.

JUNE

10

1916

The Arab Revolt began when Grand Sharif Hussein bin Ali, the guardian of the holy city of Mecca, ordered his troops to attack the Ottoman Caliphate's garrison in the city.

Through correspondence with Sir Henry McMahon, the British High Commissioner of Egypt at the time, Sharif Hussein had become convinced that a revolt by the tribes of the Arabian Peninsula would be rewarded with an independent Arabian empire stretching through the Middle East.

Hussein's troops, drawn from his own tribe, significantly outnumbered the Ottoman soldiers but were considerably less well equipped. Consequently, despite impressive initial gains, Hussein was unable to win the battle until Egyptian troops sent by the British arrived to provide artillery support. The British supported the Revolt as it distracted tens of thousands of Ottoman troops from joining other fronts in the First World War.

Captain T. E. Lawrence, known as Lawrence of Arabia following his involvement in the Revolt, did not join with the Arab forces until October 1916. Although he was just one of many British and French officers who worked closely with the Arabs during the Revolt, newspaper reports of his guerrilla tactics and close relationship with Hussein's sons Faisal and Abdullah earned him fame.

The Revolt was an enormous success, but the outcome was not what was agreed in the Hussein-McMahon Correspondence. The British and French instead divided the land according to the secret Sykes-Picot Agreement that they had negotiated between themselves in 1916. Hussein was given the Hejaz region in the Arabian Peninsula, but was driven out in 1925 by Ibn Saud.

JUNE

11

1837

The Broad Street Riot broke out in Boston, Massachusetts, between Irish immigrants and existing American citizens known as Yankees.

Due to its large seaport Boston was a key location for immigrant arrivals to America. It was a particular focal point for Irish immigrants who began arriving in large numbers from the second part of the 18th Century. Tensions between the new Catholic immigrants and the existing Protestant American citizens grew during this time.

The violence that led to the Broad Street Riot began when a company of firefighters returning to their fire station met a large group of Irish people taking part making their way to a funeral procession. The firefighters had spent some time in a nearby saloon and one of them, a nineteen year old called George Fay, either insulted or pushed some of the mourners.

The two sides began to fight in the street but, being outnumbered, the firemen were ordered to return to their station. It was there that their foreman, W. W. Miller, issued an emergency alarm that called all Boston firefighters to come and help.

The violence grew to involve around 1000 people on both sides who also broke into houses and destroyed property. Fortunately, despite the fierce street-fighting, nobody was killed before the military arrived to put an end to the carnage three hours after it began.

Despite the evident underlying racial tensions, immigrants continued to arrive in Boston. The number of Irish arrivals reached a peak during the catastrophic Potato Famine of 1845 to 1852.

JUNE

12

1942

Anne Frank received a diary as a thirteenth birthday present from her father.

The Frank family originated in Frankfurt, Germany, but moved away after the Nazi party won local elections in 1933. Anne's father, Otto, was a businessman who chose to move the family to Amsterdam after receiving an offer to start a company there. Consequently, when the German army invaded the Netherlands in 1940, the family found themselves once again trapped in a country subjected to anti-Semitic laws.

In July 1942, barely three weeks after Anne's 13th birthday, Anne's older sister Margot was ordered by the Nazi authorities to go to a labour camp. Their father instead arranged for the family to go into hiding in a so-called 'Secret Annexe' above his office building.

It was in the Secret Annexe that Anne wrote her diary, which she addressed as Kitty. Over three volumes she recorded the relationships between the Frank family, the Van Pels family, and her father's friend Fritz Pfeffer with whom they shared their confined hiding place.

An anonymous tip-off led to the discovery and arrest of the eight inhabitants on 4 August 1944. They were deported to the Auschwitz concentration camp a month later. Anne died of typhus in early 1945 after being transferred to Bergen-Belsen when she was fifteen years old.

Anne's diary, which chronicled her experiences over the two years she spent in the Secret Annexe, was published posthumously after the war under the title *The Diary of a Young Girl* and became one of the 20th Century's most celebrated books.

JUNE

13

1944

The first German attack on Britain using the V-1 flying bomb, otherwise known as the 'doodlebug', took place.

The V-1 was powered by the Argus As 014 pulsejet engine, the first mass-produced engine of its type. The noisy operation of the engine led to the bomb earning its nickname as a 'buzz bomb' or 'doodlebug'.

The pulsejet engine was simple and cheap to build and, combined with a simple fuselage of welded steel sheets and wings made of plywood, the V-1 could be produced and operated at a fraction of the cost of other bombing methods.

The bomb was specifically designed for terror bombing civilians, since its launch and autopilot system was able to identify a general target area but not hit a specific point. The very first V-1 exploded near a railway bridge in Mile End, London, killing eight civilians.

Each launch site on the French and Dutch coasts could launch up to eighteen V-1s a day, but that figure was rarely met. Furthermore due to mechanical problems, guidance system failures, and an effective system of air defences, only an estimated 25% of all V-1s hit their intended target. Within just two months of the first launch more than half of all V-1s were being intercepted. However, the V-1 was still a highly effective weapon that caused significant damage to Britain and intimidated the civilian population.

The successful Allied advance after D-Day succeeded in disabling all the launch sites on the French coast by September. This removed the threat of further attacks on Allied civilians and contributed greatly to improved morale.

JUNE

14

1777

The Second Continental Congress passed the Flag Resolution and adopted the Stars and Stripes as the official flag of the United States.

The Flag Resolution stated some general parameters for the appearance of the flag. Specifically it said that there should be thirteen alternate red and white stripes and a group of white stars against a blue background. However, it didn't specify a precise arrangement. Consequently a range of different designs, all of which met the definition, were produced. Of these, the so-called Betsy Ross flag which has the stars arranged in a circle is probably the most famous early version.

The design of the flag has changed numerous times during its history to reflect the admission of more states into the Union. In 1818 Congress attempted to bring some uniformity through the Flag Act which specified there should always be thirteen stripes to represent the original thirteen colonies that broke away from British rule, and the same number of stars as states. The 50 stars on the current flag first appeared after Hawaii joined the United States in 1959.

The flag about which the national anthem, *The Star Spangled Banner*, was written is therefore not the same design as the one in use today. That was instead a 15-star, 15-stripe flag flown at Fort McHenry in Baltimore Harbour during a bombardment by British Royal Navy ships in the War of 1812. The remains of this flag are now housed in the National Museum of American History.

The day that the Flag Resolution was passed is celebrated as Flag Day. It was proclaimed by President Woodrow Wilson in 1916, but is not an official federal holiday.

Magna Carta, one of the most famous documents in the world, was approved by King John when he added his seal to it in a field at Runnymede near Windsor in England.

Magna Carta, which is Latin for 'the Great Charter', confirmed the principle that everyone including the king was subject to the law of the land. It also gave all free men the right to justice and a fair trial. This sounds progressive, but the reality is that at the time many people in England were *not* free men – they were villeins who could only seek justice from their lord.

Although many people celebrate the advancements brought about by the 1215 Magna Carta, it ultimately failed to solve the dispute between John and some of his barons. Just ten weeks later Magna Carta was declared 'null and void of all validity for ever' by Pope Innocent III in a papal bull.

The Pope's declaration led to the First Barons War, a civil war that erupted in September and that was still being fought when John died of dysentery a year later. The war didn't end until 1217, by which time the majority of the barons had changed sides to join John's son, the nine year old Henry III.

Magna Carta was reissued many more times by subsequent monarchs, and the 1225 version was finally entered onto the statute roll in 1297. Although almost all of the clauses were repealed or superseded in the 18th and 19th Centuries, Magna Carta is still regarded as a symbol of individual freedom against despotic rulers. Four copies of the original document still exist, and these were brought together for a special exhibition at the British Museum to mark its 800th anniversary.

Hungarian Communist politician Imre Nagy was executed.

Nagy had been sacked from his position as Chairman of the Council of Ministers in April 1955 due to favouring what was referred to as a 'New Course' in socialism. Although his moderate reforms were met with hostility from the USSR, they garnered significant support within Hungary where opposition to the hard-line government of Mátyás Rákosi had grown since the death of Stalin in 1953. Nagy's popular support led to him being appointed Prime Minister on 24 October 1956, the day after the Hungarian Uprising began.

After a week of violence, Nagy recognised the crowd's desire for political change. Despite being an ardent Marxist he began moves towards introducing a multiparty political system and, on 1 November, announced Hungary's withdrawal from the Warsaw Pact and its status as a neutral country. This proved too much for Khrushchev in the USSR, who moved his troops into Budapest and seized control of most of the city by the 8 November.

Nagy took refuge in the Yugoslavian embassy, but was arrested after being given false promises of safe passage to leave Hungary on 22 November. He, and other leading members of the deposed government, were imprisoned in Romania until 1958 when they were returned to Hungary for trial. Nagy was found guilty of treason in a secret trial and executed by hanging.

News of his trial and execution were only made public after the sentence had been carried out. He was buried, face-down and with barbed wire tied around his hands and feet, in Budapest, but was reburied after the fall of communism in 1989.

JUNE

17

1885

The Statue of Liberty arrived in New York Harbour on board the French steam ship _Isère_.

The statue was designed by Frédéric Auguste Bartholdi, a French sculptor, who claimed that he was influenced by a conversation with the president of the French Anti-Slavery Society to construct a statue commemorating the Union's victory in the American Civil War and the abolition of slavery. The proposal was that France would pay for the statue and America would pay for the pedestal. The project was announced in September 1875 when the name of the statue was revealed – _Liberty Enlightening the World._

The internal structure that supports the statue was designed by French structural engineer Gustave Eiffel, who is perhaps better known for the iconic Eiffel Tower that he built in Paris a few years later. For the Statue of Liberty, Eiffel created a wrought-iron skeleton on to which the 350 separate copper plates that make up the skin were attached. The construction enables the statue to move slightly in the harbour's strong winds, reducing the risk of cracking or other damage.

The statue arrived disassembled, and remained in its 210 separate crates for 10 months while construction of the enormous pedestal it was to stand on was completed.

The completed statue was finally dedicated on 28 October 1886. As the celebratory parade, led by President Grover Cleveland, made its way past the New York Stock Exchange the traders inside spontaneously threw ticker tape onto the streets below in celebration. This marked the first occurrence of a 'ticker tape parade' in New York City.

JUNE

18

1815

Napoleon Bonaparte was defeated at the Battle of Waterloo.

Having escaped from exile on the island of Elba, Napoleon landed on the mainland of France on 1 March and successfully secured support of a small army with whom he marched to Paris. His arrival on 20 March led to Louis XVIII fleeing the city. This signalled the start of a period of Napoleonic government known as the Hundred Days.

Napoleon's return from exile was met with enormous hostility from the other European powers. Napoleon had already been defeated in 1814 and was declared an 'outlaw' by the Great Powers at the Congress of Vienna, who soon committed troops to remove him from power.

By early June, Napoleon had built an army of approximately 200,000 men. Determined to stop the separate enemy armies from combining, he marched into modern-day Belgium in an attempt to defeat each army one by one. On 16 June his army successfully defeated and drove back the Prussian army, although its soldiers were able to retreat and regroup. This Prussian recovery was to prove decisive in the Battle of Waterloo two days later.

At Waterloo the British troops led by Arthur Wellesley, Duke of Wellington, were outnumbered by the French but managed to hold them off until the Prussians arrived to break through Napoleon's right flank. The combined British and Prussian forces defeated the French, but Wellington himself said that the battle was 'the nearest-run thing you ever saw in your life'. Napoleon abdicated soon afterwards and was exiled to the island of St Helena, where he died six years later.

JUNE
19
1978

The *Garfield* comic strip was first published.

Garfield was created by Jim Davis, a cartoonist who began working for an advertising agency before developing his own comic strip. Having failed to gain a syndication deal with his first comic strip, *Gnorm Gnat*, about a group of insects, he turned to his experience of growing up on a farm with 25 cats to develop the *Garfield* strip.

Part of *Garfield*'s broad international appeal is that it focuses on ordinary household situations without turning to political or social commentary. Garfield's pessimistic and often cruel treatment of his owner, Jon, and pet dog, Odie, is also a popular feature of the cartoons.

The comic has since grown to hold the Guinness World Record for the world's most widely syndicated comic strip, being printed in just under 2,600 newspapers around the world.

The popularity of *Garfield* has led it to becoming much more than simply a comic strip. Paws, Inc., the company founded by Jim Davis in 1981 to manage the *Garfield* brand, generated merchandise revenue of $15 million in its first year. Subsequent growth of *Garfield* has included television series, video games, and even two motion pictures. Together these led to merchandise sales of up to an estimate $1 billion by the early 2000s.

Jim Davis continues to work on *Garfield* as a writer, and he still draws rough sketches of new comic strips, although his primary role is to supervise production of the cartoons by a large team of 50 artists who are responsible for inking and colouring the completed frames.

JUNE

20

1789

The Deputies of the French Third Estate swore the Tennis Court Oath in which they vowed not to separate until a written constitution had been established for the country.

Faced with enormous financial difficulties, Louis XVI was forced to call a meeting of the Estates General for the first time in 175 years. This involved representatives of the three Estates – the clergy, the nobility and the non-privileged common people known as the Third Estate – meeting with the king in the town of Versailles, close to the royal palace, on 5 May. Their objective was to solve the ongoing economic crisis.

The allocation of votes at the Estates General was deemed unfair so the representatives of the Third Estate separated themselves from the main group and met separately. On 13 June, by which time they had been joined by some nobles and the majority of the clergy, they declared themselves the National Assembly.

When the king ordered their usual meeting room to be closed and guarded by soldiers, the National Assembly feared that the king was about to force them to disband. The National Assembly instead relocated to a nearby building used for playing *jeu de paume*, a forerunner of modern tennis, where they swore the oath. The Tennis Court Oath therefore didn't really take place in a tennis court, but the name has stuck.

The Tennis Court Oath was significant for being a collective action by French citizens against their king. Faced with such opposition Louis finally relented and, on 27 June, he ordered the remaining nobles to join the National Assembly and ended the Estates General.

JUNE 21 1919

Admiral Ludwig von Reuter ordered the scuttling of the German High Seas naval fleet in Scapa Flow, a large natural harbour in the Orkney Islands in Scotland.

The High Seas Fleet had been confined at Scapa Flow under the terms of the Armistice that ended fighting in the First World War. America had suggested that the fleet be interned in a neutral country but, as neither Norway nor Sweden agreed, Britain volunteered instead.

The majority of the 74 German ships were in Scapa Flow by 27 November, where they were guarded by British Battle Cruiser Force. The fleet was manned by a skeleton crew of less than 5,000 men that gradually reduced over the next few months as they were repatriated back to Germany.

Negotiations over the fate of the ships took place at the Paris Peace Conference, where the various representatives struggled to agree on a resolution. While Britain wanted to destroy the ships in order to maintain their naval superiority, France and Italy each wanted to take a quarter each.

Concerned that the entire fleet might be shared out between the victors as the spoils of war, Admiral von Reuter, the German officer in charge of the interned fleet, began planning to purposely sink the ships.

Shortly before 11.30am on the morning of 21 June the order went out to scuttle the ships. By 5pm fifty-two of them had sunk. The sailors escaped on lifeboats, and were captured as British prisoners-of-war. Nine sailors were shot and killed, making them the last German casualties of the war.

JUNE

22

1633

Galileo Galilei, the famed scientist, was found 'vehemently suspect of heresy' by the Papal Inquisition and forced to recant his belief in the heliocentric universe.

Heliocentrism, which is the belief that the Earth orbits the Sun rather than the other way round, was originally presented by the ancient Greek astronomer Aristarchus of Samos. It gained more traction in the medieval period after Copernicus published his model in 1534.

Galileo had first visited Rome in early 1615 in order to defend his belief in heliocentrism, after complaints were made to the Inquisition. Despite his attempt to prove that heliocentrism didn't contradict the Bible, an Inquisitorial commission in 1616 unanimously declared it to be 'formally heretical since it explicitly contradicts in many places the sense of Holy Scripture'.

At that time Galileo was ordered to 'abandon completely...the opinion that the sun stands still at the centre of the world and the earth moves' but was permitted to discuss heliocentrism in theory. It was this that caused him problems when, in 1632, he published a new book called *Dialogue Concerning the Two Chief World Systems*. Although written with permission from the Inquisition and the Pope, the book implicitly defended heliocentrism. Therefore, argued the Inquisition, Galileo had broken the sentence passed down 16 years earlier and he should be forced both to recant and be imprisoned. Galileo was sentenced to house arrest where he remained for the final nine years of his life.

Nearly 400 years later, in 1992, Pope John Paul II issued a declaration that recognised and expressed regret at the way the Catholic Church had handled the so-called Galileo affair.

JUNE

23

1314

The Battle of Bannockburn began, leading to one of the most important Scottish victories in the First War of Scottish Independence.

The First War of Scottish Independence was fought intermittently from 1296 until 1328. The Battle of Bannockburn was prompted by the Scots under Robert the Bruce, who had seized the Scottish throne in 1306, besieging the strategically important English-held Stirling Castle. The constable of the castle agreed to surrender unless he received assistance from the English army to break the siege by 24 June.

Faced with the imminent loss of the castle English King Edward II successfully raised an army of around 2,000 cavalry and 15,000 infantry to march on Scotland. Robert the Bruce's army was significantly smaller than Edward's, with estimates suggesting that he commanded around half the number of foot soldiers and only a quarter of the cavalry.

Bannockburn was unusual for a medieval battle in that it lasted for two days, with the first day being notable for Bruce single-handedly killing the young English knight Sir Henry de Bohun with an axe blow to the head after he tried to charge him with a lance. The ensuing melee resulted in the English being driven back, which had a devastating effect on their morale.

The next day, after a sleepless night on marshy land next to the river known as the Bannock Burn, the English were hemmed in by the advancing Scots. Realising that they had lost, Edward was escorted away by his bodyguards. The victory secured Scotland's *de facto* independence.

JUNE

24

1374

Citizens in the German town of Aachen suddenly and mysteriously began dancing in the streets and didn't stop for many weeks.

Known variously as St John's Dance, St Vitus' Dance, or the 'dancing plague', the occurrence in Aachen was neither the first nor the last outbreaks but is one of the best documented.

Many hundreds of people were affected by the dance mania, which involved erratic movements and often involuntary shouts and screams. Of those afflicted, many would continue to dance until they dropped to the floor of exhaustion, foaming at the mouth and twitching their limbs until they had recovered sufficiently to resume the dance again. Others died of cardiac arrest or from injuries sustained during the dance.

It's understandable that people at the time were concerned about the mania and that various theories were suggested about its cause. Religion, and punishment from Saints John or Vitus, were closely associated with both the cause and the cure.

More recent theories point towards the fact that the first dancers were people on pilgrimage, not citizens of the town in which the dancing happened. The suggestion is therefore that the dancers were members of cults performing highly-planned rituals that would have seen them executed for heresy if not for the excuse that it was a mass outbreak of dancing plague. Others commentators simply suggest that the dancing was a form of mass hysteria.

It has been noted that the virtual disappearance of outbreaks by the 17th Century coincided with the spread of Protestantism and its rejection of the veneration of saints.

JUNE

25

1876

The Battle of Little Bighorn began when American Lieutenant Colonel George Armstrong Custer led federal troops against the combined forces of the Lakota Sioux, Northern Cheyenne, and Arapaho Plains Indians.

The Black Hills of South Dakota were sacred to the Plains Indians, and had been recognised as such in the Fort Laramie Treaty of 1868. However, the discovery of gold there six years later led to a gold rush of white settlers in breach of the treaty.

Sitting Bull inspired fellow Plains Indians to form an alliance against the invasion of their lands, and by late spring 1876 thousands of warriors had joined him at the Little Bighorn River in an area they referred to as the Greasy Grass.

Determined to drive the natives back to the reservations, the United States Army dispatched cavalry to engage them. When Custer, leading the 7th Cavalry Regiment, spotted a Sioux camp on 25 June he decided to attack it with his 600 men. However, the Indian forces outnumbered his troops and Custer became the victim of a pincer movement after Crazy Horse led another group of Sioux to surround him.

Within an hour Custer and his men were dead, having been overwhelmed by up to 3,000 warriors. Also known as 'Custer's Last Stand', the Battle of Little Bighorn was one of the most significant clashes of the Great Sioux War of 1876.

News of the defeat prompted outrage amongst many white Americans and, over the next year, the Sioux gradually surrendered to the Unites States Army due to continued attacks against their property.

JUNE

26

1963

American President John F. Kennedy declared US support for West Berlin with the phrase, 'Ich bin ein Berliner'.

Berlin had been a focal point for Cold War tensions ever since the Yalta and Potsdam conferences in 1945 divided both Germany and the capital city between the four leading allied powers at the end of the Second World War. When Stalin's USSR imposed the Berlin Blockade from 1948-49, the Western allies made it clear that they were not willing to back down in their support for West Berlin by airlifting supplies into the city.

Although the airlift secured West Berlin's survival, it further increased tensions between the USSR and its former allies as East Germans crossed the border in order to defect to the West. This placed an enormous economic strain on the East, which began suffering labour shortages.

In response to these problems the Soviet-supported *Deutsche Demokratische Republik*, more commonly known as East Germany, erected a barbed wire fence around its border with West Berlin. The fence soon developed into the imposing Berlin Wall, which the government claimed that it was to keep out spies and agitators rather than stop people from leaving.

It was against this background of heightened tension that Kennedy delivered his rousing speech on the steps of the Rathaus Schöneberg, the seat of the state senate of West Berlin.

While the speech effectively recognised East Berlin as part of the Soviet Bloc, it also reaffirmed America's commitment to defend West Berlin against Communist expansion.

The crew of the Russian battleship *Potemkin* mutinied in an uprising that was immortalised in Sergei Eisenstein's 1925 silent film of the same name.

Potemkin entered service in early 1905 after her gun turrets were fitted, and therefore did not take part in the disastrous Russo-Japanese War of 1904-5. Instead, by the end of June she was off the coast of Ukraine completing manoeuvres. It was here that rotten meat allegedly containing maggots was brought on board to feed the crew. Dissatisfied with the ship's doctor's opinion that the meat was fit for human consumption, the crew complained to the captain.

The ship's second in command, Commander Ippolit Gilyarovsky, confronted the sailor's delegation and killed spokesman Grigory Vakulenchuk. This triggered the mutiny, in which seven of the ship's eighteen officers including Giliarovsky and the Captain were killed. The crew chose quartermaster Afanasi Matushenko to take control.

Having hoisted the red flag, *Potemkin* set sail for Odessa where a general strike was underway. Here the crew brought the body of the revolutionary spokesman Vakulenchuk ashore and laid it on the Odessa Steps where it acted as a focal point for locals to show their support for the sailors. However, by the evening the authorities received orders from the Tsar to take firm action. Estimates say that up to 2,000 civilians were killed.

Potemkin left Odessa the next day and sailed for Constanta in Romania. The ship was surrendered to the Romanian authorities in return for the sailors receiving safe passage. *Potemkin* was later returned to the Russian navy and was renamed *Panteleimon*.

JUNE

28

1914 / 1919

28 June saw both the trigger and the definitive end of the First World War.

The assassination of Archduke Franz Ferdinand by Gavrilo Princip in 1914 had a direct effect on the outbreak of war, while the Treaty of Versailles was signed on exactly the same date five years later in 1919.

The assassination of Archduke Franz Ferdinand offers one of the most popular counter-factual debates in history: What if the heir to the Austro-Hungarian throne had not been shot dead by the Black Hand Serbian nationalist terrorist group? What if the driver of the Archduke's car had taken a different route? What if the gunman Gavrilo Princip wasn't standing outside Schiller's Delicatessen at that exact time?

The fact remains that the violent death of Franz Ferdinand directly led to a sequence of events that resulted in the First World War as it caused Austria-Hungary to declare war on Serbia. The network of pre-war alliances that bound the various states of Europe together quickly led to the conflict involving all the major powers and their empires.

The Treaty that officially ended the war was signed five years to the day of the assassination. This, however, was coincidence. The complex negotiations had taken six months to complete, meaning the final Treaty wasn't handed to the German delegation until 7 May. Having studied the 440 Articles of the Treaty with no opportunity for discussion, the German delegation rejected it as unfair.

It was only when the Allies threatened to restart the war that the German government reluctantly signed the Treaty. It went into effect on 10 January the following year.

Apple released the very first iPhone.

Although smartphones had existed before the arrival of the iPhone, they were targeted at business users. Devices such as the Blackberry incorporated full QWERTY keyboards to allow messages to be typed, which prompted other companies to introduce their own models in an attempt to compete.

This all changed when the iPhone came along with its large capacitive touchscreen instead of a bulky keyboard or stylus. Furthermore, users could customise their device by installing additional software from the App Store, which went live just a few months later.

The first iPhone required a mobile data subscription, meaning that the device also changed the way that people interacted with both information and other people. 24/7 access to data sped up the reporting of news as people were able to share large videos and still images directly from their phone. Camera phones had existed previously, but direct access to the internet meant that files were much easier to share. The installation of apps that gave direct access to social media, along with the ability to use them anywhere at any time, had a dramatic effect on the way people began to interact and communicate.

This may all seem rather exaggerated, but a number of studies have shown that a variety of cultural and social changes can be directly traced back to the launch of the iPhone. Consider, for example, that without smartphones the 2011 Egyptian Revolution might never have happened as it was organised and then shared through mobile social media.

JUNE

30

1934

The Nazis carried out a purge of their own party in the Night of the Long Knives.

By the middle of 1934 Hitler was consolidating his rule over Germany, but the relative autonomy of the SA 'stormtroopers' within the Nazi Party was a concern. As Germany became a one-party state the SA's usual political targets for street violence were removed, meaning that in a number of cases these representatives of the ruling party would instead intimidate civilians.

Such actions undermined the sense of order that Hitler was trying to project, and threatened to destabilise the party itself. The SA's leader, Ernst Röhm, was a particular concern as he sought a so-called 'second-revolution' to redistribute wealth within Germany in order to fulfil the socialist part of the Nationalist Socialist party's name. Furthermore the Reichswehr, Germany's official army, were unhappy at Röhm's desire to place the force under the command of the SA.

To remove these threats Hitler ordered the SS to murder leading figures of the SA, along with critics of the Nazi regime such as former chancellor von Schleicher.

On the morning of 30 June, the homes of Röhm and other figures who threatened Hitler's power were broken into. While some were executed on the spot, others were briefly held in prison or under house arrest first. Although the popular name suggests the purge lasted for one night, the executions went on throughout the weekend. Hitler justified the Night of the Long Knives in a public speech, claiming that during the events he acted as 'the supreme judge of the German people.'

JULY

The first Tour de France cycling race began, taking place over nineteen days and six stages.

The first Tour de France was organised as a promotional tool to boost circulation of the French newspaper *L'Auto*. It was greeted by a disappointing number of entrants, which led to the race being delayed for a month from its original start date of 1 June. The entrance fee subsequently reduced, the prize money was increased, and a promise was made to present a daily payment to every rider who completed the six stages at an average speed of 20km/h or more.

60 competitors began the race at Montgeron, south of Paris, of whom 39 were private entrants. A further 24 cyclists joined individual stages of the race, although this meant that they were not eligible for the full prize money.

When the race finished at the Paris Velodrome on 19 July, 21 competitors had successfully completed every stage and their times were totalled to give an overall result, known as the general classification. The winner, with the fastest total time over all six stages, was Frenchman Maurice Garin who finished almost three hours ahead of his nearest rival. He won the title again in 1904, but was later disqualified for unspecified reasons.

Each stage of the first Tour was more than double the length of today's equivalents, although the majority of the 2,428km course was flat. Whereas today's competition involves a series of aggressive mountain climbs throughout the race the 1903 course featured a significant ascent in just one of the six stages, although there were a number of smaller climbs.

JULY

2

1964

American President Lyndon B. Johnson signed the Civil Rights Act into law at the White House.

The 1964 Civil Rights Act originated in the Presidency of John F. Kennedy. Kennedy had actively shared statistical evidence of racial inequality with the American people, such as the fact that life expectancy for an African-American was seven years less than that of a white American.

It was also a time when Civil Rights protests were growing in size and number. In a televised speech on 11 June 1963, Kennedy made clear his intention to introduce a law that would end segregation and increase equality for all Americans.

Kennedy's assassination on 22 November 1963 led to Lyndon B. Johnson being sworn in as President, and he immediately took up the cause. In his speech, Johnson stated that the passage of the Civil Rights Act would serve as a lasting memorial to Kennedy. However opposition to the bill remained high, especially in southern and border states, whose representatives in both the Congress and the Senate did what they could to sabotage the bill including a lengthy filibuster.

Despite such attempts to disrupt it, various behind-the-scenes deals eventually helped the bill to pass through each house with the required two-thirds majority. The Act outlawed discrimination based on race, colour, religion, sex, or national origin and is consequently viewed as a landmark piece of civil rights legislation.

The Act was referred to by Martin Luther King as a 'second emancipation' and laid the foundations for later laws that expanded the legal right for all Americans to be treated equally.

The world speed record for steam locomotives was set by Number 4468 *Mallard*.

Mallard set the record of 125.88mph on a stretch of slightly downhill railway track at Stoke Band, south of the town of Grantham. The A4 Pacific Class locomotives, of which *Mallard* was one of thirty-five, were specifically designed to haul the high-speed Silver Jubilee train from London King's Cross to Newcastle.

The designer, famed steam locomotive engineer Sir Nigel Gresley, streamlined the body of the locomotive to improve its aerodynamic performance through testing and refinement in a wind tunnel.

Built at the Doncaster railway works of the London and North Eastern Railway in England four months before its record-setting journey, *Mallard* was retired in 1963. Despite being restored to working order in the 1980s, the locomotive is now a static exhibit at the National Railway Museum in York.

For its record journey *Mallard* pulled a dynamometer car fitted with various measurement instruments, along with six regular coaches, when it momentarily hit its maximum speed. Shortly after doing so the 'stink bomb' fitted in the big end bearing of the middle cylinder was released, indicating that the bearing had overheated. Consequently the remainder of *Mallard*'s record-setting journey was completed in a damaged state at very low speed.

Mallard continues to be an iconic locomotive for steam enthusiasts, but also gained enormous exposure during the Britpop era in the 1990s when a painting of it by the artist Paul Gribble was chosen to be the cover image for Blur's 1993 album *Modern Life is Rubbish*.

JULY

4

1950

Radio Free Europe, which was founded the previous year to transmit uncensored information to audiences behind the Iron Curtain, completed its first broadcast.

Although the station was uncensored in the sense that it shared information that was suppressed within the Communist Bloc, it was still a propaganda tool founded and funded by the US government.

The task facing the journalists who worked for RFE was daunting. Since they broadcast to states that suppressed a range of information and news, the gathering of intelligence to provide broadcast material was an enormous challenge. They were forced to rely on contact with émigrés and people who had travelled behind the Iron Curtain for eye-witness accounts, and closely monitored print and electronic media from the communist governments. Despite the challenge of sourcing information it has been suggested that the quality and quantity of RFE news was so comprehensive that the communist governments themselves used Radio Free Europe to gain information about what was happening within their own countries.

However, RFE was still fundamentally a broadcaster that promoted anti-communist ideas and was therefore a significant threat in the countries it targeted. The USSR tasked the KGB with establishing expensive radio jamming facilities to try to block broadcasts, while in 1981 a terrorist group funded by the Romanian regime of Nicolae Ceausescu detonated a bomb at RFE's Munich headquarters.

Despite these challenges Radio Free Europe and its partner station Radio Liberty continued broadcasting, and even after the end of the Cold War has continued to broadcast to countries where a free press is not established.

JULY

5

1948

Healthcare provision in the UK was nationalised with the launch of the National Health Service.

The Labour government of Clement Atlee won the first post-war election with a pledge to implement the recommendations of the 1942 Beveridge Report and improve the social welfare system in Britain. The idea was to bring together everyone involved in healthcare provision into a single organisation that would provide care that was 'free at the point of delivery'. Funding would come directly from taxation, meaning that people paid for the service according to their means.

A year after winning the election, Atlee's government introduced the National Health Service Act 1946 which created the NHS in England and Wales. NHS Scotland was established in 1947.

The NHS didn't appear without opposition. The Conservative Party was particularly hostile to providing universal care through taxation, while many consultants and doctors were concerned about low pay and the loss of the opportunity to top up their earnings by taking on private patients. The health minister, Bevan, recognised the seriousness of having a nationalised health system without consultants and doctors so agreed to raise the pay for consultants. He also allowed them and GPs to run their own private practices.

The first year of the NHS was incredibly expensive, costing more than twice the budgeted amount. Bevan claimed that this was due to years of under-provision and a 'rush' to take advantage in case free healthcare was later scrapped. Although costs have continued to rise with continued advances in medical science, the NHS is still a central part of the UK's identity.

JULY

6

1957

John Lennon and Paul McCartney met for the first time at the St Peter's Church garden fête in Woolton, Liverpool.

John Lennon was playing guitar with his skiffle band, The Quarrymen, who were performing on a bill alongside the Liverpool police dogs display team and the Band of the Cheshire Yeomanry. McCartney arrived at the church fête in the late afternoon, shortly after The Quarrymen began playing. According to McCartney's own recollection of the day they were halfway through a cover version of the song 'Come Go With Me' by American doo-wop group The Del-Vikings.

Following their afternoon performance, The Quarrymen went inside the church hall opposite the fête to set up for an evening 'Grand Dance' at which they had also been booked to play. It was here that the band's sometime tea-chest bass player Ivan Vaughan introduced McCartney, with whom he was at school, to the rest of the band.

McCartney demonstrated how to tune a guitar to standard tuning instead of the open G banjo tuning the band used, and then sang some rock n roll songs including 'Twenty Flight Rock', 'Be-Bop-A-Lula' and a medley of Little Richard songs. Lennon was apparently impressed with McCartney's musicianship and later that night agreed with The Quarrymen's washboard player, Pete Shotton, that they should invite him to join the band. After a Scout camp in the Derbyshire Peak District, he accepted.

Lennon and McCartney both stayed in touch with Ivan Vaughan after the Beatles achieved worldwide fame. His wife, who was a languages teacher, later helped McCartney to write the French lyrics for the *Rubber Soul* song 'Michelle'.

JULY

7

1928

Pre-sliced and wrapped bread was first sold by the Chillicothe Baking Company in Missouri.

If you have ever claimed that something was the greatest thing since sliced bread, you are indirectly referring to this particular date. The Chillicothe Baking Company's 'Kleen Maid Sliced Bread' proved incredibly popular and was advertised as 'the greatest forward step in the baking industry since bread was wrapped.' It was this slogan that led to the hyperbolic phrase we now use to describe an invention that has a huge impact on daily life.

The American inventor of the bread slicing machine was trained optometrist and former jeweller Otto Frederick Rohwedder. Having become convinced that he could invent and market an automatic bread slicing machine, he sold his three jewellery stores to finance its development. Unfortunately a fire in his factory destroyed both the blueprints and prototype in 1917, which pushed back the development of the machine by a number of years.

The first bread slicing machine was bought by Chillicothe baker Frank Bench, but demand soon increased and bakeries across the country clamoured to produce and market this new type of bread. The social impact was enormous. As well as increasing bread consumption, the arrival of pre-sliced bread also caused increased sales of automatic toasters which had first been introduced in 1926 by Charles Strite.

Sliced bread even became a political issue when, at the height of the Second World War, it was banned due to concerns over the quantity of wax paper being used to wrap it. However, the ban was lifted after just three months, and sliced bread has remained a staple food ever since.

The Dow Jones Industrial Average, which is a key indicator of the value of America's biggest companies, fell to its lowest point during the Great Depression.

From its high of 381.17 on 3 September 1929, the Dow plummeted by almost 90 per cent to 41.22. The last time it had closed that low was in June 1897.

The spectacular collapse of the Dow reflected the issue at the heart of the Great Depression. The panic selling of US stocks had wiped out private investors and many of the companies they had invested in. This had a knock-on effect outside the stock market, where those very companies were forced to lay off workers. In Cleveland, 50 per cent of the city's workers found themselves unemployed by the end of 1932. The downward economic spiral was eventually reversed, but the Dow itself didn't return to its 1929 high point until 1954.

The response of American President Herbert Hoover to the economic crisis was not viewed favourably by ordinary American people. He gave numerous radio speeches in which he attempted to reassure the population that things would improve. Although he never actually said 'prosperity is just around the corner' his speeches suggested it. But as the economic situation continued to decline, shanty towns known as Hoovervilles appeared around the country as people moved from place to place in search of work. Protesting war veterans in need of work were even attacked by the army.

With promises of a 'New Deal' Franklin D. Roosevelt went on to defeat Hoover in the 1932 presidential election and remained President until his death in 1945.

JULY

9

1877

The world's first official lawn tennis tournament began at Wimbledon in London.

The Wimbledon Championship was hosted by the All England Croquet and Lawn Tennis Club, which had only begun to set aside an area for lawn tennis two years earlier due to the declining interest in croquet.

The first Wimbledon Championship was staged in order to raise money to repair the roller that was used to maintain the lawns at the club, and only featured a Gentlemen's Singles competition. 22 amateur competitors paid 1 guinea each to take part, and ten days later 27-year-old Spencer Gore won the final in front of a crowd of 200 spectators. This was after rain had stopped play for three entire days beforehand.

As a prize, Gore received 12 guineas in cash and a sterling silver cup, valued at 25 guineas, which had been donated by the sports magazine *The Field*. Under the rules of Wimbledon's Challenge Round, the defending champion could return the next year to defend his title in the final without playing through the knock-out stages of the competition. Gore returned to defend his title in 1878, but was defeated in straight sets by his opponent. Gore never played at Wimbledon again, declaring in 1890 that tennis would 'never rank among our great games' because it was 'monotonous'.

Despite Gore's damning verdict of the game, both Wimbledon and the sport of tennis have continued to grow. The Championship's total prize fund now totals over £26.5m. In contrast, the first Wimbledon tournament generated a profit of £10 with which the club's roller was repaired.

JULY

10

1553

Lady Jane Grey was proclaimed Queen of England after her first cousin once removed, the 15-year-old King Edward VI, died of an unknown respiratory problem.

The Third Act of Succession was passed by Parliament in July 1543 and restored Henry's daughters, Mary and Elizabeth, to the line of succession after his son Edward and any children he might have. Jane was the grandniece of Henry VIII through her grandmother, Mary Tudor, Queen of France, who was Henry's sister. The Act stated that the throne would pass to her line if Henry's own children did not have any descendants.

Despite all his father's planning, Edward chose to restrict the succession further. As he lay on his death bed, he nominated the Protestant Lady Jane Grey as his successor rather than his older Catholic sister Mary. Historians disagree over how much influence Edward's chief minister, John Dudley, Duke of Northumberland and the father of Jane's husband Lord Guildford Dudley, had on this decision.

Whatever the role of Northumberland in the succession, he travelled to East Anglia after Edward's death in an attempt to intercept Mary and her supporters. During his absence the Privy Council switched their allegiance. They proclaimed Mary as queen nine days later on 19 July and imprisoned Jane in the Tower of London.

Parliament declared Jane a usurper. She was tried on charges of high treason and found to be guilty for having signed official documents as 'Jane the Queen'. She was beheaded the following February.

The world's first satellite television broadcast took place.

The Telstar communication satellite was launched almost five years after the first artificial satellite, Sputnik, was put into low Earth orbit by the USSR. For this reason Telstar is seen as being part of the Space Race between the USA and the USSR, but it's important to note that Telstar was actually the result of an international project to develop trans-Atlantic communication. The partners involved included AT&T, Bell Telephone Laboratories and NASA in the USA as well as the GPO and National PTT who were responsible for communication technology in the United Kingdom and France respectively.

Telstar was launched from Cape Canaveral in Florida the day before the first broadcast, with costs shared between the international partners. Telstar was therefore also the first privately sponsored space launch.

The satellite's first broadcast involved relaying an image of a flag outside its base station at Andover Earth Station to the Pleumeur-Bodou earth station in France. The 190 French technicians successfully tracked Telstar during the 20 minute period that Telstar was visible to both the USA and France and began watching the broadcast at 00.47am. The first public satellite broadcast took place almost two weeks later, on 23 July.

Despite partly being a product of the Cold War, Telstar was also a victim. High-altitude nuclear tests had created artificial radiation belts that overwhelmed the electronics on the satellite and led to irreparable damage that caused it to completely fail nine months later. By the time it went out of service, Telstar I had relayed over 400 separate transmissions.

JULY

12

927

Argued by many historians to be the foundation date of England, when all the kings of Britain swore an oath of peace under the overlordship of Æthelstan.

Æthelstan was the son of Edward the Elder and the grandson of Alfred the Great. His ancestors had already carved large chunks from Viking lands as far north as the River Humber which led them to refer to themselves as 'king of the Saxons' or 'king of the Anglo-Saxons'. However, without securing the submission of the other British kings Æthelstan could go no further.

His key success in 927 was conquering Viking York, which placed the kingdom of Northumbria under his control. Æthelstan went on to meet the northern kings at Eamont Bridge, near Penrith in Cumbria, where they swore the oath to him. Coins minted soon after the 927 oath referred to Æthelstan as *rex totius Britanniae* or 'king of all Britain'.

Despite the oath, Æthelstan's rule over the north of England was still fragile and in 937 he faced the combined forces of Scots, Vikings and Strathclyde Britons under the shared command of Olaf Guthfrithson, Constantine II, and Owen I. An account of the ensuing Battle of Brunanburh was recorded in a contemporary poem of the same name which was preserved in the Anglo-Saxon Chronicle.

Fifty-two other sources mention the battle, although realistically we know little about what happened other than Æthelstan and his army were victorious. This victory secured Anglo-Saxon power, and effectively laid out the map of the British Isles as we know them today.

An estimated global audience of 1.9 billion people tuned in to watch Live Aid, the 'global jukebox' concert, broadcast live from Wembley Stadium in London and John F. Kennedy Stadium in Philadelphia.

Live Aid was organised by British musicians Bob Geldof and Midge Ure with the aim of raising money to support Ethiopians suffering from an ongoing famine. They were prompted to take action after BBC news reporter Michael Buerk presented a 1984 report in which he described the situation in Ethiopia as 'a biblical famine in the 20th Century' and 'the closest thing to hell on Earth.'

Having recorded and released the all-star Band Aid charity single in December 1984 to raise funds for the same cause, Geldof was encouraged to stage a concert by Boy George of Culture Club. He had enthusiastically suggested a concert after a group of fellow stars had joined his band onstage at Wembley Arena for an impromptu performance of 'Do They Know It's Christmas' at the end of a concert.

The Live Aid concert ran for a continuous 16 hours. The performances began at noon in London and continued in Philadelphia after the London concert finished that evening. The technical requirements of the transatlantic concert made it one of the most ambitious satellite broadcasts of its time which was transmitted to 150 countries around the world.

News reports the day after the concert stated that the event had raised upwards of £40 million. Thirty years on, the legacy of Live Aid continues with the Live8 concerts of 2005 and continued CD and DVD sales generating £150 million for famine relief.

JULY

14

1789

The French Revolution began when Parisian revolutionaries stormed the Bastille, a large fortress, prison and ammunition store that acted as a symbol of the monarchy.

Despite having earlier legalised the National Assembly following the swearing of the Tennis Court Oath, King Louis XVI had ordered his royal troops to surround Paris. He also dismissed his popular finance minister, Jacques Necker. These actions led the Parisian crowd to believe that Louis was preparing to overthrow the Assembly.

The Bastille had long been a symbol of tyranny as a place for the imprisonment of people without trial, but when it was stormed it only contained seven prisoners. One was a deranged Irishman who believed himself to be both God and Julius Caesar. In addition there was another so-called 'lunatic', four forgers, and the Comte de Solages – an aristocrat who had been imprisoned at the request of his own family for allegedly committing incest.

The Bastille was not attacked in order to free these prisoners. The mob was much more interested in seizing gunpowder from the Bastille's stores to use in the 28,000 muskets they had taken earlier that day from the Hôtel des Invalides.

When the mob arrived they found the fortress guarded by 82 French soldiers and a further 32 Swiss mercenaries. Having initially attempted to calm the crowd, the Bastille's governor, Marquis Bernard-Rene de Launay, ordered the guards to open fire after 300 rioters broke into the first courtyard. A group of deserters from the French army later joined the mob, prompting de Launay to surrender to the revolutionaries. He was beheaded by the crowd.

The Tribunal of the Holy Office of the Inquisition, otherwise known as the Spanish Inquisition, was disbanded.

Originally established in 1478 by the Catholic Monarchs, the Spanish Inquisition came under the direct control of the Spanish monarchy rather than the church. This meant it was used as both a religious and political tool.

The Spanish Inquisition's main task was to regulate and maintain Catholic orthodoxy within the dual kingdoms of Aragon and Castile. Its main focus was on Jews who outwardly converted to Christianity but continued to practice Judaism. Known as Crypto-Jews or *conversos*, this group was disproportionately targeted by the Inquisition, especially after all Jews and Muslims were forced to convert to Catholicism or leave the country in decrees issued in 1492 and 1501. British historian Henry Kamen estimates that up to 90% of Inquisition trials were for *conversos*.

The Enlightenment had a significant impact on the activity of the Spanish Inquisition, as the government gradually became more secular. The fact that many Enlightenment texts were being brought in to Spain by influential nobles meant the ideas that would previously have been policed by the Inquisition had to be increasingly tolerated. Although the Inquisition made a short comeback following its earlier dissolution by Napoleon Bonaparte's older brother Joseph during his short time as king, the organisation was finally disbanded by Maria Christina of the Two Sicilies.

By the time it was abolished, up to 150,000 people had been tried by the Spanish Inquisition, of whom somewhere between two and five thousand were executed.

The atomic age began when the USA detonated the first nuclear bomb under the codename 'Trinity'.

The development of nuclear weapons by the United States Army took place in the Manhattan Project that began in 1942 at Los Alamos Laboratory in New Mexico. This was started due to concerns that Nazi Germany would develop an atomic bomb for use in the Second World War. By 1944 the American scientists had designed an implosion-type device and proposed that a test take place. The location was chosen in September, and an on-site laboratory was established.

President Truman was keen to test the bomb before the Potsdam Conference began on 18 July the next year, so the test date was chosen to give time to try again in case it failed. When the appointed hour came rain was falling, which would have increased radioactive fallout, and so the detonation time was pushed back from 4am to 5.30am to allow time for the sky to clear.

Nicknamed the 'Gadget' by the people working on it, the plutonium-based weapon was placed at Point Zero on top of a 100-foot steel tower at the Alamogordo Test Range in New Mexico.

The explosion was equivalent to about 20 kilotons of TNT, and the blast-wave was felt by civilians up to 160 miles away. To maintain secrecy, a press release was issued shortly after the successful detonation that claimed a large ammunition storage magazine had exploded.

J. Robert Oppenheimer, who was the director of the Los Alamos Laboratory, later stated that after the explosion he recalled a verse from Hindu scripture: 'Now I am become Death, the destroyer of worlds.'

The Russian Imperial Romanov family were shot dead in the basement of the Ipatiev House in the Russian city of Ekaterinburg.

The Romanov family of Tsar Nicholas II and his wife, their four daughters and their son, had begun arriving in Ekaterinburg at intervals from the 30 April onwards during the ongoing Russian Civil War. They were accompanied by a small number of servants and a doctor whose prime focus was the Tsar's haemophiliac son. The family's time inside the house was heavily regulated by the Bolshevik guards, who blocked all contact with the outside world.

As the White Army advanced on Ekaterinburg, the communist leadership became concerned that the royal family might fall into their hands and act as a rallying point for the White cause. They were also worried that the family's release could have encouraged other European nations to view them as the legitimate rulers of Russia, and thus undermine the revolutionary Bolshevik government that was struggling to establish control.

The decision to kill the royal family was therefore taken for both political and military reasons. Shortly after midnight on 17 July, the Romanovs and their entourage were woken and led to a small basement room in the house. A group of Bolshevik secret police then entered the room and read out the order for the deaths. All were shot or stabbed by bayonets, and their bodies were taken away in a truck and disposed of in a forest twelve miles north of the city.

The execution was led by Yakov Yurovsky, a member of the Bolshevik secret police known as the Cheka. He had served as commandant of the house, which by that point had become known as The House of Special Purpose.

The first volume of Adolf Hitler's manifesto *Mein Kampf*, which translates as My Struggle or My Battle, was first published.

In 1923, Hitler launched an attempted coup to seize power in Munich in Bavaria. Known as the Beer Hall Putsch, it ended in disaster for the Nazis when Hitler was arrested along with other Party leaders and charged with treason. Having been found guilty after a widely publicised 24-day trial, Hitler was sent to the surprisingly comfortable conditions of Landsberg Prison as a nationally recognised figure.

Imprisonment gave Hitler time to reflect on the future direction of the Nazi Party and dictate *Mein Kampf* to his assistant Rudolf Hess. The book laid out the blueprint for Hitler's future plans for Germany, although when it was first published it gained little following outside the ranks of the Nationalist Socialist faithful.

It was in *Mein Kampf* that Hitler clearly stated his strongly anti-Semitic views, and attempted to justify his hatred. He also outlined his intentions for a future Germany that included the destruction of the parliamentary system and the first reference to aggressive eastward expansion in order to gain *Lebensraum* 'at the expense of Russia'.

Despite its initially poor reception, *Mein Kampf* became a popular book with hundreds of thousands of copies sold each year after Hitler became Chanceller of Germany in 1933, even though he increasingly distanced himself from it. The future British Prime Winston Churchill later stated that, if world leaders had read the book, they could have anticipated the full scale of Nazi domestic and foreign policy.

JULY 19 1799

An announcement was made of the discovery of a slab of rock covered in carvings near the Egyptian town of Rashid, also known as Rosetta.

Napoleon's campaign in Egypt had begun the previous year. He had landed with the dual objectives of protecting French trade in the area and undermining Britain's access to its Indian colonies. Alongside his soldiers, Napoleon also took 167 scientists and scholars who had been tasked with various jobs including researching the geological possibilities of building a Suez Canal and creating accurate maps of the country.

It was while some of the engineers were working with the army to strengthen Fort Julien in the northern Delta area that the granodiorite block we now know as the Rosetta Stone was uncovered. French Lieutenant Pierre-François Bouchard found it as part of the excavations, and it was sent to the newly-created Institut d'Égypte in Cairo who announced the find and devised ways to make copies of the inscriptions. These copies soon made their way to universities and museums around the world.

The inscription on the stone is a decree written in three different scripts: Ancient Egyptian hieroglyphs, Demotic, and Ancient Greek. It is because the scripts effectively convey the same message that transliteration was able to take place. This provided the key to understanding hieroglyphics, although they weren't deciphered until 1822.

When the British defeated the French army in 1801 they seized a large number of French finds, including the Rosetta Stone. It has been exhibited in the British Museum ever since.

JULY

20

1969

Neil Armstrong and Buzz Aldrin successfully landed the *Eagle*, the Lunar Module of Apollo 11, on the surface of the moon.

Apollo 11 was launched from the Kennedy Space Center using a Saturn V rocket on 16 July. The crew then travelled for three days before reaching lunar orbit. Apollo 11's Command Module, known as *Columbia*, stayed in orbit throughout the landing and was piloted by astronaut Michael Collins who remained alone until Armstrong and Aldrin returned.

The descent of the Eagle was completed with just 25 seconds of fuel left, after Armstrong took semi-manual control in order to pilot to an area free of boulders. The words 'Houston, Tranquility Base here. The *Eagle* has landed' confirmed the safe touchdown at around 8:17pm GMT.

Just over 6 hours later Neil Armstrong opened the hatch of the *Eagle* and descended the ladder to become the first person to walk on the moon. Armstrong and Aldrin spent a total of 21 ½ hours on the moon's surface, of which two and a half hours were outside the spacecraft.

The flight to the moon, and the landing, relied heavily on the Apollo Guidance Computer developed at the Massachusetts Institute of Technology. Despite being the most advanced computer of its time, the AGC is dwarfed in comparison to the technology we now have at our fingertips. For example, while the AGC was able to process approximately 41.6 instructions per second, the now-superseded iPhone 6 can handle 3.36 billion Instructions per Second. In real terms, that means that a single iPhone has the processing power of 120 million Apollo Guidance Computers.

Construction was completed on the Aswan High Dam in Egypt.

A dam had already been built across the Nile near the southern Egyptian city of Aswan in 1902. This was designed to store the Nile's annual floodwater and release it during the dry season in order to irrigate the farms and settlements further downstream. Despite being heightened twice by the 1930s the dam still did not provide enough water for future development. Consequently designs for a new dam were sought.

Following the Egyptian Revolution of 1952 led by the Free Officers Movement, President Gamal Abdel Nasser began searching for funding for the new dam. The US, Britain and the USSR all initially offered financial support, but after the USSR promised funding at just 2% interest the other powers pulled out. Income from the Suez Canal following Nasser's nationalisation of the waterway provided further funds.

Construction of the High Dam took just over ten years and cost nearly $1 billion. It is estimated that this cost was recovered in less than five years thanks to income from increased agricultural production and hydroelectric generation, as well as savings from flood protection and improved navigation.

The completed dam is almost 4km long and 111 metres tall. At its centre is the monument of Arab-Soviet Friendship that commemorates it completion. The 550km long reservoir formed when the dam was flooded is known as Lake Nasser, and holds 132 cubic kilometres of water. The creation of the reservoir forced the relocation of over 100,000 people and a number of archaeological sites that would otherwise have been lost beneath the water.

JULY

22

1706

The foundations of the United Kingdom of Great Britain were laid when commissioners from England and Scotland agreed the Acts of Union.

Although Scotland and England had been under the same monarch since James I and VI, it took over a century for the two countries to be united as Great Britain. Various attempts to unite had been made in the years since James came to the throne, but each had resulted in failure.

By the start of the 18th Century both Scotland and England had found themselves in a position where political union would be advantageous. Scotland would benefit from the economic security of the union, while England hoped that a union would remove the risk of Scotland being a 'backdoor' for French attacks or a possible Jacobite restoration.

The 31 English and 31 Scottish commissioners chosen to carry out negotiations for union first met at the Cockpit, a government building at Whitehall in London, on 16 April. As well as coming prepared with their own demands, each group of commissioners also had a bargaining card: England would grant Scotland freedom of trade and access to colonial markets, while Scotland would agree to Hanoverian succession after Queen Anne.

The demands and compromises lined up incredibly well with each other and after just three days the commissioners had agreed on the basic principles of union. It took a further three months to draw up the detailed treaty before it could go to the Scottish and English Parliaments to be ratified. Royal assent was given on 6 March 1707, and on May 1 the Acts went into effect.

JULY

23

1914

Austria-Hungary issued an ultimatum to Serbia that was specifically designed to be rejected and lead to war between the two countries.

Austria-Hungary had been concerned about the growing power of Serbia, and was keen to find a way to weaken the government and stop it taking over the Southern Slavic populations of the northern Balkans. Austria-Hungary was particularly concerned about the future of Bosnia amidst the rise of pan-Slavism. To the government officials who favoured war the assassination of Archduke Franz Ferdinand, the heir to the Austro-Hungarian throne, on 28 June was the perfect catalyst.

Shortly after the assassination Germany gave Austria-Hungary assurances that it would support military action against Serbia. This is known as the 'Blank Cheque' of 5 July. Acting with the knowledge that the strongest army in Europe was on their side, the Austro-Hungarian Crown Council began to discuss how best to justify a war against Serbia. They decided that an ultimatum containing unacceptable demands would be the best course of action, and finally agreed the wording on 19 July.

The ultimatum was delivered at 6pm on 23 July by the Austro-Hungarian ambassador to Belgrade, with a deadline of 48 hours within which the Serbian government had to respond. They accepted all but one of the numerous demands, which was for Austria-Hungary to participation in the internal inquiry into the plot.

Serbia's refusal of this point led Austria-Hungary to declare war. Although it was expected to remain localised, the network of European alliances that had developed from the late 19th Century soon saw the conflict develop into the First World War.

JULY

24

1927

The Menin Gate Memorial to the Missing was unveiled in the Belgian city of Ypres.

Ypres occupied a strategic position throughout the First World War that came about as a result of its location on the route of Germany's Schlieffen Plan. Although the Allies successfully defended the city during the First Battle of Ypres in autumn 1914, they were surrounded on three sides and suffered artillery bombardments throughout the rest of the war that virtually flattened the city. Meanwhile the surrounding area was the location for four more major battles including the Second Battle of Ypres where Germany successfully used poison gas for the first time, and the Battle of Passchendaele.

After the war the city was rebuilt using reparations money from Germany, while the Commonwealth War Graves Commission constructed the memorial. The Menin Gate lies on the east side of the city, close to the route that allied soldiers would have taken to reach the front.

The Menin Gate is one of four memorials to missing British and Commonwealth soldiers from the First World War in the area around the Ypres Salient, and features more than 54,000 names. Every evening at 8pm people gather at the location for a remembrance ceremony in which buglers from the city's fire brigade sound the Last Post.

The fact that the memorial was too small to contain the names of all the missing demonstrates the scale of the destruction. The 34,000 missing soldiers killed after the arbitrary cut-off of 17 August 1917 are inscribed on the Tyne Cot Memorial 10km away.

JULY

25

1965

American singer-songwriter Bob Dylan performed at the Newport Folk Festival with an electric band.

Having come to prominence in the early 1960s with songs that chronicled the social situation in the USA, Dylan's dramatic shift away from his traditional instruments of acoustic guitar and harmonica was said to have, 'electrified one half of his audience, and electrocuted the other.'

Dylan was heralded as the 'spokesman of a generation' and released four acoustic albums in the first three years of his recording career. His fifth album, *Bringing It All Back Home*, which was released in March 1965 indicated a new direction for the musician. While one side of the record maintained his acoustic roots, the other side featured an electric backing band.

Dylan's appearances at the Newport Folk Festival reflected his album releases. In 1963 and 1964 he had been an icon of a new wave of acoustic folk music alongside female musician and on-off romantic partner Joan Baez, but on the night before his appearance at the 1965 festival he decided to go electric. Gathering together a group of musicians from the Paul Butterfield Blues Band, he frantically rehearsed a short four-song set that was performed on the Sunday evening.

Accounts of the performance, and the crowd's reaction to it, differ. While some claim that the crowd booed due to being hostile to Dylan appearing with an electric guitar, others say that it was a response to the short set and poor sound system. Whatever the case, Dylan going electric marked a watershed moment for both the folk and rock music scenes.

JULY
26
1936

Adolf Hitler informed General Francisco Franco that Germany would support his Nationalist rebellion in Spain.

The Spanish Civil War broke out on 17 July, when an army uprising against the Spanish Second Republic that began in Morocco spread to the mainland. In the face of early rebel gains, the Republican government sought assistance from France and the USSR. Meanwhile the Nationalists turned to the right-wing governments of Germany and Italy.

Benito Mussolini, the leader of Italy, agreed to intervene in the war on the Nationalist side after being encouraged to do so by Hitler. Although both countries later signed the Non-Intervention Agreement, they continued to send troops and equipment to support Franco's forces.

Hitler in particular had a number of reasons for getting involved. As well as it giving him the opportunity to take action against what he called 'communist barbarism', assisting Franco would win Germany an important ally and preferential access to Spain's natural resources. Militarily, German involvement also provided an opportunity to test the new equipment developed since the Nazi rearmament programme began in 1933.

Both Hitler and Mussolini were concerned about the risk of the Spanish Civil War escalating into a European-wide conflict, so at first their support for the Nationalists was small-scale and consisted mainly of transporting existing Spanish troops from Morocco to the mainland. As the war progressed their involvement grew. The German Condor Legion in particular began to take an active role in the aerial bombing of Republican areas, most notably the Basque town of Guernica on 26 April 1937.

Allied forces in North Africa stopped the advancing Axis powers in the First Battle of El Alamein.

Having been driven back at the Battle of Gazala in Libya the previous month, the British Eighth Army had retreated first to the Egyptian town of Marsa Matrouh that was 100 miles inside the border. They subsequently moved to the more easily defended line at El Alamein just 80 miles away from the city of Alexandria. This was effectively the Allies' final hope of protecting Egypt's Mediterranean ports, the British headquarters in Cairo, and ultimately the Suez Canal.

The Allied position at Alamein marked the narrowest defensible area between the sea and the Qattara Depression, which lay 20 miles to the south. The position ensured that Erwin Rommel, the German tank commander, would be unable to use his favoured form of attack which involved outflanking his enemy. Furthermore, the position stretched the Axis supply line perilously thin and so starved the advancing army of water, fuel and ammunition.

Despite these resource problems, Rommel ordered the 90th Light Infantry Division to begin its advance at 3am on 1 July. Although the Axis did eventually succeed in breaking through, the advance took most of the day and gave the Allies time to organise more defences along the line.

The battle continued for nearly 4 weeks and saw both sides launch attacks and counter-attacks. It eventually ended in stalemate with both sides taking time to reorganise and re-equip. Significantly, however, the Allies had stopped the previously relentless Axis advance.

JULY

28

1858

William Herschel, a British Magistrate in West Bengal in India, made the first modern use of fingerprints for identification.

Although records of finger and palm prints being used as early as 300 CE were subsequently found in China, Herschel was the first westerner to routinely take advantage of the unique nature of a person's prints to sign contracts. It was only later that their use in criminal investigations began.

Herschel had been interested in fingerprinting techniques for a number of years. Having paid in advance for an expensive contract in which local businessman Rajyadhar Konai agreed to build a new road, Herschel chose to take the full hand print of the contractor as his commitment to honour the construction. Herschel later admitted in his 1916 book *The Origin of Fingerprinting* that he simply wished to scare the contractor away from disowning a written signature.

The success of the first print led Herschel to routinely use prints to authenticate legal documents, and his increasing collection and further reference to his own fingerprints led him to publicly state his belief that a person's print pattern was unique, permanent and unchangeable. Having studied thousands of prints, he later realised that he could even stop the practice of taking a full handprint and instead take prints of just two fingers.

It was another 34 years before fingerprints were used to solve a crime. Argentinian Francesca Rojas had murdered her two young children and attempted to pin the crime on a local man. Unfortunately for her, she had left her bloody hand print on the door post to the bedroom, and this evidence directly linked to her to the crime.

JULY

29

1567

James VI was crowned king of Scotland when he was just 13 months old.

James was the only son of Mary, Queen of Scots, so immediately became heir to the Scottish throne when he was born. His mother's Roman Catholic faith caused her reign to be constantly under threat from the largely Protestant nobility and eventually contributed to her arrest and imprisonment in June 1567.

Mary was forced to abdicate in favour of her young son a month after her imprisonment. She never saw him again as he was quickly taken away to be raised in Stirling Castle as a God-fearing Protestant king.

Having been crowned king when he was barely one year old, James was understandably unable to rule Scotland himself. Power instead lay with a series of four regents who handled the affairs of government until his minority ended in 1578 when he was 12 years old. He didn't gain complete control over the government for another 5 years.

James ruled Scotland until 24 March 1603, when Elizabeth I of England – James' first cousin twice removed – died. As the great-great-grandson of Henry VII, King of England and Lord of Ireland, James succeeded Elizabeth and became the first monarch to rule all of Scotland, England and Ireland in a surprisingly smooth and peaceful succession.

Known as the Union of the Crowns, England and Scotland continued to be separate sovereign states but shared their monarch alongside Ireland. This situation only changed in 1707 when the Acts of Union created the United Kingdom.

A group of volunteer soldiers from the city of Marseille were the first to introduce and sing _La Marseillaise_ in Paris.

La Marseillaise was composed by the French army officer Claude Joseph Rouget de Lisle. Originally called _Chant de guerre pour l'Armée du Rhin_ or 'War Song for the Army of the Rhine', it had been written with the aim of rallying soldiers fighting in Strasbourg during the French Revolutionary Wars.

The song was composed at a time when the French revolutionary army was facing enormous military difficulties in the War of the First Coalition. Forced to fight against the combined forces of both Austria and Prussia, the disorganised, under-equipped, and numerically inferior French revolutionary army had suffered a number of devastating defeats in the first weeks of the war. This helps to explain the militaristic lyrics of _La Marseillaise_ as it was written at a time when France was facing the very real threat of invasion and defeat.

The song was soon adopted as the marching song of the National Guard of Marseille after one of the volunteers sang it at a patriotic gathering in the city. It became the official French National Anthem three years later, on 14 July 1795.

The song's close ties with the French Revolution meant that _La Marseillaise_ often suffered at the hands of those who were against its ideals. For example when Louis XVIII, the brother of the deposed Louis XVI, was declared king of France following the defeat of Napoleon in 1814, he banned _La Marseillaise_ outright. The song was only restored to its position as the French national anthem in 1879.

JULY

31

1970

The British Royal Navy issued the last daily rum ration, or 'tot', to sailors. The end of the daily ration became known as 'Black Tot Day'.

A daily ration of rum, sometimes referred to as 'grog', had been part of a British sailors' routine since 1655 when a half-pint measure of the spirit was introduced as a way to reduce the amount of space needed to transport pint rations of beer. The drink was issued at 6 bells in the forenoon watch, or 11am, and was marked by the call 'Up Spirits'. Due to its high alcoholic content, the size of the ration gradually decreased to an eighth of a pint of rum (70ml) per day by 1850.

As the technological systems and equipment on board ships became more and more complex, concerns over sailors drinking alcohol were raised. In December 1969 the Admiralty Board, which meets in order to administer the Royal Navy, published a written statement that said issuing rum was 'no longer compatible with the high standards of efficiency required'.

The following month the 'Great Rum Debate' took place in the House of Commons during which MP James Wellbeloved put forward a passionate argument that rum helped sailors to 'face the coming action with greater strength and greater determination'. His argument didn't convince his fellow MPs, however, who voted that the rum ration should end.

On Black Tot Day itself the last pouring of rum was marked with funerary significance as some sailors wore black armbands or, in the case of the Royal Naval Electrical College, by conducting a mock funeral procession.

AUGUST

AUGUST

1

1834

The Slavery Abolition Act came into force in the United Kingdom.

Parliament had outlawed the slave trade in the Slave Trade Act of 1807, but that Act only served to stop the creation of new slaves. It did not address the issue of existing slaves who were already in the colonies.

It was these slaves that the new Slavery Abolition Act sought to address, and it received royal assent in 1833. The Act outlawed slavery throughout the British Empire although the impact took a long time to be felt. There were also some exceptions such as in areas controlled by the East India Company.

A key problem facing the government was what to do with the former slaves. The Act addressed this issue by stating that former slaves over the age of six became 'apprentices' and continued to work on the same plantations in largely the same conditions as before. Many of them were only fully emancipated six years later in 1840, although all slaves in Trinidad were fully emancipated ahead of schedule in 1838.

The position of the former slave owners themselves was also addressed in the Slavery Abolition Act. It's important to remember that the Act effectively stripped slave-owners of their property. The Act therefore compensated the slave-owners for their loss of property. This was done by the Slave Compensation Commission that awarded the equivalent of £17bn in today's money, funded by the taxpayer, to 46,000 slave owners.

A searchable online database of every slave-owner who was awarded compensation by the Commission is available to view at www.ucl.ac.uk/lbs.

AUGUST

2

1934

86 year old German Reichspräsident Paul von Hindenburg died of lung cancer allowing Adolf Hitler to become both the Führer and Reich Chancellor of the German People.

The move by Hitler effectively merged the offices of both the President and Chancellor into one role, and therefore completed what the Nazis referred to as *Gleichschaltung* (or 'Co-ordination') by establishing Hitler as both Germany's head of state and head of government.

Interfering with the post of President was illegal under the terms of the 1933 Enabling Act, and although merging the two positions under Hitler removed any political checks and balances of his personal domination of Germany, a plebiscite held seventeen days later on 19 August saw an 90% of people approving of the change.

Hitler's assumption of the role of Führer also allowed the Nazi Party to more actively pursue its promotion of the ideology of *Führerprinzip*. This stated that Hitler possessed absolute control over the German government. Supported by a propaganda machine that relentlessly pushed the slogan *Ein Volk, ein Reich, ein Führer* which translates as "One People, One Empire, One Leader", the *Führerprinzip* also confirmed the Nazi Party's complete control over every element of German society.

Nazi influence ranged from local government to factories and even to the management and control of schools, although in terms of government it sometimes meant that officials were reluctant to make decisions without Hitler's personal input or approval. The *Führerprinzip* was also used by Nazis at the Nuremberg Trials to argue that they were not guilty of war crimes since they were only following orders.

AUGUST

3

1492

Christopher Columbus set sail from the Spanish port of Palos de la Frontera on the voyage that would take him to the Americas.

Columbus captained the *Santa María* while the Pinzón brothers who were Palos natives captained the *Pinta* and the *Santa Clara*. which The latter ship is better known by its nickname the *Niña*. A third Pinzón brother was the master of the *Pinta*.

None of the ships belonged to Columbus himself and, despite the voyage officially being supported and financed by the Catholic Monarchs Ferdinand and Isabella, they forced the inhabitants of the port to contribute towards the costs associated with supplying and equipping them. In the case of the *Pinta*, its owners had even been forced to send the ship on the voyage against their wishes, with led to suspicions that they had sabotaged the craft when the rudder broke after just three days at sea.

Columbus' small fleet sailed first to the Canary Islands which were ruled by the Kingdom of Castile. Here they ensure the broken rudder of the *Pinta* was repaired for the longer voyage. They also restocked the ships with provisions for the Atlantic crossing, which they began on 6 September from the port of San Sebastián de la Gomera.

Palos de la Frontera holds the official title as the starting point of Columbus' transatlantic voyage. The town also played a significant role in the later Christianisation of the New World since it continued to be a departure point for later westward voyages, and was the location of the Franciscan Rábida Monastery that sent some of the first missionaries to the Americas.

AUGUST

4

1693

Legend says that French Benedictine monk Dom Pérignon invented champagne.

There is no evidence that Pérignon ever exclaimed the phrase attributed to him, 'Come quickly, I am drinking the stars' after tasting sparkling wine. The earliest known use of that phrase is in a champagne advertisement from the 1880s, nearly 200 years after the monk's apparent exclamation. Secondly, and most importantly, Dom Pérignon did not invent champagne. As the cellar master at the Benedictine abbey in Hautvillers he actually dedicated much of his time to researching how to avoid making sparkling wine.

Sparkling wine was a problem for Dom Pérignon and his contemporaries because the build-up of carbon dioxide from a secondary fermentation inside the bottle could cause it to explode without warning. In a cellar, the proximity of the exploding bottle to other bottles could set off a devastating chain-reaction which led to sparkling wine becoming known as *le vin du diable* or 'the devil's wine'.

Developments in English glassmaking in the 17th Century created bottles could withstand the additional pressure of sparkling wine. Records from the time, including a paper presented to the Royal Society in 1662, suggest that it was the English scientist Christopher Merret who first developed the process of making sparkling wines through secondary fermentation.

Although Pérignon did not invent champagne, he did make a significant contribution to the development of the drink as we know it today. In particular, he mastered the technique that allows winemakers to produce white wines from red grapes – something that is an important part of the champagne process.

238

Nelson Mandela was arrested near the South African town of Howick and imprisoned facing charges of inciting workers' strikes and for leaving the country without a passport.

Mandela was a leading figure of the anti-apartheid movement and sought to protest peacefully against the racist system. However, having been imprisoned after being found guilty of treason, he adopted more militant tactics on his release and soon became a wanted man. His arrest came after he spent six months travelling in disguise around Africa and to London in order to win support for the movement.

Mandela's trial began on 15 October. He represented himself and used his defence speeches as a way to promote the African National Congress' 'moral opposition to racism'. In his 'black man in a white man's court' speech, for example, he said he would serve the sentence handed down by the court but would continue to fight against racial discrimination.

Having been sentenced to five years' imprisonment, within a nine month period Mandela was jailed in Pretoria, moved to Robben Island, and then sent back to Pretoria again. Shortly after his return to Pretoria he and nine other defendants were charged on four counts of sabotage and conspiracy to violently overthrow the government and were put on trial in what became known as the Rivonia Trial.

The Rovonia Trial brought international attention to the anti-apartheid struggle but, having been found guilty, Mandela and his co-defendants were sentenced to life imprisonment. He was finally released in 1990 after twenty-seven years, six months and five days of imprisonment of which he spent 18 years on Robben Island.

AUGUST

6

1945

The United States dropped an atomic bomb nicknamed 'Little Boy' on the Japanese city of Hiroshima from the B-29 aircraft *Enola Gay.*

The Potsdam Declaration issued on 28 July by the Allies had called for the unconditional surrender of Japan. If the government did not surrender, they were threatened with 'the complete destruction of the Japanese armed forces and...utter devastation of the Japanese homeland'. Having completed the successful Trinity atomic test on 16 July, the USA felt that the atomic bomb could quickly end the War in the Pacific.

Hiroshima was chosen as a target due to its industrial and military significance. The city was the command centre for the defence of southern Japan and contained approximately 40,000 military personnel.

Enola Gay and six accompanying aircraft had a 6-hour flight from the air base at North Field, Tinian before reaching the city where they released the bomb at 8.15am. It exploded 600m above the city as planned, with the equivalent to 16 kilotons of TNT. Virtually all buildings within a mile of the blast were flattened.

70,000 people were killed instantly as a result of the explosion, of whom 20,000 were military personnel. Approximately another 70,000 died over the following months due to radiation sickness, burns, and other injuries directly related to the explosion.

Following the explosion, President Truman warned that, if Japan did not surrender, 'they may expect a rain of ruin from the air, the like of which has never been seen on this earth'. Japan did not surrender. A second bomb was dropped on Nagasaki three days later.

AUGUST

7

1964

The Gulf of Tonkin Resolution was passed by the United States Congress.

The Resolution was a response to the Gulf of Tonkin Incident that had taken place just a few days earlier, in which the North Vietnamese Navy was blamed for attacking US ships on two separate occasions. While it is accepted that USS *Maddox* did exchange fire with three enemy torpedo boats on 2 August, the claim that the ship was attacked again on 4 August is now known to be false.

Even at the time it was acknowledged that the second attack may not have actually happened. Captain John J. Herrick, the commander of *Maddox*, had spent four hours firing at enemy ships picked up on radar. However, he sent a message just a few hours later saying that no enemy boats had actually been sighted and so the radar may have malfunctioned.

President Lyndon B. Johnson was not informed of Herrick's message suggesting malfunctioning radar before he went on national television to announce that US ships had been attacked. His desire to retaliate led to the Resolution, which led in turn to the USA escalating its involvement in the Vietnam War.

The Gulf of Tonkin Resolution granted powers to President Johnson to use American military force to assist countries in Southeast Asia that were facing so-called 'communist aggression'. Many critics of the war condemned Congress for granting Johnson a 'blank cheque' to escalate American military involvement in the Vietnamese conflict. At the time it passed unanimously through the House of Representatives and only two Senators opposed the resolution.

The Great Train Robbery took place when a gang of 15 men attacked a Royal Mail train heading from Glasgow to London.

A core team of five men with backgrounds in organised crime had planned the robbery over a number of months. They later drafted in support from another group of criminals with specific experience in train robberies. Central to the plan was information about the amount of money carried on Royal Mail trains, and this was supplied by a Salford postal worker known to the gang as 'The Ulsterman'.

On the night of the robbery, the gang tampered with the signal at Sears Crossing in the Buckinghamshire hamlet of Ledburn in order to stop the train. Having overpowered the driver and the second crew member, the gang then drove the train half a mile to a location where they could load the stolen bags of money onto a waiting Austin Loadstar truck.

Forcing their way in to the High Value Packages coach, the gang met only little resistance from the five postal workers inside the carriage and so ordered them to lie down on the floor in the corner while the bags of money were removed.

Having set themselves a time-limit of thirty minutes to carry out the robbery, eight bags were left behind on the train when the gang drove to their hide-out at Leatherslade Farm. Here they divided the loot, and the robbers dispersed before the police could find them.

The robbers succeeded in stealing over £2.6 million in cash. Worth £50million today, the vast majority of the money was never recovered. Most members of the gang were subsequently arrested and convicted, although two of them later escaped prison.

Richard Nixon resigned as President of the United States of America while facing impeachment and the almost certain removal from office due to the Watergate Scandal.

The Watergate Scandal began when five men were arrested inside the Democratic National Committee headquarters in Washington D.C.'s Watergate building on June 17, 1972. It was soon discovered, thanks primarily to two journalists at the *Washington Post* and an anonymous informant nicknamed Deep Throat, that the men were connected to the Committee for the Re-Election of the President that was in charge of Nixon's campaign.

Although Nixon probably didn't know about the break-in in advance, he did later attempt to cover up the details by getting the CIA to force the FBI to abandon its investigation. Despite this attempt, details later emerged of the Republican Party's connection to the break-in and of other 'dirty tricks' carried out against the Democrats in the run-up to the Presidential election.

The release of taped conversations held in the Oval Office between Nixon and his aides provided more evidence of wrong-doing. When the so-called 'Smoking Gun Tape' was released on 5 August, in which Nixon was heard personally agreeing that the CIA should ask the FBI to stop the investigation, any remaining support for the President disappeared. He announced his resignation in a televised speech on 8 August and it took effect from noon the next day.

Nixon's impeachment trial was not completed due to his decision to resign. However it is still the only time in American history that impeachment has resulted in the departure from office of its target.

AUGUST

10

1792

French revolutionary troops stormed the Tuileries Palace in Paris in what some historians refer to as 'the Second Revolution'.

The French royal family had lived in the Tuileries since they were brought back to Paris from Versailles during the October Days of 1789. Louis XVI and his family were virtually imprisoned, as proved when crowds barred them from moving to their summer residence in April 1791. This may have influenced Louis to carry out the failed Flight to Varennes two months later, after which the family were more officially held under house arrest in the Tuileries Palace.

The relationship between the royal family and the people of Paris continued to decline throughout 1792. Louis did himself no favours by vetoing a range of decrees passed by the Legislative Assembly, and the situation grew worse with the threat of invasion from foreign armies.

With the subsequent issuing of the Brunswick Manifesto on 1 August in which Charles William Ferdinand, Duke of Brunswick, issued a declaration that lent foreign support to the royal family, the crowds of Paris held Louis and the concept of monarchy in absolute contempt.

On the morning of 10 August, crowds massed outside the Tuileries. Louis opted to shelter his family in the Legislative Assembly building and left the Swiss Guard to defend the palace. They were eventually overrun after they ran out of ammunition. Approximately 800 people on the king's side were killed and Paris was put in the hands of the revolutionaries. The new government suspended the monarchy and the royal family were sent to the Temple prison.

The Weimar Republic was officially established when Friedrich Ebert signed the new constitution into law.

The Weimar Republic was born amid the civil strife and open revolt that had engulfed cities across Germany in the closing weeks of the First World War. The November Revolution actually began at the end of October 1918, but spread from the port of Kiel to eventually reach as far as the southern Bavarian city of Munich by 7 November.

The German Republic was declared on 9 November, shortly after the abdication of Kaiser Wilhelm II was announced. Power was swiftly transferred to Friedrich Ebert who reluctantly accepted the role of Reichspräsident and formed a coalition government known as the Council of the People's Deputies.

It was therefore Ebert's government that signed the Armistice of Compiègne on 11 November, and which authorised the brutal suppression of the Spartacist Uprising in January 1919. Just four days after the deaths of Spartacist leaders Rosa Luxemburg and Karl Liebknecht elections for the National Assembly took place, which convened in Weimar in order to avoid the unrest in Berlin.

Although the state of Germany from the inauguration of the new constitution until Hitler became Führer is generally referred to as the Weimar Republic, its official name continued to be *Deutsches Reich* or 'German Empire' which had first been adopted in 1871.

It took the best of part of seven months for the delegates of the National Assembly to agree on the terms of the new constitution, which Ebert signed into law whilst on holiday in Schwarzburg.

Joseph Lister carried out the world's first antiseptic surgery using the chemical phenol, otherwise known as carbolic acid.

To understand the importance of Lister's achievement, it's important to remember that in the 19th Century up to 50% of all hospital patients died of infection. This often occurred after surgery, during which time patients developed 'ward fever' – a non-specific range of secondary infections caused through poor hygiene in hospitals at a time when surgeons weren't required to wash their hands or even their stained operating gowns.

Having read the work of the Frenchman Louis Pasteur regarding the spread and growth of bacteria, Lister became interested in finding a way to remove infection-causing microorganisms from hospitals. Germ theory of disease was only just becoming more widely accepted but, after discovering that carbolic acid, which is also referred to as phenol, had successfully been used to reduce the smell of raw sewage Lister began experiments using it as what became known as an 'antiseptic'.

On 12 August Lister used a piece of lint doused in carbolic acid to cover the compound fracture wound of a seven-year-old boy. Over a period of six weeks the wound healed without developing gangrene. Developments in surgical hygiene followed. As well as surgeons wearing gloves, they began to wash their hands in carbolic acid, as well as washing their instruments in Lister's 5% solution and spraying it liberally around the operating theatre.

Lister is consequently remembered among the greats of medical science for being the first person to identify the link between clean hospital conditions and infection rates.

Members of the East German police and army began to close the border with West Berlin.

The border between East and West Germany had been closed since 1952 although the crossing between East and West Berlin remained open. This easy access proved highly problematic for the communist government of East Germany, since many people who compared the two parts of the city found West Berlin to be much more appealing.

Berlin became a focal point for East Germans who wanted to move to the West, and by 1961 an estimated 20% of the entire population had emigrated. The majority were young, educated, and skilled professionals. This so-called 'brain drain' seriously depleted the workforce, and was hugely damaging to the political credibility of East Germany.

The erection of the Berlin Wall was intended to put a stop both of these problems, although it was presented to the East German people as the 'Anti-Fascist Protection Rampart'. The East German leader, Walter Ulbricht, had even denied any intention of building a wall just two months earlier despite pressuring USSR Premier Nikita Khrushchev to support him doing just that.

Over the following years the barbed wire and mesh barrier that was constructed overnight was gradually replaced with a virtually impregnable ring of reinforced concrete that ran 155km around West Berlin.

The construction of the Wall turned Berlin from the easiest way to cross between East and West into the most difficult. It cut people off from their jobs, and divided families. The crossing was not opened again to unrestricted access for 28 years.

Electrician Lech Walesa led a strike by workers at the Lenin Shipyard in the Polish city of Gdańsk and triggered the formation of the Solidarity trade union.

A decade of economic and political crises preceded the 1980 strike in Gdańsk, which quickly spread throughout Poland and galvanised various other strike committees to join together for a common goal.

The trigger for industrial action was the firing of a popular worker at the shipyard, a female crane operator and activist called Anna Walentynowicz. Just five months before her planned retirement, she was sacked for being a member of an illegal trade union. This move proved highly unpopular with the shipyard workforce, who demanded that she be reinstated.

Just a week after the strike began, a governmental commission began negotiations with the strikers and, on 30 August, they and representatives of the Gdańsk workers signed an agreement in which many of the strikers' demands were met.

The fact that political change, including the resignation of the Polish Communist Party's General Secretary, had come about thanks to the workers' action emboldened the people of Poland and fuelled the formation of the national labour union *Solidarity*.

Within two years up to 80% of the entire Polish workforce had joined *Solidarity* or one of its suborganisations, and they regularly used strikes to achieve political change. In March 1981, the crippling effects of 12 million people going on a four-hour warning strike demonstrated that the Communist Party was no longer the most powerful force in the country.

The last execution at the Tower of London took place when German spy Josef Jakobs was killed by firing squad.

Jakobs had served in the German Army during the First World War and, following the German defeat, became a dentist in the interwar period. Due to a decline in business following the worldwide depression that came about as a result of the Wall Street Crash, he instead turned to selling fake gold. He was later arrested and served two and a half years in jail.

After his release Jakobs became involved in providing counterfeit passports to German Jews fleeing Hitler's regime. This led to him being arrested in 1938 and sent to a concentration camp from which he was released in 1940.

Within six months Jakobs had begun training with the intelligence wing of the Germany Army, known as the Abwehr. He was parachuted into England on 31 January 1941 dressed in a business suit. Having broken his ankle due to a bad landing, he was found the next morning in a field near Dovehouse Farm in Huntingdonshire after he signalled for help.

Jakobs was taken into custody and was held at Dulwich Hospital in London while his ankle was treated. Eventually he was transferred to Wandsworth Prison where he was formally charged with espionage. He was tried by General Court Martial in early August as he didn't have British nationality and was a formal member of the Germany Army.

Found guilty, he was taken to the miniature firing range at the Tower of London where he was strapped to a wooden Windsor chair and killed by firing squad at 7:12am.

AUGUST

16

1819

An estimated 15 people died in the Peterloo Massacre at St Peter's Field in Manchester when a group of over 60,000 protesters were charged by cavalry.

The protesters had gathered to hear the radical speaker Henry Hunt demand parliamentary and social reform. Britain was caught in the midst of economic depression and the textile industry, which was concentrated in the industrial centres of northern England, was particularly badly hit. Factory owners cut wages by as much as two-thirds which, combined with the increased price of grain due to the Corn Laws that imposed tariffs on cheaper imports, led to workers facing famine as they could no longer afford to buy food.

The workers also lacked political representation. The millions of people who lived in the Lancashire mill towns were represented by just two Members of Parliament due to out-of-date constituency boundaries and, due to the limitations of voting rights, they weren't eligible to vote anyway. These inequalities became a target for political reformers who quickly gained working class support.

Contemporary accounts say that the crowds were peaceful and in good spirits when they assembled on the morning of 16 August. However, the chairman of the magistrates was concerned by the enthusiastic reception when Henry Hunt arrived and ordered the local Yeomanry to arrest him. Unable to move through the dense crowd, the cavalry began hacking with their sabres. The melee was interpreted by the magistrates as the crowd attacking the yeomanry, and more cavalry were sent in. The crowd dispersed within ten minutes, but eleven people died on the field. An estimated fifteen people died as a result of the day's events and approximately 700 others were injured.

AUGUST
17
1982

The very first commercial compact disc was produced in the German town of Langenhagen.

Having initially created separate prototype digital audio discs, engineers at electronics giants Philips and Sony came together in 1979 to develop a standardised format. Interestingly, this happened while they sat on opposite sides of the VHS-Betamax war over home video formats.

In 1980 the engineers agreed on and published their 'Red Book' standard which is still used, with some minor amendments, as the basis for all compact discs. Having agreed on this, marketing could then begin.

The first public demonstration was given in 1981 on *Tomorrow's World*, a BBC television program about new science and technology, in which presenter Kieran Prendiville smeared strawberry jam on a CD of the Bee Gees' album Living Eyes to demonstrate the supposedly indestructible nature of the new format.

A year later the first CD was produced to be sold commercially, although a number of months went by before the disc was available to purchase in stores. Chilean pianist Claudio Arrau's recording of Chopin waltzes was pressed at Philips' Polydor Pressing Operations plant, with the pianist himself starting the machine. Philips apparently believed that classical music fans were generally more affluent and therefore more likely to pay the hefty price tag for CDs and their players.

The first 'pop' music compact disc to be produced was the *The Visitors* – the last album recorded by the Swedish musical super-group ABBA.

AUGUST
18
1612

The trials of nine Lancashire women and two men known as the Pendle Witches began.

The trials of the Pendle Witches are not only some of the most famous but also some of the best recorded witch trials in British history. This is due to a published account called *The Wonderfull Discoverie of Witches in the Countie of Lancaster* by Thomas Potts, the clerk to the Lancaster Assizes where all but one of the trials took place.

One interesting aspect of the trials is that the majority of the defendants self-identified as witches, or at least as village healers who practised what they referred to as 'magic' in return for payment. A number of the accused even admitted to Roger Nowell, the justice of the peace for Pendle and chief prosecutor at the trials, that witchcraft had been practised by a number of people in the area around Pendle Hill for many years.

Accused of the murders of various people in and around the area, twelve people were charged. One of there was found not guilty and another died in prison before going to trial. The other ten were found guilty and executed by hanging.

In historical terms, the Pendle Witch trials were significant for their scale. Despite a popular belief that witch trials were a common occurrence in the early modern period, only around five hundred people were executed for witchcraft throughout the 300 year period when they were carried out.

Statistically, this means that the ten found guilty in Pendle represented two per cent of all British witches to face trial over three centuries.

Mikhail Gorbachev, the President of the Soviet Union, was placed under house arrest in what is known as the August Coup.

The leaders of the coup were opposed to Gorbachev's reforms and believed that the new Union of Sovereign States, which had been approved in a union-wide referendum, threatened the complete disintegration of the USSR. A number of members had already declared their independence, but the New Union Treaty would devolve much of the Soviet Union's remaining power to individual states.

It was while Gorbachev was on holiday in Foros, a resort in the Crimea, that the coup was launched. On 17 August, the coup's leaders met with Gorbachev and demanded that he either declare a state of emergency or resign. Although the specific details of the conversation are unclear, the outcome was that Gorbachev refused.

Gorbachev was placed under house arrest and the leaders of the coup – known as the Gang of Eight – created the State Committee of the State of Emergency to govern the USSR due to Gorbachev suffering from an 'illness'.

The changes in government were announced on state media on the morning of 19 August but, having chosen not to arrest Russian President Boris Yeltsin, the coup faced a blow when he began speaking against it. Two days later, the military supporting the coup failed to take control of the Russian parliament building in the face of civil resistance. The coup collapsed two days later and left the USSR seriously weakened. Just over four months later the Soviet Union was officially dissolved.

AUGUST

20

1968

Troops from the USSR, Bulgaria, Poland and Hungary entered Czechoslovakia in an invasion that brought the Prague Spring to an end.

The Prague Spring had begun in early January, shortly after Dubček became the leader of Czechoslovakia. Keen to push forward with a policy of de-Stalinisation within the country, he granted greater freedom to the press and introduced a programme of 'socialism with a human face' through which he intended to decentralise parts of the economy and introduce some limited democratic reforms.

This new openness led to criticisms of the Czechoslovakian government appearing in the press, which concerned the other Warsaw Pact countries. János Kádár, the leader of Hungary who came to power after the fall of Imre Nagy in 1956, even warned that the situation in Czechoslovakia seemed 'similar to the prologue of the Hungarian counterrevolution'.

Concerned that Dubček's reforms might spread to other Eastern Bloc countries and threaten the USSR's security, the Soviet leader Leonid Brezhnev chose to open negotiations with the Czechoslovakian leadership. The talks lasted until August and ended in compromise, but Brezhnev remained unhappy with the situation and began to prepare military intervention.

Overwhelmed by the military invasion by almost half a million Warsaw Pact soldiers, Dubček asked his people not to resist. 72 Czech and Slovak soldiers and 108 civilians were killed, while a further 500 civilians were injured. It later emerged that members of the Czechoslovakian government had asked for Soviet assistance against Dubček's reforms.

Leonardo Da Vinci's *Mona Lisa* was stolen from the Louvre.

The man who stole the portrait, Italian Vincenzo Peruggia, had previously worked at the Louvre. Acting alone, he hid in a cupboard inside the museum on the evening of 20 August and exited on the morning of Monday 21 August – a day when the museum would be closed for cleaning – wearing a smock identical to all the other museum employees. With the museum deserted of visitors, he entered the Salon Carré where the painting hung and simply removed it from the wall.

Making his way to a stairwell, Peruggia removed the glass that had only recently been fitted to protect the painting from vandalism, and discarded the frame. Leaving both the glass and the frame behind he went back through the door with the painting and walked out of the museum unchallenged. Described by some as the greatest art theft of the 20th Century, the museum itself didn't even realise that the painting had been stolen until the next day. Contrary to some reports it is likely that he wrapped the 53cm x 76cm painting in his smock, rather than concealing it up his shirt, as the painting on its solid plank of poplar wood would have been too big.

The *Mona Lisa* lay hidden in Peruggia's apartment in Paris for two years before he decided to take it to Italy in 1913. Here he made contact with Alfredo Geri, a gallery owner, on 10 December who in turn contacted the director of the famous Uffizi gallery. The two men took the painting 'for safe keeping' and informed the police.

Peruggia served just six months in jail for the robbery, and was hailed by many Italians as a nationalist hero for returning the *Mona Lisa* to her real home although it was later returned to France.

AUGUST

22

1485

King Richard III was killed at the Battle of Bosworth, and the forces of Henry Tudor brought the Plantagenet dynasty to an end.

Wishing to capitalise on Richard III's diminishing support following the disappearance of the Princes in the Tower and the death of his wife, Henry Tudor prepared to invade England from his base in Brittany and fight him for the throne. Funded by Charles VIII of France, and supported by three times as many French mercenary soldiers as his own troops, Henry set sail on 1 August with 2,000 men. He landed at the Welsh port of Milford Haven and secured the support of the influential Welsh landowner Rhys ap Thomas on his march to England.

Richard's army gathered in Leicester from 16 August and, on the night of 21 August, camped on Ambion Hill near the town of Market Bosworth with 10,000 men. The next morning, facing Henry and his force of around 5,000 soldiers, the Yorkists were defeated after their allies from the Stanley family switched sides. The Stanleys surrounded and killed Richard after the king chose to break ranks and target Henry himself. Henry was crowned under an oak tree near the site.

Henry secured his reign as Henry VII soon afterwards by marrying Elizabeth of York, the niece of Richard III and daughter of Edward IV. This united the two warring houses and was symbolised through the creation of the Tudor rose.

Richard's body was taken to Leicester by the Lancastrians where it was buried in an unmarked grave in Greyfriars church. The church was demolished after its dissolution in 1536, but the grave was found again in 2012 as the result of an archaeological dig on a site that had been turned into a council car park.

AUGUST

23

1939

Soviet foreign minister Vyacheslav Molotov and German foreign minister Joachim von Ribbentrop signed the Nazi-Soviet Pact.

Stalin and the USSR deeply distrusted Nazi Germany, suspecting that Hitler ultimately intended to invade and annex Russia. Similarly, Britain distrusted Stalin due a fear of communism. Although talks took place between Britain and the Soviet Union in early August 1939 regarding a possible alliance against Hitler, they were never taken seriously by the British who sent their representative by a slow boat and did not grant him authority to make any decisions or sign any agreements on behalf of the government.

Frustrated by Britain's reluctance to agree to a deal, Stalin's government received Ribbentrop later that month. He proposed the Nazi-Soviet agreement which, in the face of continued British reluctance to form an alliance, was accepted.

Officially called the Treaty of Non-aggression between Germany and the Union of Soviet Socialist Republics, on the surface the pact guaranteed that neither side would fight against the other in war. However a 'secret protocol' also outlined how Eastern Europe would be divided between the two countries in the future. This ensured that the USSR would not intervene in the Nazi invasion of Poland that began just nine days later.

The Soviet government almost certainly knew that Hitler would break the non-aggression pact at some point by invading Russia, but the pact delayed that and gave time to prepare. Nazi forces invaded the Soviet Union in Operation Barbarossa on 22 June 1941. All the territory gained by the USSR under terms of the 'secret protocol' was lost in just a matter of weeks.

AUGUST
24
79

The eruption of Mount Vesuvius wiped out numerous Roman settlements including Pompeii and Herculaneum.

There is considerable debate over the accuracy of this date due to archaeological discoveries and recent meteorological research, but the majority of scholars continue to favour 24 August. This, by unnerving coincidence, was just one day after the annual Roman festival of *Vulcanalia* which was held to honour the Roman god of fire.

An eyewitness account of the eruption has survived in the shape of two letters from Pliny the Younger. Through them it is known that the eruption lasted for two whole days. The eruption released thermal energy that was hundreds of thousands times greater than the atomic bomb dropped on Hiroshima.

Beginning at around 1pm on 24 August, Mount Vesuvius sent gas, volcanic ash, and pumice into the stratosphere for up to 20 hours. This was followed by a pyroclastic flow that carried gas and molten rock down from the volcano and which then buried the previously fallen ash.

The discovery of the astoundingly well-preserved settlements of Pompeii and Herculaneum has provided scholars with detailed evidence about daily Roman life. It's believed that the majority of the 1,500 people whose remains or impressions have been discovered died of thermal shock during one of the pyroclastic surges. Others may have suffocated, or been hit by falling rocks and collapsing buildings.

There is still a lot of archaeological work to be done, especially at Herculaneum, but digging has been put on hold to focus on the preservation of the areas already uncovered.

The Nazi German garrison in Paris surrendered the city to the Allies.

A series of actions by the Nazis against French political prisoners and members of the resistance had previously sparked mass civil unrest. This began on 15 August and climaxed three days later with a general strike. However, having been ruled by the Nazis for over four years, the liberation of the capital was not a priority for the forces under General Dwight D. Eisenhower. Furthermore, the Allied commanders were unwilling to risk the destruction of the city since they were aware that Hitler had said it 'must not fall into the enemy's hand except lying in complete debris.'

Having received reports that the US Third Army led by General Patton was close to Paris, but unaware that they did not intend to attack the city Von Choltitz, the Nazi military governor, ordered explosives to be placed at strategic points. The Nazis never had the chance to detonate them.

The German military withdrew down the Champs Élysées on the morning of 19 August. At this point the French Forces of the Interior, otherwise known as the French resistance, seized the opportunity to begin a full-scale uprising. Barricades were erected the next day, with fighting reaching a peak three days later. It was this that persuaded Eisenhower to change his plan and allow Allied troops to enter Paris.

Over 800 resistance fighters died before the Free French 2nd Armoured Division led by Captain Raymond Dronne arrived to assist the uprising just before midnight on 24 August. On 25 August the US 4th Infantry Division entered the city. Von Choltitz surrendered later that day.

AUGUST

26

1346

The Battle of Crécy, one of the most decisive battles in the Hundred Years War, was won by the army of the English king Edward III.

The battle was fought against the French army of King Philip VI and led to the port of Calais becoming an English enclave for over two centuries.

Determined to unseat Philip from the French throne and claim it for himself, Edward had already been involved in a series of conflicts across the Channel. The invasion force he brought in 1346 was notably different to previous campaigns due to its large number of longbow archers who made up between half and two-thirds of the approximately 15,000 men in the army.

The key advantage of the longbow was its ability to be fired over long distances and so disrupt the enemy without any threat to one's own troops. Research has since shown that longbow arrows could only pierce the plate armour worn by knights at a distance of 20 metres, but they were highly effective against their horses and the lighter armour worn on a knight's limbs. Being able to bring down knights before the onset of hand-to-hand combat was incredibly important. Furthermore, the psychological effect of thousands of arrows raining down is known to have affected the fighting spirit of the enemy.

Having forced over 4,000 Genoese crossbowmen in the service of the French to retreat, Philip's cavalry were similarly overwhelmed by the archers. He abandoned the battle around midnight and his remaining knights and men-at-arms fled the field soon afterwards. French losses numbered in the thousands while the English lost barely a hundred.

AUGUST

27

1928

Germany, France and the United States signed the General Treaty for Renunciation of War as an Instrument of National Policy otherwise known as the Kellogg-Briand Pact.

Jointly created by the US Secretary of State Frank B. Kellogg and French foreign minister Aristide Briand, the Pact stemmed from France's desire to protect itself against possible future German aggression. The United States government was unwilling to join what could be interpreted as a military alliance, so Kellogg suggested that they instead invite all countries to sign a condemnation of war unless in self-defence.

The United States' involvement meant that the Pact was signed outside the League of Nations, of which America was not a member. This means that it is still in force today. A total of 62 nations eventually went on to sign the agreement, which promised to never use war as a way to settle conflicts.

At the time it was optimistically hoped that the signing of the Pact would stop any future wars, but the impact of the Great Depression in the 1930s led nations such as Japan and Italy to launch invasions of Manchuria and Abyssinia respectively. Both offensives began without the aggressor ever declaring war but, despite this, the Pact was ineffective anyway since it provided no way to enforce its terms.

Despite its shortcomings the Kellogg-Briand Pact did act as the legal basis for the notion of a crime against peace, and in turn became the foundation for many of the key prosecution arguments in the Nuremberg Trials and the Tokyo Trials that followed the Second World War.

AUGUST
28
1963

American Civil Rights leader Martin Luther King Jr. delivered his iconic 'I Have a Dream' speech from the steps of the Lincoln Memorial in Washington D.C.

Designed to demonstrate mass support for President Kennedy's Civil Rights legislation, the March on Washington saw approximately 250,000 people from across the United States converge on the National Mall. Taking place on the centenary of President Lincoln signing the Emancipation Proclamation, in which he declared the freedom of slaves, 'I Have a Dream' was the sixteenth of eighteen speeches given by different orators that day and is regularly described as one of the best speeches of the 20th Century.

Martin Luther King's speech paid homage to Lincoln's Gettysburg Address in which had reiterated the Declaration of Independence's principals of human equality. Claiming that America had not fulfilled the promises made in the Declaration of Independence towards black people, the 'I have a dream' refrain presented the ideal of an integrated and equal America.

King had already included this refrain in a number of earlier speeches, and hadn't intended to make it part of his speech in Washington. He made the choice to deviate from his prepared speech after gospel singer Mahalia Jackson, who had performed 'I Been 'Buked and I Been Scorned' directly before King took to the podium, called out 'Tell them about the dream, Martin!'

Extensive media and television coverage of the March on Washington meant that the speech was witnessed across the nation and encouraged Kennedy's administration to push forward with its Civil Rights legislation.

The Soviet Union successfully detonated its first nuclear weapon, codenamed RDS-1 and nicknamed *First Lightning*.

The USSR started its nuclear program in 1943 after discovering that the USA, Britain and Canada had already begun research into the development of an atomic bomb. Assisted by intelligence from sources inside the USA's Manhattan Project, the USSR's program developed quickly as the Soviets were able to replicate American successes while avoiding some of their costlier mistakes. Although the majority of Cold War academics accept that the USSR's success had a lot to do with domestic expertise, they also recognise that foreign intelligence helped to reduce the time it took for them to develop the bomb.

Work was accelerated after the bombings of Hiroshima and Nagasaki and took place in secret, purpose-built cities dedicated to the nuclear program known as *Atomgrads*. By 1949 the Soviets had developed two types of bomb and opted to detonate the simpler of the two designs first since it was similar in design to the successful *Fat Man* bomb that was dropped on Nagasaki.

The RDS-1 test was conducted in secret in an attempt to avoid the USA increasing its own nuclear program. The explosion had the power of 22 kilotons of TNT, and was 50% more destructive than its designers had expected. Despite the USSR's attempts to maintain secrecy the US Air Force detected radioactive fallout from the explosion a few days later and tracked the trail.

The USSR's successful detonation occurred four years ahead of American estimates, and the knowledge that the Soviets now had 'the bomb' dramatically increased tensions in the early years of the Cold War.

AUGUST

30

1918

Bolshevik leader Vladimir Ilyich Ulyanov, better known as Lenin, was the victim of a failed assassination plot.

The assassination was attempted by Fanya Kaplan, a member of the anti-Bolshevik faction of the Socialist Revolutionary Party. She believed that Lenin was a 'traitor to the revolution' as he had dissolved the Constituent Assembly and banned other left-wing political parties. She fired three shots at him as he left the Hammer and Sickle factory in Moscow. One bullet hit Lenin's arm and lodged in his shoulder while the other went through his neck and is reported to have punctured part of his left lung.

Made unconscious by the attack, Lenin was taken to his living quarters in the Kremlin from where he refused to move in case other would-be assassins attacked him. Without the medical facilities of a hospital, his doctors were unable to remove the bullets and, although Lenin did survive, the injuries he sustained may have contributed towards the strokes that led to his death in 1924.

In retaliation for the attack on Lenin, which had occurred barely two weeks after the successful assassination of Moisei Uritsky, the head of the Cheka in Petrograd, the Bolsheviks issued a decree beginning the Red Terror. Designed to crush counter-revolutionary action against the Bolsheviks, the Red Terror is generally accepted to have lasted throughout the period of the Civil War until 1922. Meanwhile, the Communist Party newspaper *Pravda* used the attack as an opportunity to print propaganda that promoted Lenin.

Kaplan was executed on 3 September, but over the next four years tens if not hundreds of thousands of Bolshevik opponents were killed in a huge political clampdown.

AUGUST

31

1888

Mary Ann Nichols, who was commonly known as Polly, became the first confirmed victim of Jack the Ripper when she was murdered in the Whitechapel area of London.

As well as cutting Polly Nichols' throat, her murderer had mutilated her body. Her corpse was left in shadow next to a gate in Buck's Row, which is now known as Durward Street, and was discovered by cart driver Charles Allen Lechmere as he walked to work.

It took three weeks for the inquest to be completed, by which time a second murder with a similar *modus operandi* had been committed. On studying the body of the new victim, Annie Chapman, the coroner noted that 'the similarity of the injuries in the two cases is considerable'.

Nichols was 43 years old when she was murdered, having found herself forced to live in boarding houses and workhouses after her alcoholism led her husband to leave her. She turned to prostitution as a way to earn money and, in the early hours of the night she was murdered, had gone out to make money to pay for her bed in a boarding house at 18 Thrawl Street.

An hour before her murder, Nichols' friend and roommate Nelly Holland spoke to her as she walked the streets. She had already spent her night's earnings on drink, and so continued to search for customers. Holland was the last person to see her alive before her body was found by Charles Cross at 3.40am.

Nichols' killer was never found, and debate continues about the identity of the Whitechapel murderer who was given the nickname 'Jack the Ripper'.

SEPTEMBER

SEPTEMBER
1
1939

German forces invaded Poland in a move that was to trigger the Second World War.

During the night of 31 August, Nazi SS troops dressed themselves in Polish uniforms and staged an attack on the Gleiwitz radio tower in Upper Silesia. This 'false flag' operation was part of a wider series of staged attacks on Germans and German property called Operation Himmler that was designed to make it appear as if Poland was exercising aggression against Germany.

Just hours after the Gleiwitz incident, at 4.45am on 1 September, the first of approximately 1.5 million German troops launched their attack on Poland. This led to the encirclement of Polish forces thanks to the launch of coordinated attacks from the north, south and west. The attack from the south came across the border with Slovakia, which had declared its independence in March under pressure from Hitler.

Known as the Battle of the Border, Germany's three-pronged ground attack was supported by air raids that targeted key Polish cities. It took just 5 days for German troops on the ground to force the Polish army to retreat to their secondary defensive lines. The German government had already ensured that the Soviet Union would not respond aggressively to the invasion by signing the Nazi-Soviet Pact a week earlier. In accordance with the 'secret' protocol' of this agreement, the USSR launched its own invasion of Poland from the east on 17 September, and this crushed Polish hopes of victory.

The Polish government refused to surrender to Germany and instead evacuated the country to form a government-in-exile in Allied countries.

SEPTEMBER

2

1666

The Great Fire of London began at a bakery in Pudding Lane.

London in the 17th Century was a sprawling and disorganised conurbation, with the thousands of buildings inside the old Roman wall that lay at its heart. This area – known confusingly as 'the City' – may well have been the centre of English commerce but was also an enormous fire hazard due to its narrow warrens of houses and workshops. The ballooning population ignored the law that banned the use of wood and thatch, and continued to construct up to six- or seven-storey buildings with over-hanging 'jetties' whose roofs would often meet.

It is generally accepted that the Lord Mayor should have acted more decisively when pressed to authorise the demolition of buildings to create a fire-break. Having failed to cut off the fire in the early hours of Sunday morning, it spread to the south and west thanks to the wind.

By lunchtime most residents had given up any hope of extinguishing the flames themselves, and instead were fleeing the fire. The mass of refugees in the narrow streets made it almost impossible for professional fire crews to reach the blaze, further slowing down attempts to extinguish the flames.

The catastrophic fire blazed for more than three days and destroyed over 13,000 houses, churches and government buildings. Historians believe that the fire was only brought under control thanks to the use of gunpowder to create large firebreaks, which coincided with the previously strong winds dying down. Then the biggest challenge began: trying to rebuild the city from the smouldering ruins.

SEPTEMBER

3

1939

The Second World War officially began when France and the United Kingdom, together with Australia and New Zealand, declared war on Germany.

Nazi forces had invaded Poland two days earlier, claiming to be acting in self-defence following a 'false flag' operation. However, although both France and Britain had each signed pacts with Poland regarding mutual assistance in case of invasion, no significant military action was taken for eight months against Germany. As a result, this period became known as the Phoney War.

To call the war 'phoney' ignores some key elements of this period. The French, for example, launched the Saar Offensive against Germany. This major attack across the German border failed and the French troops were forced to pull back to their defensive Maginot Line on 17 October when it became clear that a full-scale assault would not be successful.

Further action took place at sea, where both the British and French navies began to blockade Germany's ports the day after the declaration of war. The previous evening the British passenger ship *SS Athenia* was hit by torpedoes fired from a Nazi U-boat off the coast of the Hebrides. 128 civilian passengers and crew were killed as a result of the attack, and it is seen by some as marking the start of the Battle of the Atlantic.

On 10 May 1940, British Prime Minister Neville Chamberlain resigned and was replaced by Winston Churchill on Chamberlain's own suggestion. This coincided to the day with Germany's invasion of the Low Countries using the tactic of blitzkrieg, and effectively marked the end of the Phoney War.

SEPTEMBER

4

1957

A group of nine black schoolchildren were prevented from entering the previously segregated Little Rock Central High School by the Arkansas National Guard acting on the orders of Governor Orval Faubus.

The desegregation of American schools began after the United States Supreme Court declared it unconstitutional to segregate public schools on the grounds of race in the historic ruling on Brown v. Board of Education of Topeka, Kansas in 1954. Little Rock School District subsequently declared its intention to begin integrating Little Rock Central at the start of the 1957 school year under the terms of the Blossom Plan, drawn up by school superintendent Virgil Blossom.

Speaking against the plan, Governor Faubus claimed that there was danger of 'tumult, riot and breach of peace and the doing of violence to persons and property' if the black students who had enrolled were allowed into the school. Consequently he ordered the National Guard to prevent them from entering, effectively overruling the Supreme Court.

The Little Rock Crisis gained national attention, and was only resolved when President Eisenhower intervened. Almost three weeks after Faubus had put the National Guard in position President Eisenhower issued proclamation 3204 that ordered the National Guard to stand down. This order on 23 September was ignored and so Eisenhower removed control of the National Guard from the state and placed it in the hands of the federal government.

The 101st Airborne Division were sent to Little Rock the next day, and on 25 September the nine students were finally able to enter the school for good.

SEPTEMBER

5

1698

Tsar Peter I of Russia, more commonly known as Peter the Great, imposed a tax on beards.

Determined to modernise and westernise Russia following the death of his brother Ivan, with whom he had jointly ruled Russia until 1696, Peter returned from the Grand Tour and immediately began a series of dramatic reforms. Military, political, economic and social changes were imposed that were designed to catapult Russia into the modern world and place it amongst the great powers of Europe.

Peter's war on beards began as soon as he returned to Russia. In a meeting with numerous nobles and senior members of the government, he is said to have begun shaving his guests with a barber's razor.

The long flowing beards of Russian tradition, which were closely associated with Orthodox Christianity, were presented with a progressive tax that charged up to an eye-watering 100 roubles. In return, the wearer would receive a small copper token indicating that the tax had been paid but which declared 'the beard is a superfluous burden'. Only members of the clergy and peasants were spared the demand to have a clean-shaven face.

The decision to ban beards was unpopular, not only because it was a significant challenge to tradition but also because shaving a beard was interpreted by some Orthodox Christians as being sinful. Although he had initially ordered officials to shave anybody they found who did not comply with the new decree, Peter soon realised that taxing beards would create valuable income for the Treasury thanks to some of his subjects' unwillingness to shave. The tax wasn't abolished until 1772.

Nine Israeli Olympic athletes were killed in the Munich massacre by Palestinian terrorists from the Black September group.

Security at the 1972 Munich Olympics was kept purposefully low-key in an attempt to shed the military image of Germany portrayed in Nazi propaganda from the 1936 Berlin Olympics. The consequent lack of heavy security allowed the eight Black September members to gain access to the Olympic Village by climbing over a fence in the early hours of 5 September. Here they entered apartments where members of the Israeli team were sleeping.

The terrorists were seeking the release of 234 Palestinian prisoners who were held in Israeli jails. They also called from the release of two leading members of the Baader-Meinhof Gang held in Germany. A total of nine Israeli hostages were held in the apartment block at 31 Connollystraße for over twelve hours before the German authorities agreed to the captors' demands to arrange transport to Cairo where negotiations would continue.

The hostages and their captors were shuttled by helicopter from the Olympic Village to the Fürstenfeldbruck airfield, a short distance outside Munich. Landing shortly after 10:30pm, a gun-battle broke out between the gang members and police snipers which ended after the kidnappers found cover behind and beneath the helicopters.

The status quo held for a short time, but it became clear to the terrorists that their mission was probably going to fail when German armoured personnel carriers arrived at the airport around midnight. At that point the captors turned on the hostages and killed them with machine guns and a grenade.

SEPTEMBER

7

1497

The Second Cornish Uprising of 1497 began when Perkin Warbeck landed at Whitesand Bay near Land's End.

Warbeck had convinced his followers that he was Richard, Duke of York, the younger of the two 'Princes in the Tower'. Soon after his arrival Warbeck declared himself King Richard IV.

Warbeck's career as a pretender to the throne began shortly after he arrived in the Irish city of Cork in 1491. It was here that he was first identified as a member of the York dynasty. He quickly adopted his new identity, and travelled around the royal courts of Europe securing support for his claim. The French King Charles VIII lent him support, as did Margaret of York – the aunt of the Princes in the Tower.

Warbeck had attempted an invasion of England from France in 1495, but it went disastrously wrong. After finding little support in Ireland he instead headed to Scotland where he stayed for two years and married the Scottish King's cousin. Another failed invasion of England led to him being invited to join with Cornish rebels in what was to be his final failed assault.

Having landed in Cornwall, Warbeck soon surrendered to the significantly more powerful forces of Henry VII in Hampshire. Warbeck was held by Henry in relative luxury, even though he confessed to being an imposter. His admission that he was actually the son of a prosperous family in Tournai, in what is now Belgium, was subsequently proven by the 19th Century historian James Gairdner who had access to the town archives. Two years after his capture, Warbeck was hanged at Tyburn in London on 23 November 1499.

SEPTEMBER

8

1888

The very first Football League games were played in England.

The Football League was the brainchild of William McGregor, a director of Aston Villa, who hoped to provide a system whereby all the member clubs would play a guaranteed number of games each season rather than have to rely on ad-hoc arrangements between individual teams.

The idea was simple: each member of the League would play a home game and an away game against every other League team. Two points would be awarded for a win and one point for a draw and, at the end of the season, the team with the highest number of points would be declared the Champions of England.

Twelve teams from across the Midlands and the North West of England made up the very first Football League. Preston North End finished the season without suffering a single defeat and became the first ever League champions. They also went on to win the 1889 FA Cup which made them the first ever team to win the League and Cup double.

Based on post-match reports that reveal the delayed kick-off times of each of the matches, it's now generally accepted that the first ever Football League goal was scored by Bolton Wanderers striker Kenny Davenport against Derby County just 2 minutes after the match began.

If a league table had been printed at the conclusion of the first day's games it would have shown West Bromwich Albion at the top based on the calculation of 'goal average' that acted as the tie-break criteria. If the modern rules of 'goal difference' that were introduced in 1976 were used instead, Derby County would have been top of the table on the first day.

The first literal computer 'bug' was found in the Harvard Mark II electromechanical computer.

The bug at Harvard was very literal since it was a moth trapped between the points inside an electromagnetic relay. Its presence led to problems in the functioning of the whole computer which were resolved when the moth was removed. The relays inside the Mark II were used for logic calculations using the Boolean system, but if the relay didn't switch in the correct way the algebraic function would be incorrect.

Development of the Harvard Mark II was financed by the United States Navy, which explains the involvement of Grace 'Amazing Grace' Hopper. She had previously been assigned to work as one of the very first programmers of the Harvard Mark I during the Second World War when she was a member of the US Navy.

Urban legends suggest that the discovery of the moth inside the Mark II caused the use of the terms 'bug' and 'debugging' in computer programming. However, the word 'bug' is known to have been used to describe malicious beasties since medieval times, and was well-known in the world of electrical engineering since at least the time of the telegraph. Even Hopper, who is credited with popularising the term 'debugging' to find problems in computer code, regularly stated that the moth simply fitted with existing terminology.

The preservation of the moth in the log-book of the Mark II alongside the label 'First actual case of bug being found' is further proof that computer scientists were already aware of the term 'bug' to describe a fault in a computer.

SEPTEMBER

10

1989

The Hungarian government announced the opening of the border with Austria to allow thousands of East Germans to leave the Communist Bloc.

Hungary had been inundated with East Germans since the government began removing the border fence in May. Inspired by the Hungarian government's moves towards a more democratic political system, numerous East Germans travelled to Hungary as tourists but then sought refuge in the West German embassy. A 'friendship picnic' held on the Austrian-Hungarian border on 19 August had already seen East Germans using the border as a way to escape and, before long, thousands of East Germans refugees were living in Hungary.

Unwilling to 'become a country of refugee camps', Hungarian Foreign Ministrer Gyula Horn made the announcement that the East Germans would be permitted to enter Austria. As well as allowing the refugees to cross the border, the announcement led to an exodus of an estimated 70,000 more East Germans who made their way to Hungary.

Hungary's decision was met with incredible anger from the East German government who were facing increasing opposition at home. The first of what were to become weekly 'Monday demonstrations' had started in the East German city of Leipzig earlier that week, and the Hungarian announcement encouraged others to begin protesting in favour of democracy. Within a month up to 70,000 people a week were making their way to the Leipzig protest, and by the end of October over 300,000 were taking part every week. The Berlin Wall fell on 9 November.

SEPTEMBER

11

1978

Janet Parker became the last recorded person in the world to die from smallpox.

Parker was a medical photographer working at the University of Birmingham Medical School and was infected with smallpox from a nearby lab. It is believed the disease was spread by air currents through service ducts within the building.

At the time of her infection, the World Health Organisation had almost completed its successful international smallpox eradication programme. Although the last naturally occurring infection had been recorded the previous year, various laboratories around the world – including one at the University of Birmingham Medical School – were continuing research on strains of the virus that were a threat to eradicating the disease.

Parker's darkroom in the hospital was directly above a laboratory where research on live smallpox viruses was carried out. It's believed that the virus had spread through ventilation ducts while being handled in the laboratory on 24 and 25 July. Parker is known to have spent longer than normal in the room where the ducting connected on those days.

She first became ill on 11 August, but nine days passed before she was admitted to hospital and her infection was identified as smallpox. Transferred to the Catherine-de-Barnes Isolation Hospital outside Solihull, she and a number of other people with whom she had had contact were placed in quarantine. Parker died on 11 September, but her death was preceded by that of her father who died of cardiac arrest shortly after visiting his daughter. The scientist in charge of the laboratory at the University of Birmingham committed suicide.

SEPTEMBER

12

1919

Adolf Hitler officially joined the German Workers' Party (DAP).

At the end of the First World War, Hitler began work as an army intelligence officer and was tasked with infiltrating the German Workers' Party. Through attending their meetings he became attracted to the angry rhetoric of the founder, Anton Drexler. During a party meeting in the first floor restaurant of the *Sterneckerbräu* beer hall in Munich on 12 September Hitler himself put forward a passionate argument denouncing the views of another speaker. In *Mein Kampf* Hitler describes Drexler as being impressed by his oratorical skills, which resulted in him being invited to join the Party.

At the time no membership cards were issued but, when they were made available in January 1920, Hitler was given membership number 55. He later claimed in *Mein Kampf* to have been the seventh person to join. Hitler was actually the seventh executive member of the Party's central committee and his membership card identified him as member number 555. Numbering had been started at 500 in order to make the Party appear to have more members than it really did.

Despite members of the army not being permitted to have membership of a political party, Hitler had been given special permission to join the DAP. Before long his role in the Party began to eclipse his role in the military. He was discharged from the army on 31 March 1920 after which he began working full-time for the renamed National Socialist German Workers Party.

The *Sterneckerbräu* building still exists in Munich as a registered monument on the Bavarian monument list. The beer hall has now gone and the building is instead used for residential and commercial purposes.

SEPTEMBER

13

1985

The *Super Mario Bros.* video game was released in Japan.

The Italian-American plumber Mario, and his younger brother Luigi, had first appeared in a video game called simply *Mario Bros.* in 1983. *Super Mario Bros.* was therefore a pseudo-sequel that featured the same characters, but implemented dramatically different gameplay. Although not the first game of its type, it popularised side-scrolling platform games and spawned a whole series of successors.

Originally only available for the Japanese Family Computer, it took nearly another two years for the game to be available worldwide. This happened following the release of the 8-bit Nintendo Entertainment System home video game console, more commonly known as the NES.

The success of *Super Mario Bros.* played a major role in reversing the early-1980s crash in the American video games industry, and confirmed its creator Shigeru Miyamoto's position as one of the leading forces in video game design.

Super Mario Bros. received positive reviews on its release, and is still regarded as one of the best video games of all time. This has led to it spawning a vast number of successors and being re-released on a number of occasions for subsequent Nintendo gaming platforms. In some cases even the original bugs have been left in place for the sake of authenticity.

As well as appearing in video games, Mario and Luigi have also starred in their own TV show and a feature film. Even the music from the game is iconic, with the three-bar introduction to the first level being proclaimed the most memorable video game theme in history.

The poem that was to provide the lyrics for the United States' national anthem was written by 35 year-old Francis Scott Key.

The poem *Defence of Fort M'Henry* provides an account of the British attack on the United States during the Battle of Baltimore. The War of 1812 had already been raging for two years when the British launched their seaborne invasion of Baltimore.

At the time of the invasion, Key was aboard one of the British Navy ships lying off the coast. He had sailed to the flagship HMS *Tonnant* the previous week in order to negotiate a prisoner exchange, and was present when the British officers discussed war plans. Since he was aware of the plans the British did not permit him to return to his own boat, as it was assumed he would pass intelligence to the American military.

When the British began their attack, Key was only able to watch as Fort McHenry was subjected to an enormous bombardment from the ships. A number of Congreve rockets fired from HMS *Erebus* provided inspiration for the 'rockets' red glare' in the fifth line of the poem. However, bad weather combined with the poor accuracy of the British munitions being fired at their maximum range meant that little damage was done to the fort.

When dawn came and the skies above Baltimore cleared, Key could clearly see a large American flag flying over the fort. He claimed that this sight inspired him to write the poem. It was published a week later alongside a note instructing readers to sing it to the melody of 'The Anacreontic Song'. This was the official song of a gentlemen's club of amateur musicians although, ironically, the club and the song were English.

SEPTEMBER

15

1935

The German Reichstag passed the Nuremberg Laws that legally discriminated against Jews.

Since coming to power in 1933, the Nazi Party had produced large amounts of propaganda that discriminated against minorities, and which encouraged people in Germany to view Jews in particular as belonging to a separate race to other Germans. The Nuremberg Laws enshrined this discrimination in the legal framework of the country through two pieces of legislation.

The Law for the Protection of German Blood and German Honour focused on individual relationships by banning marriages and sexual relationships between Jews and Germans. Furthermore it strengthened the concept of 'German' racial superiority in law by banning German women under the age of 45 from working in Jewish households. Meanwhile the Reich Citizenship Law stripped Jews and many other racial minorities of their German citizenship since it stated that only people with German or related blood could be citizens of the country.

The Reich Citizenship Law relied on a clear definition of 'Jewishness', which was not actually agreed upon until November. In the end, Hitler declared that anyone with three Jewish grandparents was to be classed as Jewish; anyone who had two Jewish grandparents would be considered Jewish under the law if they practised the faith or had a Jewish spouse. Proving racial heritage therefore became a vital part of life in Nazi Germany.

Due to concerns about how the international community might interpret the laws, prosecutions did not begin until after the 1936 Berlin Olympics.

SEPTEMBER

16

1978

Filming began on *Monty Python's Life of Brian*.

Life of Brian was the third motion picture to be released by the Monty Python comedy troupe, and is said to have had its origins in the publicity circuit accompanying their previous film *Monty Python and the Holy Grail*. The box-office success of *Holy Grail* had proved that there was significant demand for feature-length creations from the group, and soon the idea of lampooning organised religion became a focus for development.

Two members of Monty Python, Eric Idle and Terry Gilliam, dismissed the idea of a direct satire of Jesus Christ as they agreed that – despite both being non-believers – there was nothing to mock in his teachings. Therefore they settled on the idea of his neighbour, Brian, being mistaken for the Messiah despite not wanting the attention.

It took just over a year for the script to be completed, during which time EMI Films had been lined up to fund the project. However, just two days before filming was due to begin the funding was withdrawn on direct orders of the company's chief executive.

Faced with catastrophe, Eric Idle confided in his friend, ex-Beatle George Harrison, who stepped in to save the film by providing £3 million. He did this through his production company HandMade Films, which was set up specifically to finance the film. *Life of Brian* grossed over $19 million in America alone during its first year of release.

Claimed by its fans to be the greatest comedy film of all time, *Life of Brian* has courted controversy since its release due to its satirical portrayal of religion that is interpreted by some as blasphemous.

The Camp David Accords, which led to the first ever peace treaty between Israel and an Arab state, were signed by Egyptian President Anwar El Sadat and Israeli Prime Minister Menachem Begin.

Brokered by United States President Jimmy Carter, the two frameworks that were agreed upon gained their name from the Presidential retreat at Camp David where the negotiations took place. Having accepted Carter's invitation to attend the talks, Begin didn't expect to leave with anything more than an outline for future meetings. Egypt and Israel had been at war for a number of years, and the likelihood of there being any agreement between the two nations was slim.

Over a period of thirteen days, the three leaders engaged in a number of heated discussions that became so hostile that Carter was forced to meet with each leader separately. At times both leaders threated to scrap the talks, but Carter repeatedly succeeded in to salvaging the situation and keep them at Camp David. The political cost of leaving without an agreement was certainly in the forefront of each man's mind as nobody wanted to shoulder the blame for the collapse of the Middle East peace process.

The talks concluded with the signing of two separate agreements – 'A Framework for Peace in the Middle East' and 'A Framework for the Conclusion of a Peace Treaty between Egypt and Israel'. The first of these was condemned by the UN for being conducted without involvement of the Palestinians, and the second led to Sadat's assassination by Islamic extremists who were angered that he had made peace with Israel.

SEPTEMBER

18

1931

The Manchurian Crisis, also known as the Mukden Incident, began when Japanese soldiers blew up a section of their own railway in the Chinese region of Manchuria.

The South Manchuria Railway had been controlled by Japan since the end of the Russo-Japanese War, but the relationship between the local Chinese population and the Japanese soldiers who guarded the line was tense. Following the onset of the Great Depression, some renegade members of the Japanese Kwantung Army believed that a conflict in the area would be beneficial for Japan.

Japanese troops detonated a small quantity of dynamite near the tracks at around 10.20pm on the evening of 18 September. The explosion caused such little damage to the railway line that a train was able to travel over the same section of track ten minutes later without any problems. Despite having carried out the explosion themselves, the Japanese blamed Chinese rebels for the blast. Within hours the resident Japanese forces had driven a nearby Chinese garrison from their barracks in apparent retaliation for the alleged attack.

Over the next few days the Japanese army took control of towns and cities along the entire railway line, acting independently of the government in Tokyo. The politicians, unable to rein in the army, eventually lent their support and sent additional troops to support the invasion.

The Chinese government appealed to the League of Nations for assistance, and the League promptly passed a resolution calling for the withdrawal of Japanese troops. Japan ignored the League, and ruled Manchuria as a puppet state.

SEPTEMBER
19
1970

The first Glastonbury Festival took place at Worthy Farm in Somerset.

Organised by dairy farmer Michael Eavis, the event was billed as the *Pilton Pop, Blues & Folk Festival* and attracted 1,500 people who paid a pound each to see a number of bands on a single stage and drink unlimited quantities of milk.

The two-day music festival was inspired by Eavis' earlier visit to the nearby Bath Festival of Blues and Progressive Music, but was run on a much smaller scale. Described by performer Ian Anderson as 'ramshackle' the festival was a very laid-back event that featured a stage constructed of scaffolding and plywood and security provided by local Hell's Angels. There was no indication from the first festival that the event would grow to the size and significance of the modern day incarnation, especially after the Kinks pulled out from the headline spot.

It is reported that the Kinks' Ray Davies had got a doctor's note to say he had a throat infection and couldn't sing, after reading in Melody Maker that the event was only a 'mini-festival'. However, Eavis struck lucky by securing the band T.Rex as a replacement headliner just as 'Ride a White Swan' was about to take the number 1 spot in the charts.

Despite Eavis' stroke of luck, singer and guitarist Marc Bolan's experience of the first festival wasn't entirely positive. His velvet-covered car ended up getting covered in mud due to the poor condition of the ground, and Eavis was only able to pay his fee in instalments. The festival ultimately lost £1,500 and only took place the next year thanks to an injection of money from its supporters.

The Norwegian king Harald Hardrada defeated his northern English enemies at the Battle of Fulford.

The origins of Hardrada's invasion lie in the conflicting claims to the English throne after the death of Edward the Confessor. As one of the claimants, Hardrada had allied himself with Harold Godwinson's banished brother Tostig. Having been blown across the North Sea by the very winds that famously left William's fleet stuck on the Normandy coast, Hardrada met up with Tostig's forces and they made their way to York.

The battlefield at Fulford was largely flat marshland so was far from an ideal place to undertake armed combat. However, the English took advantage of the nearby River Ouse on one side and the marshier ground on the other to arrange their troops and secure their flanks. Despite this, the fierce fighting that initially saw the Norwegians being driven back gave way to a counter-attack that led to Hardrada's victory.

The Norwegians made their way to the city of York, which surrendered to Hardrada on condition that the city wasn't forcibly entered. The loss of the city, and the defeat of Harold Godwinson's northern earls, was disastrous for the new English king. He was forced to rush north and face Hardrada himself in order to avoid losing his realm.

The Norwegians had set up camp at Stamford Bridge, and it was here that they were surprised by Harold's forces five days later. The English secured victory at Stamford Bridge, but the defeat at Fulford had depleted their army. This had a major impact on William the Conqueror's successful invasion that occurred just a few weeks later.

J. R. R. Tolkien's fantasy novel *The Hobbit* was first published in the United Kingdom.

Tolkien was an academic linguist who held the position of Rawlinson and Bosworth Professor of Anglo-Saxon at the University of Oxford, where he was friends with fellow academic and novelist C. S. Lewis. Alongside his academic pursuits he had a creative mind that saw him produce a series playful poems and stories for his children. Tolkien combined both these areas in *The Hobbit*. While it is primarily a children's book, part of its appeal is the rich fantasy world that Tolkien created by drawing upon his knowledge of Old English literature and early Germanic mythology.

Tolkien is said to have taken up to two years to write the original manuscript for the book, copies of which he lent to various friends. Through contact with one of his students at Oxford, the publisher George Allen & Unwin Ltd. obtained a copy, which was given a positive review by the 10-year old son of the owner and encouraged Unwin to publish it.

The initial run of 1,500 copies sold out within three months, and further runs proved similarly popular. Arguably *The Hobbit's* greatest legacy is that it spawned the creation of *The Lord of the Rings*, the sequel that Tolkien was encouraged to write after the runaway success of *The Hobbit*.

The Hobbit has remained in print ever since it was first published, although Tolkien made a number of revisions to the text over the course of the next thirty years. This was done to bring plot elements into line with the storyline of the subsequent *Lord of the Rings*, and also to retain copyright in the United States.

The longest conventional war of the 20th Century began when Iraq launched an invasion of Iran.

Having become President of Iraq in 1979, Saddam Hussein was keen to consolidate the power of his minority Sunni Muslim Ba'ath government. At almost exactly the same time, Ayatollah Khomeini came to power in Iran in a revolution that overthrew the Shah. Khomeini installed a Shi'ite Muslim theocracy in Iraq's neighbour and called for the overthrow of Saddam's regime. This was met with enormous hostility in Iraq, especially after Shi'ite militants assassinated 20 Ba'ath Party officials in April 1980.

Iraq also wanted to push Iran back from the Shatt Al-Arab waterway in order to secure its own oil exports. If the army was successful, Iraq could even increase its own oil reserves by capturing some of Iran's oil fields.

Iran was poorly prepared for war as its army had recently been purged of officers and soldiers loyal to the former Shah. Furthermore, the country's economy was in tatters as a result of western countries boycotting trade due to the ongoing hostage crisis at the American Embassy. At first Saddam consequently dubbed the Iran-Iraq War the 'Whirlwind War' in which he expected Iran to be defeated relatively swiftly.

Despite Saddam's expectations of a quick and easy victory, however, Iran mobilised its revolutionary population and soon the front lines were filled with enthusiastic volunteers who pushed the Iraqis back to their own border. The war persisted for nearly eight long and bloody years, leading to the deaths of an estimated half a million soldiers and the same number of civilians.

The world's first teletext service went live when the BBC began transmitting its Ceefax service.

Teletext was the name given to a system that could broadcast text-based information during the overnight 'close-down' of television services. It was the dominant medium for accessing breaking news until the arrival of the World Wide Web.

A system for broadcasting text had been developed by the BBC during the 1960s, but it was a noisy and technically limited mechanical system that only ever made it as far as internal tests. The advancement of digital technology in the early 1970s led to the emergence of a new system that was originally developed to encode subtitles for viewers who were deaf.

Launched slightly before the competing ORACLE system that had been developed by the Independent Broadcasting Authority, The BBC's Ceefax system was launched with thirty pages of information. However, this quickly grew to the point where hundreds of pages of up-to-the minute information were being shared. At times Ceefax pages were even broadcast as conventional television images in order to fill gaps between programming.

Within two years the creators of Ceefax and ORACLE had settled on a standard teletext system that became known as World System Teletext that was used by a host of international broadcasters. However, the rapid rise of the World Wide Web and the arrival of digital television in the first decade of the 21st Century saw Ceefax and related teletext services become redundant as the information was available elsewhere. Ceefax itself was switched off shortly after 11.30pm on the evening of 23 October 2012.

SEPTEMBER

24

1946

Clark Clifford and George Elsey presented a report to US President Truman in which they recommended 'restraining and confining' Soviet influence.

The report helped to shape Truman's decision to follow a policy of containment. It had a direct impact on the introduction of the Truman Doctrine and the Marshall Plan, and on the formation of NATO.

The report was a detailed appraisal of relations between the USA and the Soviet Union, elaborating on the points raised in the 'Long Telegram' that had been composed by George F. Kennan at the US Embassy in Moscow. Kennan's telegram highlighted the USSR's 'perpetual war' with capitalism, stating that the communist and capitalist worlds could never peacefully coexist.

These warnings were picked up by Clifford and Elsey, who also noted Kennan's comments regarding the likelihood that the Soviets would back down from any direct conflict in their attempts to expand communism. Consequently they recommended 'restraining and confining' Soviet influence in an attempt to maintain some form of coexistence. Elsey suggested that this could be achieved by persuading the USSR that the USA was 'too strong to be beaten and too determined to be frightened'. The term 'containment' was first used to describe this approach in an expanded essay in the *Foreign Affairs* journal.

Ten copies of the report were printed, the first of which was presented to the President. Truman's daughter Margaret wrote that, having stayed up most of the night to read it, her father ordered all copies to be brought to him and locked away since the content was a serious threat to US-Soviet relations.

Spanish explorer Vasco Núñez de Balboa became the first European to successfully lead an expedition to the Pacific Ocean from the New World.

Balboa had first sailed to the New World in 1500, and in September 1510 established the first European settlement in the mainland Americas. Within a year he had expanded his power and become the governor of the province of Veragua by usurping his rivals.

Over the next few years Balboa added to his territory and built up significant stores of gold. It was during an argument between his men over the size of their share that Balboa heard of a kingdom on 'the other sea' that was rich in gold.

In order to find what was then known as the 'South Sea', Balboa and his men first needed to cross the Isthmus of Panama – the narrow strip of land between the Caribbean Sea and the Pacific Ocean.

The expedition departed the settlement of Santa Maria on 1 September 1513. Having sailed along the coast to find a good landing point, Balboa and his men began the land crossing on 6 September. The journey involved battling with native tribes and forging a way through thick jungle, before reaching the mountain range along the Chucunaque River.

It was from this summit that Balboa first saw the Pacific Ocean on the morning of 25 September. It then took the expedition another four days to descend to sea level, where Balboa claimed it for the Spanish sovereigns.

German Chancellor Gustav Stresemann ended passive resistance in the Ruhr and resumed the payment of First World War reparations.

The 1921 London Schedule of Payments had set out both the reparations amount and the timetable over which Germany was expected to pay for its defeat in the First World War. However, from the very start of the payments Germany missed some its targets. Failure to provide the full quota of coal and timber in December 1922, provided the excuse for France and Belgium to occupy the Ruhr on 11 January 1923.

Occupation was met with passive resistance and the striking workers were paid with money printed by the government. This contributed to the rampant hyperinflation that had begun to cripple the economy from before the occupation began. Stresemann was aware that the situation was unsustainable and, despite having been Chancellor for only six weeks, called off passive resistance and started to pay reparations again.

By ending the strikes and restarting reparations payments, Stresemann was able to slow down the economic crisis that was enveloping the country and show that he accepted the international realities of the new era. This marked the start of Germany's international rehabilitation, although within Germany it was met with opposition from both Left and Right extremists. For that reason, Stresemann asked President Ebert to announce a state of emergency under Article 48 of the constitution on the same day.

Despite the anger from some Germans, Stresemann's actions laid the foundation for the economic recovery that Germany experienced up until the onset of the Great Depression.

SEPTEMBER

27

1908

The first Model T Ford automobile rolled out of the Piquette Avenue factory in Detroit.

Although some sources claim that the first Model T was built four days later on 1 October, research has shown that this was the date on which the new model was made available for delivery.

The new Model T wasn't the first automobile to be produced by the Ford company, but it was significant for being the first one that was widely-affordable. While the low cost was ultimately achieved thanks to an innovative 'assembly line' process, the first models were built and assembled largely by hand in a more traditional way. Consequently only 11 cars were completed in the first month of production.

Ford's development of the assembly line used the concept of the division of labour to split the construction of the car into 84 distinct phases. This meant that the knowledge and skills a worker had to master was reduced. Conveyor belts moved the vehicle from labourer to labourer who would perform his or her specialism before the car moved on to the next. As the assembly line was refined, a new Model T rolled off the line every three minutes. This speed of construction was so quick that the paint barely had time to dry. It was for this reason that Ford only painted the car in japan black, as it was the only coating that dried quickly enough.

The Model T was enormously successful, and at one point half of all automobiles on the road were not just Ford cars but Model Ts. Even as other companies began competing, the Model T continued to be produced in enormous numbers. Production was only halted in 1927, nineteen years after the first one rolled out of the factory.

SEPTEMBER

28

1928

The bacteriologist Alexander Fleming laid the foundation for a revolution in modern medicine when he accidentally discovered penicillin.

Fleming discovered the world's first antibiotic after returning to his laboratory from a family holiday. He found that a petri dish containing staphylococci bacteria had been contaminated with an unidentified fungus. The bacteria around the fungus had been destroyed, whereas bacteria that were further away survived. He allegedly remarked 'that's funny' and began investigating the fungus.

Over time Fleming identified that the fungus came from the genus *penicillium*, and laboratory tests indicated that it could be used to destroy a variety of disease-causing bacteria. However, despite his best efforts he was never able to cultivate the fungus in any significant quantity or isolate the active ingredient. The work of subsequent scientists was therefore vital to the development of the antibiotic, although without Fleming there would have been no fungus to investigate.

Fleming originally referred to his discovery as 'mould juice' and it initially met with little attention or enthusiasm from the medical establishment. This changed in the early 1940s when research by Howard Florey and Ernst Boris Chain at the Radcliffe Infirmary in Oxford raised the profile of the drug. Their developments led to its mass-production to treat Allied casualties in the Second World War.

Fleming was very modest about his contribution to the development of penicillin, and often referred to the 'Fleming myth' surrounding the drug. However, as the first person to identify the antibiotic properties of the active substance he earned the right to name it.

Adolf Hitler, Neville Chamberlain, Benito Mussolini and Édouard Daladier reached an agreement on the Nazi annexation of the Sudetenland areas of Czechoslovakia.

As a result of the Treaty of Versailles at the end of the First World War, Germany had lost territory to the newly-created state of Czechoslovakia. Following his rise to power in Germany, Hitler set about reuniting ethnic Germans and laid his sights on the Sudetenland. After the Czechoslovakian government turned down the Sudetenland's branch of the Nazi Party request for autonomy from the rest of Czechoslovakia, which had been encouraged by Hitler, tensions between the two countries rose.

By the autumn of 1938 the situation had become a crisis, and Britain's Prime Minister Neville Chamberlain had begun to engage Hitler in discussions aimed to avoid war. Britain and France were both desperate to reach a peaceful resolution and, when faced with Hitler's demand to annex the Sudetenland in return for making no further territorial demands in Europe, the leaders eventually agreed.

Seen by many as the ultimate act of failed appeasement, the Munich Agreement was tabled on 29 September and signed in the early hours of the next day. Czechoslovakia had no option but to agree to the terms, despite not being involved in the discussions. Meanwhile Chamberlain returned to Britain and made the famous speech in which he referred to the Munich Agreement and the related Anglo-German Declaration as securing 'peace for our time'.

The agreement was broken by Hitler the following March when he annexed the rest of Czechoslovakia. Britain declared war on Germany less than six months later.

The words '...And, good morning everyone. Welcome to the exciting new sound of Radio 1' launched the BBC's new popular music station.

Radio 1 was created to compete with the numerous successful offshore 'pirate' radio stations that had been outlawed by an Act of Parliament. 'Flowers in the Rain', a song by The Move, was the first to be played when the station launched in 1967. Radio 1's target demographic was, and has continued to be, the 15-29 year old age group which means the music it broadcasts has evolved throughout the station's history.

The first voice on the station, that of DJ Tony Blackburn, had previously been heard on the pirate stations Radio Caroline and Radio London. Blackburn moved to the BBC earlier in 1967, and his cheery presenting style made him the perfect person to host the Radio 1 breakfast show. He did so until 1973 when he took over the weekday mid-morning slot.

Blackburn's own personal dislike of heavier rock music made him unpopular with some listeners. They were disappointed that the BBC had managed to get the pirate stations banned by the government, but then didn't fill the hole in the airwaves with equivalent music.

Adding to the complaints from listeners, the existence of so-called 'needle time' meant that Radio 1 featured more DJ talk than the pirate stations. This legally imposed limit on the amount of commercial music the station could play was initially a problem for the station, but it led to the station making a large number of live broadcasts and session recordings that have since become prized in their own right.

OCTOBER

OCTOBER

1

1928

The Soviet Union introduced Joseph Stalin's first five-year plan.

The plan set a series of economic goals to be achieved between 1929 and 1934, with the intention of rapidly industrialising the USSR in case of war with the West. Based on Stalin's policy of Socialism in One Country, the five-year plan called for a complete change in the culture of the Soviet Union that affected agriculture just as much as industry.

A vital ingredient in being able to fulfil the industrial goals of the five-year plan was an increase in agricultural productivity. Improved agricultural output would release peasants and farm labourers from the land and allow them to become industrial workers. The first five-year plan is therefore probably most famous for the introduction of the policy of collectivisation, where hundreds of peasants were put together to work on enormous farms that covered thousands of acres.

The dramatic increase in food output per peasant as a result of mechanisation on collectivised farms freed up former agricultural workers to move to the new factories instead. This led to the number of industrial workers almost doubling between 1928 and the end of the plan in 1932. However, significant opposition to the process of collectivisation meant that overall productivity remained low in many areas and caused widespread famine in the countryside as Party officials seized food for the cities yet left the agricultural workers with nothing.

In the factories, however, production soared. Although the targets were constantly revised to the point where they could never be achieved, the first five-year plan firmly set the USSR on the road to becoming a world superpower.

The Siege of Jerusalem came to an end when Saladin captured the city from the crusaders who had ruled the city since 1099.

Having been defeated at the Battle of Hattin on 4 July 1187, the majority of the forces of the Crusader Kingdom of Jerusalem fled to the city of Tyre in modern Lebanon. The Kingdom was left with only its capital city having not been captured by Saladin's armies, although King Guy had been taken prisoner alongside various other members of the nobility. This left Balian of Ibelin as the most senior noble in the Kingdom.

Balian secured permission from Saladin to travel to Jerusalem to rescue his wife Maria Comnena, Queen consort of Jerusalem, and their family. On arrival he was persuaded to stay and lead the defence of the city. This meant breaking an oath he had sworn to Saladin that he wouldn't stay in Jerusalem for more than a day.

Arriving at the city on 20 September, Saladin provided an escort for Balian's wife and children who were moved to safety in Tripoli. Meanwhile, he began a relentless assault on the city that eventually led to a breach in the wall. Although the attacking army was unable to gain access to the city, the lack of knights available to maintain the city's defence led Balian to negotiate the surrender after twelve days of siege.

In return for the crusaders' unconditional surrender, Saladin agreed that anyone who paid a ransom would be able to leave the city in safety. Balian paid for the freedom of 7,000 people, while Saladin himself later freed thousands more who were unable to pay. Despite this, approximately 15,000 inhabitants were enslaved. The Third Crusade was launched two years later in an attempt to reconquer the Holy Land from Saladin.

OCTOBER

3

1990

Germany was reunified when the territory of the communist German Democratic Republic joined with the Federal Republic of Germany.

Large cracks had begun to show in East Germany's communist regime from the middle of 1989 and eventually led to the fall of the Berlin Wall in November that year. This encouraged the ongoing Peaceful Revolution in the East, which succeeded in bringing about free elections in March the following year.

The West German Chancellor, Helmut Kohl, had already called for greater cooperation between West and East in November 1989. Furthermore the election of the new East German parliament, known as the Volkskammer, in March 1990 ensured that both sides now had governments who were considering reunification.

The GDR's economy had begun to collapse as the structures of communist control were removed. The replacement of the East German Mark with West Germany's Deutsche Mark as the official currency in June ensured a secure economic framework for political union.

By the end of August the Volkskammer had passed a resolution in favour of reunification and signed the German Reunification Treaty. This was approved by large majorities in the legislative chambers of each country on 20 September, and at midnight on 3 October the black, red and gold flag of West Germany was raised above the Brandenburg Gate which had previously divided the two sides.

3 October is now an official public holiday in Germany, and is known as The Day of German Unity.

OCTOBER

4

1582

Pope Gregory XIII implemented the Gregorian calendar.

By the 16th Century a sizable drift had developed between the Julian calendar, the lunar calendar, and the real moon. Consequently the date on which the church celebrated Easter had begun to move away from the time that it had been celebrated by the early church. The Catholic Church disliked this seasonal drift, and so decreed the papal bull *Inter gravissimas* in early 1582. This was intended to reform or, in the words of the Latin text, 'restore' the calendar to align with that at the time of the First Council of Nicaea in 325.

Thirteen centuries' worth of accumulated variations between the existing and new calendars meant that the change to the Gregorian calendar would lead to the deletion of ten days. Consequently, in the territories that adopted the new calendar, the day after 4 October 1582 became 15 October although the day of the week did not change.

The Gregorian calendar was originally only planned to be adopted by the Catholic Church and the Papal States, since to become a nation's official calendar it had to be approved by the civil authorities. Other Catholic territories did implement it on the specified date, however, such as those territories governed by Philip II of Spain and the Polish–Lithuanian Commonwealth. Many more Catholic countries adopted it soon after, but Protestant governments rejected the change.

Despite this slow uptake, by the end of the 18th Century most of the countries of Western Europe including the sizeable British Empire had switched to the Gregorian calendar to ease international trade. The Gregorian calendar is now the most widely used calendar in the world.

Two cultural icons made their first appearance when *Dr No*, the first of the *James Bond* series of films, hit cinema screens on the same day as the Beatles released their debut single 'Love Me Do'.

Most Hollywood studios at the time were not interested in making the *James Bond* films because they were seen as being 'too British'. Eventually United Artists agreed to provide $1 million dollars to fund the film. *Dr No* was jointly produced by two expatriate Americans in Britain, Harry Saltzman and Albert R. 'Cubby' Broccoli, but the money only covered the most basic production. For example there was only one sound editor, and sets were built on a shoestring budget.

The Beatles' debut single, meanwhile, was recorded on three separate occasions due to problems with the drums. More precisely, the problem was the drummer. Producer George Martin had been unhappy with the loose R&B drum of the band's first drummer, Pete Best, when he played at an artist test in June. By the time the band arrived for their first official recording session Ringo Starr had replaced Best in the band, but a further session with professional session drummer Andy White was arranged because Martin didn't like Ringo's drum sound. Very early pressings of the single for 'Love Me Do' featured Ringo's drumming, but later ones used the White recordings instead.

Both the *James Bond* films and the Beatles went on to be huge worldwide successes from their humble low-budget beginnings in Britain, and their legacy as dominant forces in film and music continues to this day.

Egyptian President Anwar Sadat was assassinated by members of the Egyptian Islamic Jihad, a terrorist group that was angered by the peace treaty he had negotiated with Israel.

Three years prior to his assassination, Sadat had signed the Camp David Accords and jointly received the Nobel Peace Prize with Israeli Prime Minister Menachem Begin. The Accords led to Egypt signing the Egypt–Israel Peace Treaty in 1979, which marked the first time that an Arab nation had formally recognised the existence of the state of Israel.

The Treaty ended forty years of almost continuous war between the two nations, but it was met with hostility by some people in Egypt who felt that Sadat had betrayed both his national honour and the Palestinian cause.

With growing hostility to his rule at home, Sadat was surrounded by security as he observed the 6 October parade in Cairo that marked the Egyptian crossing of the Suez Canal at the start of the Yom Kippur War. The assassins were on board an artillery truck in the procession, which stopped directly in front of Sadat. They climbed down from the truck and were able to approach the President. Believing that this was part of the proceedings, Sadat stood to salute the men but was killed in a hail of grenades and indiscriminate firing of AK-47s. He died in hospital two hours later.

The assassins were arrested, put on trial and executed, while the death of the President led to Vice President Hosni Mubarak being sworn in as the new President eight days after the assassination. He went on to rule for almost 30 years before he stepped down during the 2011 Egyptian Revolution.

The German Democratic Republic, known as East Germany, was founded in the Soviet occupied zone of Germany.

The establishment of the GDR ensured that the division of Germany that had been implemented in 1945 was made permanent. West Germany had already gained independence from the occupying powers earlier in 1949, and the creation of East Germany meant the same for the former Soviet controlled zone. Although independent, the ruling Socialist Unity Party of Germany maintained close ties with the USSR and was therefore seen as a satellite state.

The constitution that was adopted by the government of the GDR bore striking similarities to the Weimar Constitution of 1919 and was based largely on a draft written from 1946 that was intended for a united Germany. Consequently a new constitution was adopted in 1968 that more accurately reflected the socialist government of the country.

The position of head of state was originally taken by Wilhelm Pieck, who was President until his death in 1960. In reality authority lay with the General Secretary of the Socialist Unity Party who, in 1950, was Walter Ulbricht who had lived in exile in France and the USSR until the defeat of the Nazis. On Pieck's death the office of President was dissolved and was replaced by the State Council. Since the chairman position was commonly held by the General Secretary, this gave Ulbricht and his successors ultimate power in the GDR.

Following 1989's Peaceful Revolution and the fall of Berlin Wall, East Germany experienced the first truly democratic elections that dramatically reduced the power of the Socialist Unity Party and led to the reunification of Germany that took place on 3 October 1990.

OCTOBER

8

1829

Robert Stephenson and Company's steam locomotive *Rocket* won the Rainhill Trials to secure a prize of £500 and the contract and to produce locomotives for the new Liverpool and Manchester Railway.

A specific set of rules had been produced for the Rainhill Trials which, among other things, emphasised speed, reliability, and a low weight. *Rocket* was built specifically to take account of these rules, with Stephenson realising that the relatively light haulage demands meant that a small and nimble locomotive with only moderate pulling power would be more successful than a heavier engine with greater strength.

The approximately 1-mile stretch of track at the Rainhill section of the line was straight and flat so, although it posed no significant challenges to the competitors, it allowed the judges to see all locomotives in an identical setting. Each engine was required to run up and down the section twenty times, meaning that they travelled a distance roughly equivalent to the full journey from Liverpool to Manchester.

Of the ten locomotives entered into the competition only five turned up to the first day on 6 October. By the end of the competition *Rocket* was the only engine to complete the full course without suffering any damage, despite reaching speeds in excess of 25 miles per hour while hauling a train of 13 tons. Consequently Stephenson secured the contract to manufacture locomotives for the Liverpool and Manchester Railway that opened the following year. Although not the world's first steam locomotive, *Rocket* is notable for being the first to bring together a number of innovations that made it the basic template for subsequent steam engines.

OCTOBER

9

1967

The Marxist revolutionary icon Ernesto 'Che' Guevara was executed in Bolivia after being caught by CIA-assisted forces during his attempt to provoke a revolution.

Guevara was born in Argentina and, during a motorcycle journey around South America while he was studying medicine at the University of Buenos Aires, began to become associated with left-wing organisations. Guevara joined the 26th of July Movement after meeting Fidel and Raul Castro during their exile in Mexico and rose to prominence in the Cuban Revolution that deposed Batista. He took on various governmental positions in the years that followed, and continued to refine his socialist views.

Having left his Cuban government post in April 1965, which some believe was the result of a disagreement with Castro over economic and foreign policy, Guevara eventually made his way to Bolivia where he gathered a group of guerrilla fighters to incite revolution and establish a socialist state.

Despite securing some initial victories, Guevara was captured during a huge operation on 8 October. This was carried out by Bolivian Special Forces acting on the advice of Félix Rodríguez, a Cuban exile-turned-CIA operative. 1,800 Special Forces troops surrounded his camp in the Yuro ravine, and Guevara surrendered after being wounded in a firefight.

He was transported to a nearby schoolhouse where Bolivian officers tried but failed to interrogate him. The next morning the Bolivian President ordered his execution. Guevara was shot nine times in a way designed to make the injuries look like they had been caused during a battle with the Bolivian army.

OCTOBER

10

1903

The Women's Social and Political Union, whose members came to be known as suffragettes, was founded at the Manchester home of Sylvia and Emmeline Pankhurst.

Frustrated by the lack of progress made by the National Union of Women's Suffrage Societies from whom the group had split, the WSPU soon became known for its militant and sometimes violent actions under the motto 'Deeds, not words'.

The WSPU sought votes for women on the same basis as votes for men rather than universal suffrage. Many men at the time were denied the vote due to property qualifications, which meant the proposals by the WSPU were seen by some not as 'votes for women' but 'votes for ladies'. The WSPU even split from the Labour Party after Labour voted in favour of universal suffrage, leading the suffragettes to became more explicitly middle-class.

The actions of the suffragettes soon brought into question the traditional ideas of ladylike behaviour as they were routinely arrested for activities that were designed to shock the refined members of the establishment. Actions such as window breaking, arson and the sending of letter bombs routinely saw members of the WSPU imprisoned, where they would often go on hunger strike and be subjected to force-feeding by the authorities. The best known militant action is probably that of Emily Davison who was killed after stepping in front of the King's horse at the 1913 Epsom Derby.

Daily Mail newspaper reporter Charles Hands introduced the term 'suffragette' to describe the WSPU's members as a way to distinguish their violent actions from those of the less militant suffrage groups.

OCTOBER

11

1521

Pope Leo X granted the title *Defender of the Faith* to King Henry VIII of England.

The Pope granted the Latin title *Fidei defensor* to Henry after he published the book *Assertio Septem Sacramentorum*. In the book he defended Catholic doctrine against the criticisms levelled at it by Martin Luther in his *Ninety-five Theses* during the early stages of the Protestant Reformation. Known in English as the *Defence of the Seven Sacraments*, and dedicated to Pope Leo X, Henry began the book as a direct criticism of Luther's *Ninety-five Theses*. In response Luther wrote his own book in called *Against Henry, King of the English (Contra Henricum Regem Anglie)*.

Henry's book was published throughout the 16th Century and remains an important early example of anti-Protestant argument. Two of the key points related to the sanctity of marriage and the supremacy of the Pope. It is notable, therefore, that Henry was later stripped of the title *Defender of the Faith* in 1530 by Pope Paul III after he broke from Rome and established himself as the head of the new Church of England following his divorce from Catherine of Aragon.

Although he was excommunicated from the Catholic Church, Henry was later re-awarded the title *Defender of the Faith* by the English Parliament in relation to defending the new Anglican faith. All of Henry's successors, except for his Catholic daughter Mary, have held the title.

The British monarch is therefore the Supreme Governor of the Church of England and is superior even to the Archbishop of Canterbury. To this day, British coins are inscribed with the abbreviations F D or FID DEF in reference to the original Latin phrase *Fidei defensor*.

OCTOBER

12

1810

The first Oktoberfest took place in Munich to celebrate the marriage of Crown Prince Ludwig to Princess Therese of Saxe-Hildburghausen.

For the newly-married royals, the most important part of the festivities was a horse race held on the final day. The decision to repeat the race the following year led to the establishment of the annual festival at which beer halls and carnival stalls soon began to dominate. Key elements of the original event, such as the procession from Maximilian Strasse to the festival ground, continue to be staged. Since its foundation, the festival has only not taken place 24 times in over 200 years.

The fairground on which the Oktoberfest is held takes its name from the original event. Known as *Theresienwiese* or 'Theresa's meadow' in honour of Ludwig's wife, the land used to lie outside the city gates but is now such an important part of the city that it even has its own station on the U-Bahn underground railway network. Covering an area of 420,000 square metres and now housing 14 large tents and 20 smaller beer tents in addition to a huge fairground, the site hosts in excess of 6 million people a year.

Visitors to the Oktoberfest invariably travel to enjoy the beer, a special brew that is 2% stronger than most conventional beer. Rules state that the beer must be brewed within the city limits of Munich and adhere to the *Reinheitsgebot* or German Beer Purity Law decreed by Duke William IV in 1516.

The last Oktoberfest horse race, the part of the event that was responsible for establishing the annual celebration, took place in 1960.

OCTOBER

13

1792

The cornerstone of the White House, which at the time was to be known as the United States Executive Mansion, was laid.

The White House was built as part of the development of the Federal City – a national capital founded under the terms of the 1790 Residence Act. A competition, organised by Thomas Jefferson, led to the White House being built according to a design by Irish-born James Hoban, during which time Philadelphia in Pennsylvania served as the temporary capital. Hoban's design was greatly influenced by Dublin's Leinster House alongside various other Georgian-era buildings in Ireland.

The foundations of the White House and the main residence were built by African-American slaves, alongside some freemen and employed Europeans. Other work, such as the dressing and laying of the sandstone walls, was completed by immigrant masons who came primarily from Scotland.

According to the White House Historical Association, slave labour was used for the building due to the poor response to adverts for paid construction workers, although records show that slaves were hired from their masters rather than being owned by the government itself. Construction of the building took eight years, and John Adams was the first President to take up residence when he moved in on Saturday 1 November 1800.

The sandstone walls of the White House get their familiar colour and name from whitewash applied after construction. The story that the building was painted white to hide damage inflicted during the 1814 Burning of Washington is not true. However, following damage caused by the British attack, the White House did have to undergo a major reconstruction project that lasted until 1817.

OCTOBER

14

1066

The Battle of Hastings was fought between Duke William II of Normandy and the Anglo-Saxon king Harold Godwinson.

To call the battle the Battle of Hastings is actually misleading, since it was actually fought seven miles away from Hastings. Its true location is near the modern town of Battle, although the 1087 Domesday Book ordered by William the Conqueror did describe it as the Battle of Hastings.

Less than four weeks before the battle, the northern English army had been defeated by King Harald Hardrada of Norway during the Battle of Fulford. Harold had been waiting on the south coast, expecting an invasion by William, but Hardrada's invasion and seizure of the city of York forced him to rush north. Here he defeated the Norwegians at the Battle of Stamford Bridge on 25 September.

Conscious of an imminent Norman invasion, Harold was forced to immediately march his battered and depleted army south again. On this exhausting journey the soldiers had to cover an average distance of 27 miles a day. Having received news of William's arrival on the way, Harold arrived at the battleground and took up a defensive position on top of Senlac Hill.

Contemporary accounts of the battle frequently contradict each other, so specific details are not known. However, most historians accept that the Anglo-Saxons formed a shield wall that was broken after the Norman knights staged a feigned retreat. Harold was killed on the battlefield and, although his exact cause of death isn't known, it signalled the collapse of the English forces. William was crowned King of England on 25 December at Westminster Abbey.

The Rentenmark was introduced in Weimar Germany in an attempt to stop the hyperinflation crisis that had crippled the economy.

The French and Belgian occupation of the Ruhr that began on 11 January 1923 had been met with a policy of passive resistance by the German government. Although this succeeded in frustrating the occupying powers who sought to extract reparations payments in the form of natural resources, it also brought the economy in the Ruhr to a shuddering halt.

As the strike had been called for by the government, the strikers and their families were eligible to receive income support. However, falling tax revenues due to the lack of trade meant that the government struggled to keep up with payments. In response they began printing money despite there being no product to base it on. The Papiermark went into freefall as hyperinflation took hold, and the cabinet resigned in favour of a new one formed under Gustav Stresemann.

Stresemann's finance minister, Hans Luther, introduced the Rentenmark to replace the crisis-hit Papiermark in a plan devised jointly with Hjalmar Schacht at the Reichsbank. Schacht later went on to be the Minister of Economics in the early years of Hitler's rule.

The new currency was backed by land that was used by businesses and agriculture, and was introduced at the rate of one Rentenmark to one trillion Papiermarks. With the currency now tied to something with physical value, hyperinflation was stopped in its tracks. The more commonly known Reichsmark was introduced the following year at the same value.

Marie Antoinette was executed by guillotine in the Place de la Revolution in Paris.

Marie Antoinette and her children had continued to be held prisoner in the Temple following the execution of her husband, the former King Louis XVI. Calls for her trial grew louder following the creation of the Committee of Public Safety during the period known as the Terror. This became the National Convention's preferred policy following the fall of the more moderate Girondins at the end of May.

Marie Antoinette was moved to an isolated cell in the *Conciergerie*. Meanwhile her son, Louis-Charles, was sent to live with a Jacobin cobbler as a form of revolutionary re-education. While imprisoned in the *Conciergerie* the former queen plotted a failed escape attempt known as 'The Carnation Plot' which is believed by some to have convinced the Committee of Public Safety to bring her to trial in front of the Revolutionary Tribunal on 14 October.

Although the guilty verdict was a foregone conclusion, Marie Antoinette had expected to be sentenced to life imprisonment or exile. Having been found guilty of treason, she was instead sentenced to death and transported to the guillotine in an open cart. It's widely reported that she showed courage throughout the remaining hours of her life including in the face of extreme verbal abuse she suffered on the hour-long journey to the Place de la Revolution.

While climbing the steps to the scaffold the former queen accidentally stepped on the foot of the executioner. She reacted by saying, 'Pardon me, sir, I meant not to do it'. These were her last words before the blade fell at 12.15pm. She was buried in an unmarked grave in the Madeleine cemetery.

Eight people were killed when nearly one and a half million litres of beer swept out of London's Horse Shoe Brewery.

The brewery, which was owned by Meux and Company, had first been established in 1764 on the site of a tavern at the corner of Tottenham Court Road and Oxford Street. The area soon developed into one of dense slum housing known as St Giles Rookery, and was immortalised in the work of the artist William Hogarth who used it as the inspiration for his Gin Lane.

Although some citizens had expressed concern over the presence of large quantities of beer so close to a residential area, there was no response from the company or the authorities. Even when one of the metal hoops that held the huge brewing vats together broke earlier in the day, nothing was done to improve the safety of the vessels.

The weakened vat later broke, and the force of the escaping beer led to a chain reaction that ruptured neighbouring vessels to form an alcoholic tidal wave that swept down Tottenham Court Road. The flood rushed with such force that two houses were completely destroyed.

Once the beer began to pour into the street, it quickly began to fill the cellars of nearby houses in which families lived. Some of these drowned when they became trapped underground in the sea of beer. Despite the destruction the flood was declared to be an act of God by both judge and jury, so the brewery was able to resume production shortly afterwards. Beer continued to be brewed on the site until 1921 when it was cleared to make way for the Dominion Theatre.

The British Broadcasting Company was established.

In the early 1920s, radio set producers in Britain were keen to expand their market. However, at the time the government only granted occasional 'experimental' radio licenses which meant that there were large periods when the airwaves were completely silent. This was no use to radio manufacturers themselves who needed regular broadcasts in order to make their products worthwhile.

As more and more requests were submitted for the 'experimental' licenses, the government instead chose to grant a single broadcasting license to a consortium of the UK's leading radio manufacturers. The six companies held an equal amount of shares in the new venture, which hired John Reith, later to become a Lord, as its first Managing Director.

The new broadcasting company was jointly funded through a royalty on the sale of radio sets sold by the member producers and a license fee. However, the number of amateur electronics enthusiasts who began building their own sets meant that the income did not produce adequate funds. Consequently the member companies found themselves running at a loss, and this contributed to their desire to extricate themselves from the arrangement. Having successfully negotiated an exit deal, the company later became the British Broadcasting Corporation when it transferred to government ownership under the Postmaster General, the ministerial position that was responsible for the postal system and telecommunications.

By the time the BBC had begun its first experimental television broadcasts in 1932, the company had been publicly funded for five years.

The League of Nations voted to impose sanctions on Italy after it invaded Abyssinia.

The Italian invasion began without a declaration of war on 3 October 1935, although the two nations had previously been embroiled in a territorial dispute over the Walwal oasis throughout which both countries had acted aggressively. However, the decisive invasion of Ethiopia by Italian troops stationed in nearby Eritrea saw the League of Nations declare Mussolini's country the aggressor four days later.

The League imposed limited sanctions which failed to restrict oil sales to Italy and access to the Suez Canal, which was used by Italy to transport troops, equipment and supplies. Therefore, although the speed at which the League acted was considerably quicker than during the Manchuria Crisis in which the League took a year to respond, the sanctions themselves were virtually worthless.

Concerned about the rise of Hitler in Germany and the increasing danger of a European conflict, Britain and France were reluctant to punish Italy in case they were driven to ally with the Nazi dictator. They even began to formulate the secret Hoare-Laval Plan that would have granted large parts of Abyssinia to Italy, but were forced to cancel this when details became public and were met with popular opposition.

Even after it became evident that Mussolini was using chemical weapons against Abyssinia, the League continued in its failure to impose stringent sanctions. Hitler's remilitarisation of the Rhineland in March 1936 had made France desperate to keep Mussolini as an ally. When Abyssinia was finally captured on 5 May, all the sanctions were dropped.

The 6,000 mile Long March by the Red Army of the Communist Party of China ended when the troops led by Mao Zedong arrived in Shaanxi.

The communists had been fighting a Civil War against the nationalist Kuomintang since 1927 and, by 1934, the Jiangxi Soviet was surrounded by Chiang Kai-shek's anti-Communist troops. Facing certain starvation if the siege was allowed to continue, the communists opted to abandon the Soviet in a controlled breakout that began on 16 October 1934.

Numbering nearly 100,000 people, the fleeing Red Army faced almost daily assaults from the Nationalists as they struggled north on a year-long journey that covered up to sixteen miles a day. Although the primary aim of the march was to establish a safe base away from Nationalist interference, the Long March also served as a useful propaganda tool as Red Army troops came into direct contact with the local peasantry. The Eight Points of Attention, a set of orders for the good behaviour of troops, was central to this. The Eight Points ensured that the Red Army treated peasants with respect and gratitude, in stark contrast to the Nationalists who were known to confiscate property and supplies.

Although the three armies involved in the march didn't fully unite until two days after the arrival of the first troops, their journey to the foot of the Great Wall marked the successful end of the Red Army's flight to safety.

It was during the Long March that Mao Zedong emerged as the best person to lead the Chinese Communist Party, and his survival alongside less than 10% of the original troops mythologised him and reinforced his authority.

The British Navy under the command of Vice Admiral Horatio Lord Nelson defeated the combined fleets of the French and Spanish Navies in the Battle of Trafalgar.

The War of the Third Coalition, which was part of the wider Napoleonic Wars, had seen the British Navy blockade France since early 1805. The enemy fleet under Admiral Pierre-Charles Villeneuve successfully managed to leave port during a storm, and this made Nelson keen to engage them.

By the middle of October, Nelson had assembled his fleet off the Spanish coast at Cadiz where Villeneuve had chosen to harbour. Realising his numerical inferiority to the combined French and Spanish force, and wishing to achieve a conclusive victory, Nelson developed a tactic that flew in the face of established naval battle tactics.

The Combined Fleet left Cadiz on the evening of 20 October, and was quickly pursued by the British. By the next morning they were just over twenty miles away from Cape Trafalgar and the two fleets began to prepare for battle. Just before midday Nelson's flagship, HMS *Victory*, flew the flag signal, 'England expects that every man will do his duty' and the battle began shortly after with the British fleet divided into two columns that sailed through the French-Spanish line at right-angles. During the mêlée that followed, Nelson was hit by a musket ball from a French infantryman on board the *Redoutable*. He died three hours later, but the British went on to win the battle.

The Battle of Trafalgar secured British supremacy of the seas and saw the victorious fleet sail away without having lost a single ship.

The Granville–Paris Express train ran across the station platform, crashed through a 60cm wall, and fell 10 metres to the street below after it overran the buffer stop at the Gare Montparnasse terminus.

131 passengers were on board the express as it left its final stop behind schedule. The heavy train of six passenger coaches, three luggage vans and a post van was being driven by Guillaume-Marie Pellerin. Despite nineteen years of experience he was concerned that he was running late as he approached Montparnasse.

In an attempt to claw back some time, Pellerin drove much faster than normal into the station and applied the Westinghouse air brake, which operated the brakes of each carriage, in an attempt to slow down the train.

Unfortunately the Westinghouse brake failed and the locomotive's own brakes were insufficient to stop such a heavy train travelling at high speed. The conductor on board was preoccupied with paperwork and realised the danger too late to be able to apply his own handbrake. As a result the train ran through the buffer stop and crashed through the wall onto the street below.

Falling masonry hit and killed a woman selling newspapers on the street outside, but amazingly she was the only person who died. The fireman, two guards and two passengers sustained injuries, but everyone else was left unharmed. The driver was later found guilty of driving too fast and fined 50 francs.

The event is now probably best known thanks to the proliferation of posters showing the train standing on its nose in the street having crashed through the station wall.

England declared war on Spain in what became known as the War of Jenkins' Ear.

Robert Jenkins commanded the British merchant brig *Rebecca* and was involved in trade with Spanish America. Although Spain had granted permission for Britain to transport limited goods and slaves, numerous smugglers took advantage and brought additional items into port. Spanish patrol boats therefore routinely boarded British ships, and it was on one of these occasions in 1731 that Jenkins was accused of smuggling.

The Spanish crew tied Jenkins to the mast and his left ear was cut off with a sword. The captain, Julio León Fandiño, then told him to inform the British king that the 'same will happen to him if [he was] caught doing the same'.

Although Jenkins returned to Britain and relayed the message to the king, his disfigurement was greeted with little interest. However, when opposition politicians began pushing for war against Spain seven years later Jenkins was invited to address Parliament where he recounted his experience on the *Rebecca* and reputedly showed his carefully preserved severed ear. Press reports of Jenkins' testimony ignited public passions against the Spanish and put pressure on Prime Minister Robert Walpole to respond with aggression. War was declared on 23 October 1739.

Although it later became subsumed into the War of the Austrian Succession, the War of Jenkins' Ear is notable for coinciding with the first performance of the song 'Rule, Britannia!' The writer Thomas Carlyle is credited with giving the conflict its name in his 1858 biography of the Prussian King Friedrich II.

OCTOBER

24

1929

The Wall Street Crash began, and the day assumed the name Black Thursday.

Signs of an impending financial crisis had been identified many months before the crash. For example, on 25 March the Federal Reserve had issued a stark warning of the dangers of speculation on the stock market. This warning coincided with a slowing down of the American economy, but investors continued to purchase stocks that gradually pushed the market to a peak of 381.17 points on 3 September.

By late September many of the larger investors had begun to grow nervous at the continued growth of the markets and started to sell their shares. By the middle of October the market was in freefall as more and more people began panicking about the plummeting prices. Black Thursday saw selling of shares on the New York Stock Exchange on an unprecedented scale. Over 12.8 million shares were sold on that one day alone which resulted in the market losing 11% of its value.

Although Black Thursday was the first day of large-scale panic selling, the losses were dwarfed by those the following week when around 16 million shares were sold. Within just a few days of trading, $30 billion dollars had been wiped off the stock market. This was the Wall Street Crash.

Although the scale of panic selling did slow down, the market continued its downward trajectory for over 2 years, finally reaching an all-time low on 8 July 1932. By that time the effect of the Great Depression had crept around the world, acting as a catalyst for the Second World War that was to follow. The market didn't return to its pre-crash level until 1954.

OCTOBER

25

1415

The English king Henry V celebrated a major victory in the Hundred Years War when he defeated the numerically superior French army at the Battle of Agincourt.

Having landed in northern France on 13 August, Henry sought to regain control of lands that had once come under the rule of the English kings. However, it took longer than planned to capture the town of Harfleur which meant that Henry was not able to mount an effective attack on the French.

Instead the English troops marched to Calais as a 'show of force', but were shadowed by the French who continued to raise an army en-route. By 24 October both armies had gathered at Agincourt, and the next morning Henry began the battle.

Henry's archers launched an initial volley that incapacitated many of the French army's horses and forward troops. The French forces behind these ranks struggled to find a way through this mass of dead bodies and across the muddy field that separated them from the English. Furthermore, the French cavalry was unable to advance efficiently due to a number of wooden stakes that had been driven into the ground to protect the English archers.

The French advance became more and more densely packed, making the forward French knights less and less able to fight efficiently. Over 8,000 French troops are estimated to have been killed in the battle while the English army's losses were less than 500.

Famous as a result of the decisive role of the English and Welsh longbowmen, the Battle of Agincourt is sometimes claimed to have provided the origin for the 'two finger salute' (V sign) as an offensive gesture in England. There is no contemporary evidence to support this claim.

OCTOBER

26

1860

Giuseppe Garibaldi met with Victor Emmanuel II, the King of Sardinia, at Teano and handed him control of southern Italy.

Garibaldi landed with his 'Thousand' – also known as the Redshirts – on the island of Sicily on 11 May. The number of troops under his command quadrupled within just three days and so, on 14 May, Garibaldi proclaimed himself dictator of Sicily in the name of Victor Emmanuel II of Italy.

Within a fortnight he had besieged the Sicilian capital of Palermo, where many of the inhabitants joined with him and began to attack the Neapolitan garrison. Despite the arrival of 25,000 reinforcements the Neapolitans surrendered the city following an armistice facilitated by a British admiral, but not before the city had been virtually reduced to rubble.

Further difficult battles followed, but by the start of September Garibaldi had crossed to the mainland and taken control of Naples. The king fled with his army, but he had had not been defeated and still had the support of around 25,000 soldiers. At the Battle of Volturno, Garibaldi's Redshirts were only successful against these forces thanks to the arrival of the Piedmontese Army who made it clear that they would not allow Garibaldi to march on Rome. When Victor Emmanuel arrived on 26 October, Garibaldi chose to hand over his territory.

Hailing him as King of Italy, Garibaldi's surrender of the Kingdom of the Two Sicilies effectively ended any hope for an Italian republic but was one of the most significant events in the unification of the peninsula. Garibaldi subsequently retired to the island of Caprera.

American singer Ben E. King recorded the renowned song 'Stand By Me'.

Released the year afer it was recorded, 'Stand By Me' was King's second solo single after he quit the American R&B and doo-wop band The Drifters. The song went on to be voted one of the Songs of the Century by the Recording Industry Association of America. According to BMI – the largest performing rights organisation in the USA – it was the fourth most performed song of the 20th Century.

Accounts of the recording of 'Stand By Me' differ. Some reports claim that, having been in the studio to record what was to become his debut solo hit, 'Spanish Harlem', King had some spare time at the end of the session. The producers asked if he had any other songs and liked 'Stand By Me' enough to call the session musicians back in to the studio and record it.

Other accounts, including that of co-writer and producer Mike Stoller, claim that 'Stand By Me' was jointly written by King, Stoller and Mike Leiber in their office. Stoller attributed King's inspiration for the song to an older spiritual. Stoller and Leiber were already renowned songwriters who had written a range of hit songs such as 'Hound Dog' and 'Jailhouse Rock' that were recorded by Elvis Presley. Many people therefore believe that Stoller's account is more likely to be accurate.

Stoller and Leiber were hugely influential record producers who mentored Phil Spector before he went on to become an influential songwriter and record producer in his own right. By coincidence, Spector later produced John Lennon's cover version of 'Stand By Me' that was released in 1975.

OCTOBER

28

1962

The Cuban Missile Crisis ended when Soviet Premier Nikita Khrushchev agreed to remove Russian nuclear missiles from the island of Cuba.

Cuban President Fidel Castro had met with Khrushchev in July 1961, and the two men had agreed to station short-range nuclear missiles on Cuba. America already had a number of nuclear missiles in Italy and Turkey that threatened the USSR, and had supported the failed Bay of Pigs invasion in April 1961.

Although the missiles were identified by American reconnaissance on 15 October, the thirteen days of the crisis officially began when President John F. Kennedy was informed the following morning.

Threatened by the discovery of the missiles on Cuba, which lay barely 90 miles from the coast of Florida, the USA responded by enforcing a naval blockade around the island in an attempt to stop any more missiles being delivered. The Soviet Union initially refused to recognize the blockade, but the ships carrying missiles later turned back while Kennedy and Khrushchev continued a series of tense negotiations.

An agreement was eventually struck in which the USSR would publicly remove the missiles from Cuba while the USA would secretly remove its own from Turkey and Italy. The Soviet Union broadcast its intention to remove the missiles on Radio Moscow on the morning of 28 October, and the first dismantled missiles were shipped out of Cuba on 5 November.

Because America's part of the agreement was kept secret, Khrushchev appeared to have 'lost'. The reality is that both sides made concessions.

OCTOBER

29

1956

Israel invaded the Egyptian Sinai and began the military phase of what became known as the Suez Crisis.

Egyptian President Gamal Abdel Nasser had nationalised the Suez Canal on 26 July. He had been careful to pay compensation to shareholders of the Suez Canal Company after the nationalisation, but both Britain and France were concerned about the potential economic and political problems that might ensue if Egypt chose to limit their access to the canal. They were particularly worried about access to oil from the Persian Gulf. Meanwhile, Israel was angry that Egypt had closed the canal to their shipping and blockaded the Gulf of Aqaba.

Months of tense negotiations failed to reassure Britain and France who secretly began preparing a military response to take back control of the canal in alliance with Israel. An agreement between the three allies was concluded at Sèvres in France on 24 October. The Protocol of Sèvres called for a full-scale Israeli assault on Egyptian Sinai on 29 October, which would be followed the next day with calls from Britain and France for the two sides to withdraw from the Canal Zone. Their troops would then move in to the area and place it under Anglo-French control.

The Israeli invasion took place on 29 October as agreed, and Nasser rejected the demands to withdraw his troops from the canal. In response British and French forces invaded the Egyptian city of Port Said on the night of 5-6 November.

The invasion was met with international condemnation that pressured British Prime Minister Anthony Eden into calling a ceasefire just a day later.

Orson Welles directed and narrated a radio adaptation of 'The War of the Worlds' as part of the *Mercury Theatre on the Air.*

The Mercury Theatre on the Air was a series of weekly one-hour radio plays created by Welles and broadcast on the CBS Radio network. 'The War of the Worlds' was the seventeenth episode of the radio show, and was adapted by American playwright Howard E. Koch who is probably best known for later co-writing the film *Casablanca* starring Humphrey Bogart and Ingrid Bergman.

For the radio play of 'The War of the Worlds' Koch took the general story arc from H. G. Wells' original novel but substituted 19th Century Europe for 20th Century America by changing the names of locations and personalities to ones that were more familiar and contemporary. He was only asked to write the script a week before the broadcast and earned $50, but was permitted to keep the rights to the finished script.

Before the live broadcast had even finished on the night of 30 October, CBS began to receive telephone calls from concerned listeners. Announcements were made before, during and after the performance that the events were fictitious, but it was clear that these warnings went unheeded by many. Although the listening figures were relatively small, news of the alien invasion spread through a country nervous about impending war.

Within hours of the broadcast the billboards in New York's Times Square flashed with reports of mass panic caused by the play, although most reports were based on anecdotal accounts from the Associated Press. Subsequent research suggests that the public response was nowhere near the scale claimed at the time.

The foundations of the Protestant Reformation were laid when Martin Luther reputedly nailed his *Ninety-five Theses* to the door of All Saints' Church in Wittenberg.

Officially titled *The Ninety-Five Theses on the Power and Efficacy of Indulgences*, Luther had sought to engage the church authorities in a debate over the effect of earthly deeds on a soul's salvation. As a 'disputation' the theses were designed to be points for theological debate around the practice of selling indulgences. However, the political and religious climate of the time, combined with the recent invention of the printing press, meant that Luther's document was circulated to a much wider audience and soon gained attention across Europe.

The popular story that Luther angrily nailed a list of grievances to the door of the church in the German state of Saxony-Anhalt is highly unlikely. Modern scholars instead suggest that Luther wrote to his bishop, Albert of Mainz, on 31 October with a copy of the *Ninety-five Theses*. After failing to receive a response, he began circulating copies amongst his friends.

Luther's particular concern was the church practice of selling indulgences with a promise that a buyer's sins would be absolved. In Thesis 86 he also shone light on the Papacy's extraction of money from the poor in order to build St Peter's Basilica, rather than using its own financial reserves. It is therefore no surprise that the *Ninety-five Theses* made their way to Rome, where the Pope condemned them. Two years later Pope Leo X issued a papal bull that led to Luther's excommunication but failed to stop the Protestant Reformation.

NOVEMBER

The world's first aerial bombing took place when Italian Lieutenant Giulio Gavotti dropped four grenades on Turkish troops in Libya.

The weakness of the Ottoman Empire demonstrated by Italy's later victory in the Italo-Turkish War is seen by some historians as a contributing factor to the rise of Balkan nationalism that preceded the First World War. The First Balkan War was actually launched while Turkey was distracted by ongoing fighting against the Italians in Libya.

The Italo-Turkish War was also significant for its impact on the use of aircraft for military purposes. As well as carrying out the world's first aerial bombing, the Italians were also responsible for conducting the first ever aerial reconnaissance mission a week earlier.

Unmanned balloons had already been used by Austrian troops to carry bombs in their war against in Venice in 1849. However, Gavotti was the first to drop explosives from a manned aeroplane. He was flying a reconnaissance mission when he decided to drop the four separate 4-pound grenades from his Taube monoplane.

Although nobody was injured during the attack, the Ottoman Empire complained that aerial bombing contravened the Hague Convention of 1899. Italy argued that the agreement specifically stated that bombs could not be dropped from balloons and said nothing about bombs dropped from aircraft. However, it's important to note that the aeroplane hadn't even been invented when the agreement in question was signed. Within three years of Gavotti's attack, aerial bombing had become an established part of modern warfare.

NOVEMBER

2

1795

The Directory was established in France following the Thermidorian Reaction.

The Thermidorian Reaction had begun on 27 July 1794 in which the National Convention turned against the increasingly radical Jacobin leaders of the French Revolution. It ended the dominance of the Committee of Public Safety and resulted in the arrest and execution of Robespierre and 21 other leading members. Their executions were followed by a purge of other radicals in what became known as the White Terror.

Having alienated itself from the radical left-wing, the National Convention also faced threats from the right that culminated in a Royalist attack on 13 Vendémiaire. This uprising was put down by Napoleon Bonaparte with 'a whiff of grapeshot'.

Prior to the Royalist uprising, the National Convention had ratified a new constitution known as the Constitution of the Year III. This established a bicameral legislature and a five-man Directory that wielded executive power. Although it survived for four years, the Directory was generally unsuccessful at dealing with the domestic problems facing France. Even the numerous military victories against foreign enemies were not enough to secure much support. In response the Directory used the Army to repress its opponents, which only fuelled the opposition further and gave the Army increasing power within France.

By 1799 even the government realised that it could not continue for much longer. On 9 November, Napoleon launched the coup of 18 Brumaire. This replaced the Directory with the Consulate and effectively brought the French Revolution to an end, ten years after it began.

NOVEMBER

3

1957

Laika the dog became the first animal to enter orbit around the Earth when she was launched into space on board the Soviet spacecraft Sputnik 2.

Laika was a stray dog who was found on the streets of Moscow. Strays from Moscow were specifically chosen for the mission on the assumption that they had already learned how to deal with extreme temperatures and prolonged periods without food. Despite this pre-conditioning, Laika and two other dogs selected by the scientists still had to undergo extensive training ahead of the mission. This included having to endure long periods of time in cramped conditions, extreme G-forces on centrifuges, and exposure to loud noises to simulate the conditions of spaceflight.

Laika was never intended to return to Earth as the technology to re-enter the atmosphere had not yet been developed. Despite this, the launch of a canine into space was seen by the Russian scientists as a precursor to human spaceflight in order to determine the effect of launch and prolonged weightlessness on a living passenger.

Throughout the mission, scientists on the ground monitored data coming from sensors attached to Laika. The readings indicated significant stress, but she survived the launch and made four circuits of the Earth before dying of overheating as a result of a malfunction in the temperature control system. The exact cause of her death was only confirmed in 2002.

Laika's death raised ethical questions about the use of animals in scientific research as the spacecraft was not designed to be retrievable. She was, therefore, knowingly sent on a mission from which she would not return.

The Iran hostage crisis began when a group of Iranian students from a group called the Muslim Student Followers of the Imam's Line stormed the American Embassy in Tehran.

The origins of the crisis lay in the declining relationship between the United States and Iran as a result of the rule of Mohammed Reza Shah Pahlavi. In 1953 the American CIA joined with MI6 from Britain to orchestrate a coup that would install the Shah as ruler of Iran. The aim was to protect British and American oil interests in the region. Although the coup was successful, many Iranians opposed the Shah's repressive rule and found a leader in Ayatollah Ruhollah Khomeini under whose guidance the Shah was overthrown in July 1979.

Three months later, on 22 October, the Shah was granted entry to the United States to access medical treatment for lymphoma. Although President Jimmy Carter was initially reluctant to grant entry to the Shah, he eventually did so on humanitarian grounds. The political repercussions of Carter's apparent sheltering of the Shah were huge. Khomeini stirred up anti-American feeling by referring to the USA as the 'Great Satan' and began hinting that the CIA was plotting another coup to return the Shah to power.

Shortly after the Shah landed in New York on 4 November, a student demonstration outside the gates of the American Embassy in Tehran stormed the building. The students seized 66 hostages, 14 of whom were released before the end of the crisis. The other 52 hostages were held for 444 days. They were set free shortly after Ronald Reagan concluded his inaugural address as the new President of the USA on 20 January 1981.

NOVEMBER

5

1605

The Gunpowder Plot was foiled when Guy or Guido Fawkes was discovered guarding 36 barrels of gunpowder that had been placed in an undercroft beneath the House of Lords in London.

The Gunpowder Plot was conceived at a time of significant religious tension in the British Isles. Less than a century had passed since Henry VIII broke from Rome, and Catholics continued to be persecuted after James VI of Scotland was crowned James I of England.

A group of thirteen Catholics led by Robert Catesby conspired to blow up the House of Lords during the State Opening of England's Parliament, when James would be inside the building. Having killed the king, they planned to then initiate a revolt that would bring James' young daughter Elizabeth to the throne as a puppet queen. However, the plot was revealed in an anonymous letter and a search of the undercroft beneath the Palace of Westminster was conducted late in the evening of the 4 November.

The failure of the plot and subsequent convictions and executions of the conspirators has since been commemorated in Britain on what is known as Guy Fawkes Night or Bonfire Night. The event traditionally involves effigies of Guy Fawkes being burned on a bonfire amidst large firework displays.

Most people know that Guy Fawkes, along with the other surviving conspirators, was found guilty of high treason and sentenced to execution by being hung, drawn and quartered. What is less widely known is that he managed to leap from the gallows and break his neck. Fawkes was therefore already dead by the time the executioner began to carry out the more gruesome parts of his sentence.

NOVEMBER

6

1975

The Sex Pistols played their first gig at St Martin's College of Art in London.

The Sex Pistols had developed from a band called The Strand, who had been managed by British impresario and provocateur Malcolm McClaren. Having returned to the UK after a period working with the New York Dolls, McLaren developed the image for a new line-up which added bass guitarist Glen Matlock and singer Johnny Rotten to the band.

The St Martin's College gig was arranged by Matlock, who was studying there. The Sex Pistols supported pub rock band Bazooka Joe and played a few cover songs on equipment borrowed from the headliners, but the plug was pulled after twenty minutes.

The band had only played five songs, and their dismissal from the stage led to a short fist fight. Hazy memories of people who were there mean that there are different recollections over who exactly chose to end the set. However, everyone agrees that the Sex Pistols' performance was not very polished but incredibly loud.

The bassist with Bazooka Joe, Stuart Goddard, was the only member of the band to be impressed by the Sex Pistols. Energised by the rawness of the punk sound and image, he soon quit the band and formed a new group under his new stage name of Adam Ant. Daniel Kleinman, another member of Bazooka Joe, is now better known for designing seven of last eight *James Bond* title credits.

Despite their popularity on the 'pub rock' circuit, Bazooka Joe failed to find commercial success and broke up soon after the St Martins gig. The Sex Pistols went on to become one of the most influential bands in rock music.

NOVEMBER

7

1917

Red Guards entered the Winter Palace in St Petersburg in a defining event of the Bolshevik Revolution.

Sometimes referred to as the October Revolution, 7 November is the date from the modern Gregorian calendar that aligns with 25 October on the older Julian calendar, from which the revolution got its alternative name.

On the night of 6 November, Bolshevik revolutionary Leon Trotsky led the Red Guards to take control of key government buildings and communication points such as post offices, bridges and the State Bank. Although the Red Guards were armed, historians generally accept that the takeover was carried out without bloodshed or indeed any shots being fired.

Throughout 7 November large crowds of troops sympathetic to the Bolsheviks began to surround the Winter Palace. The actual attack on the palace began after a signal shot fired from cruiser ship *Aurora*. Soviet accounts of the night, portrayed most powerfully in Sergei Eisenstein's film re-enactment, present the takeover of the Winter Palace as a huge battle. However, this popular image is a fabrication. The large number of Red Guards marching towards the palace led the Cossacks who were guarding the palace to desert their posts, while the remaining Cadets and volunteers from the Women's Battalion laid down their weapons and surrendered after the Red Guards found their way inside the palace through an open door.

The remnants of the Provisional Government were discovered in a small dining room and were arrested. Meanwhile the wine cellar was looted, leading to what historian Orlando Figes suggested was perhaps, 'the biggest hangover in history'.

NOVEMBER

8

1923

The Beer Hall Putsch took place when Adolf Hitler and First World War hero Erich Ludendorff led an attempted coup against the Weimar Government in the Bavarian city of Munich.

The Beer Hall Putsch was conceived at a time when the Weimar Republic was politically, socially and economically crippled. Hyperinflation had reached its worst level since the occupation of the Ruhr, and many 'patriotic associations' sought to emulate Mussolini's successful March on Rome that had taken place the previous year in order to wrest control away from the seemingly useless Weimar government.

Having led a group of approximately 600 brown-shirted Nazi stormtroopers from their meeting point in the *Bürgerbräukeller*, Hitler burst into a meeting at which Gustav von Kahr, the state commissioner, was speaking. Threatening him at gunpoint, Hitler demanded support for the putsch.

Having made a speech that was met with uproarious approval from the 3,000 members of the audience, Hitler then called on Ludendorff to further press Kahr to support the coup. The state commissioner eventually agreed, and he and his fellow politicians were allowed to leave. They immediately alerted the police and army who began to move against the putsch.

Sixteen Nazis and four policemen were killed in a brief firefight the next day. Hitler was injured and escaped capture, but was arrested two days later and put on trial for high treason. He got revenge on Kahr eleven years later when he ordered his murder as part of the Night of the Long Knives.

The East German government opened the Berlin Wall after Central Committee spokesman Günter Schabowski mistakenly announced that GDR citizens could cross into West Berlin with immediate effect.

Communist Hungary had opened its border with Austria in September, and this had encouraged East Germans to push for reform in their own country. Weekly 'Monday protests' attracted hundreds of thousands of people and eventually forced the government to prepare a new travel policy.

Although the new policy had been agreed by the Politburo on the afternoon of 9 November, their intention was to implement it the next day so that border guards could be briefed and crossings managed in a controlled manner. However, Schabowski had not been at the Politburo meeting and so was only able to base his announcement on notes from a piece of paper handed to him shortly before the press conference. This explains his mistake over the timing of its introduction.

The announcement led huge crowds to begin gathering at the checkpoints. Surprised border guards, who had been given no information about the new rules, were overwhelmed by the appearance of thousands of East Germans who wanted to cross. Although the border remained closed for around three hours, by 11pm the checkpoint at Bornholmer Strasse had been opened. Others followed soon after.

West Berliners still had to have a visa in order to cross to the East. Therefore, for a few weeks after the Wall was opened, East Berliners actually had greater freedom of movement than their West German counterparts.

The American children's television show *Sesame Street* was broadcast for the first time.

Sesame Street was first conceived in 1966 as a way to provide low-income, inner-city children with an educational foundation ready for when they began formal schooling. Creators Joan Ganz Cooney and Lloyd Morrisett wanted the show to appeal to all young children and worked closely with educational psychologists and other experts for a number of years in order to devise a format that would educate and entertain. Extensive use of research was made to shape and direct each episode, resulting in what became known as the CTW (or Children's Television Workshop) model of planning, production, and evaluation.

The producers decided to cast a majority of black actors in order to fit with the original intention of appealing to underprivileged urban children in America. However, this decision met some opposition when the show was made available for broadcast in different states. In Mississippi, for example, a state commission was pressured to reverse its decision not to broadcast the show after it was leaked that they felt 'Mississippi was not yet ready' for a racially mixed cast.

Despite such controversies, *Sesame Street* was met with almost universal acclaim. It quickly became a part of early-years culture with its combination of education, human characters, and Muppets created by Jim Henson's production company.

Sesame Street has now been broadcast for more than 45 years in over 120 different countries and has won over 150 Emmy Awards and 8 Grammy Awards, making it the most awarded children's show on television.

NOVEMBER

11

1918

Fighting on the First World War's Western Front ended when representatives from the Allies and Germany signed the Armistice of Compiègn.

President Woodrow Wilson of the USA had outlined his war aims in the Fourteen Points that he announced in a speech in January 1918. These provided a framework for peace, and were a key factor in encouraging Germany to enter negotiations.

By the end of September, the German High Command had realised that the German cause on the Western Front was doomed. The Kaiser was informed of the situation on 29 September, and by 5 October the German government had contacted President Wilson of the United States to begin preparations for negotiating an armistice. However, the two sides didn't come together until 8 November because Britain, France and Italy were unwilling to enter discussions based on the 14 Points. By this time the German Revolution was about to result in the abdication of Kaiser Wilhelm II.

The treaty negotiation wasn't really a negotiation as the German delegation was presented with the terms and had no option but to sign. Named after the location in which it was signed, the armistice was signed at around 5:00 a.m. in a railway carriage that was part of Allied supreme commander Ferdinand Foch's private train. Designed to be implemented at 11:00 a.m. Paris time, the armistice was extended three times before the Treaty of Versailles finally came into force on 10 January 1920.

The same railway carriage in which the First World War armistice was signed was later used by Hitler for France's surrender to Nazi Germany in 1940.

NOVEMBER

12

1990

British computer scientist Tim Berners-Lee published the first formal proposal for the World Wide Web.

At the time of his invention Berners-Lee was working at CERN, the European Organization for Nuclear Research, in Switzerland. He had initially been based there as a communications engineer but, after three years working for another company in Britain on a computer networking project, returned to CERN as a fellow.

During his previous tenure, Berners-Lee had developed a way to use hypertext to improve the way that researchers could share and update information within the facility. By the time he returned to CERN the internet (the name given to the global connection of different computers and networks) was expanding exponentially. He later described the creation of the World Wide Web as putting the internet's existing TCP/IP technology together with other previously developed technologies such as hypertext and DNS.

In less than two months Berners-Lee had developed the first four key parts of his 'Hypertext project': a piece of software known as a browser called 'WorldWideWeb' (which he spelled as one word without spaces), a web editor, a web server, and the first ever web pages.

The World Wide Web initially met with a muted response outside CERN, so was only used internally until it made its debut on the Internet on 6 August 1991 following a post by its inventor on a newsgroup. Within five years the World Wide Web began to be adopted by people and companies that weren't connected with science or academia, and it has seemingly been dominated by photographs of cats ever since.

NOVEMBER

13

1002

English King Æthelred the Unready 'ordered slain all the Danish men who were in England' in what became known as the Saint Brice's Day Massacre.

Æthelred came to the throne sometime between the ages of ten and thirteen following the assassination of his half-brother Edward the Martyr. Suspicions over Æthelred's involvement in his brother's death led to distrust of the new king, and meant that he did not secure the full loyalty of all his subjects.

By this time Danes already dominated large areas of northern and eastern England in a region known as the Danelaw, where Danish settlers had practised self-rule since 878. Some Danes later settled in Æthelred's kingdom, of which a portion exploited the existing divisions among the king's subjects by raiding towns on the south coast. Combined with raids by new arrivals from Scandinavia, Æthelred found his kingdom under attack every year.

The king paid significant amounts of silver and gold to the new Danes as Danegeld in an attempt to stop the attacks but, in 1002, received information that they planned to 'beshrew him of his life, and afterwards all his council, and then have his kingdom without any resistance.' In response Æthelred ordered the killing of all Danes in England, although it is unlikely that the killing extended into the Danelaw. While it is believed that there was considerable loss of life, actual numbers of Danes who were killed following the order are unknown.

For Æthelred, the massacre had little effect other than to provoke a brutal retaliation by Sweyn Forkbeard, King of Denmark, who invaded the following year.

NOVEMBER

14

1990

Margaret Thatcher's fifteen year leadership of the British Conservative Party was challenged by Michael Heseltine, a former cabinet minister.

Thatcher became Prime Minister of the United Kingdom following the General Election of 1979 but by the late 1980s her popularity, along with that of her party, was plummeting. Interest rates had been raised to 15% in an attempt to bring rampant inflation under control, and the economy was suffering as the first stages of recession took hold. Regular opinion polls had put the Labour Party ahead of the Conservatives for the eighteenth consecutive month by autumn 1990.

Amidst internal party disagreements over Britain's relationship with the European Economic Community, Deputy Prime Minister Geoffrey Howe resigned from the cabinet on 1 November. He made his resignation speech to a packed House of Commons on 13 November. In the speech he portrayed Thatcher as a divisive and confrontational leader, and his criticisms are seen by many to have been the catalyst for Heseltine to mount his leadership challenge the next day.

Although Thatcher won the leadership election that took place on 20 November, she did not do so with a sufficiently large majority to result in an outright victory. She needed to secure a margin of 56 votes over Heseltine and came in four below that.

Initially determined to contest the second ballot, Thatcher consulted with a range of Cabinet members who gave mixed responses on her chances of winning. Consequently she withdrew her candidacy and resigned from the leadership of the Party on 22 November. John Major went on to win the leadership election.

NOVEMBER

15

1917

Georges Clemenceau was appointed Prime Minister of France for the second time.

Clemenceau first had served as Prime Minister until 1909, after which he spent much of his time criticising the government in his radical newspaper. However, by 1917 France had experienced three separate wartime Prime Ministers. President Raymond Poincaré, with whom Clemenceau had a frosty relationship, was frustrated by the government's instability and began to believe that Clemenceau's desire to defeat Germany made him the best replacement.

Throughout 1917 the French government had become increasingly divided over whether to negotiate peace with Germany. Clemenceau was a fierce critic of this approach, having held a deep-seated hatred of Germany since France's loss of Alsace-Lorraine in the Franco-Prussian War five years before he was first elected. His appointment therefore heralded a marked change in government as he sought to consolidate French support behind its troops.

In a speech three days after his appointment, Clemenceau declared, 'Nothing but the war. Our armies will not be caught between fire from two sides. Justice will be done. The country will know that it is defended.' This coincided with a clampdown on pacifist opponents and suspected traitors, and he continued to speak in favour of 'war until the end' until Germany's surrender in November 1918.

Victory was a double-edged sword: Clemenceau now needed to negotiate the terms of the peace treaty with Wilson and Lloyd-George, which he described as like being 'between Jesus Christ on the one hand, and Napoleon Bonaparte on the other.'

NOVEMBER

16

1945

The United Nations Educational, Scientific and Cultural Organisation (UNESCO) was founded.

UNESCO was created to promote international collaboration in education, science and culture as a way to contribute towards world peace and security. The organisation therefore has an enormous remit, seeing it operate across five major areas: education, natural sciences, social and human sciences, culture and the arts, and communication/information.

Although part of the United Nations, UNESCO has its origin in the earlier League of Nations which aimed to 'contribute to the building of peace, the eradication of poverty, sustainable development and intercultural dialogue through education, the sciences, culture, communication and information'. Its original constitution was signed by 37 countries.

UNESCO is best known for its cultural work in which it confers World Heritage status on places with special cultural or physical significance. Its first major scheme was to physically move the Abu Simbel temple in Egypt to avoid the flood waters of the Aswan Dam. However, UNESCO's work extends beyond cultural preservation and has seen it engage in literacy, technical, and teacher-training programmes; international science programmes, and support for freedom of the press.

Since its inception UNESCO has found itself involved in a number of controversies. South Africa withdrew in 1956 amid claims that the organisation was interfering in the country's domestic policies through declarations regarding race. More recently, when 107 member states voted in favour of Palestine becoming a UNESCO member, the United States and Israel withdrew their funding.

NOVEMBER

17

1558

Elizabeth I succeeded her half-sister Mary to become Queen of England.

Elizabeth was the daughter of Henry VIII and Anne Boleyn and, despite being declared illegitimate following the annulment of her parents' marriage, came to the throne as the next in line behind her Catholic half-sister under the terms of the Third Act of Succession. Elizabeth became queen when she was twenty-five years old, and relied heavily on a group of advisers led by Robert Cecil. Despite this she is generally seen as having provided stability through her long reign, in comparison to her two siblings.

Soon after assuming power she introduced the Elizabethan Religious Settlement. Although its two Actos of Parliament resolved much of the Protestant/Catholic divide that had characterised the years before and after her reign, it did little to appease the Catholic Philip II of Spain who launched the Spanish Armada against England in 1588.

Elizabeth never married, nor had any heirs, which led to her becoming known as the Virgin Queen. When she died in 1603, the lack of an heir caused the end of the Tudor dynasty and the beginning of the Stuarts after her closest living relative James VI of Scotland became James I of England.

As the last monarch of the Tudor dynasty, Elizabeth's reign is seen by many as a 'golden age' in English history. She oversaw a period of relative political and religious stability, alongside unprecedented foreign exploration and expansion. The English Renaissance also brought about enormous cultural developments such as the rise of the playwright William Shakespeare.

NOVEMBER

18

1916

The Battle of the Somme ended when German troops retired from the final large British attack at the Battle of the Ancre amid worsening weather.

By the end of the battle the Allies had advanced more than six miles into German-held territory. The Somme had offered the opportunity for them to refine their use of aircraft and had also introduced the tank for the first time.

Following the withdrawal of the German troops Field Marshal Sir Douglas Haig called a halt to the operation, claiming the Somme offensive to have been successful. In his dispatch from the front, Haig stated that 'Verdun had been relieved; the main German forces had been held on the Western front; and the enemy's strength had been very considerably worn down.' He went on to state that 'any one of these three results is in itself sufficient to justify the Somme battle.'

The Somme offensive, and the enormous number of casualties that totalled more than a million men on both sides, has drawn fierce criticism ever since. British Prime Minister David Lloyd George wrote in his *War Diaries* that 'over 400,000 of our men fell in this bullheaded fight and the slaughter amongst our young officers was appalling.'

German losses were also high, however, and some historians have since claimed that the battle left Germany unable to replace its casualties like-for-like, which contributed to their ultimate defeat through a war of attrition. However it was to be another two years before the war finally ended following Germany's signing of the Armistice of Compiègne on 11 November 1918.

United States President Abraham Lincoln delivered the Gettysburg Address at the dedication of the Soldiers' National Cemetery in Gettysburg, Pennsylvania.

Opening with the famous line 'Four score and seven years ago,' Lincoln made the speech to an assembled crowd of approximately 15,000 people including six separate state governors. The President's ten-sentence speech was only ever intended to be 'dedicatory remarks.' Lasting just over two minutes, it linked America's founding principles, as written in the Declaration of Independence, to the struggles of the Civil War.

The main address at the dedication came from famed orator Edward Everett in a 13,000 word speech that directly preceded the President. Everett wrote to the President the next day, stating that the Lincoln had delivered a better address in two minutes than he had in two hours.

Not everyone was so complimentary. Newspaper reports at the time were divided along party lines, with Democrat-leaning newspapers such as the *Chicago Times* dismissing Lincoln's 'silly, flat and dishwatery' speech. Meanwhile, Republican newspapers were overflowing with praise.

The exact location, and even the exact wording, of the Gettysburg Address continue to be points of disagreement. Five manuscripts exist of the speech, but there are a number of notable differences between each of them. Even the inclusion of the words 'under God' are disputed. Furthermore, the manuscripts also differ from reports by people present at the address itself. Despite this, the Gettysburg Address is still seen as one of the most important English-language speeches of all time.

The first of the Nuremberg Trials began.

The Allies announced their intention of punishing German war crimes while the Second World War was still being fought. They did this through a number of declarations, all highlighting their resolve to prosecute those who committed crimes during the war. These were declared again at both the Yalta and Potsdam conferences that took place in 1945.

Procedures for the trials were finally agreed under the London Charter of the International Military Tribunal on 8 August 1945. This defined three types of crime: crimes against peace, war crimes, and crimes against humanity, and stated that members of the military and civilians could be brought to trial.

The first trial was of twenty-four defendants and a number of Nazi organisations, and began on 20 November at the Palace of Justice in Nuremberg. Organised by the Allies to bring senior Nazis to justice for their part in the war crimes committed by the regime, it lasted for almost a year.

Martin Bormann was tried and sentenced *in absentia*, although it was later discovered that he had committed suicide many months previously. Another defendant, Robert Ley, committed suicide a week after the trial began. All but three of the defendants were found guilty, of whom twelve were sentenced to death. The highest ranking of these was Hermann Göring, who committed suicide the night before his execution.

Although criticised by some for being a form of 'victors' justice', the Nuremberg Trials laid the foundations for a permanent international criminal court.

American inventor Thomas Edison announced his phonograph, the world's first practical machine that could record and play sound using a cylinder.

Frenchman Charles Cros had presented plans for a sound recording and reproduction machine called a paleophone earlier in 1877, but his machine was never actually built. Edison made the first demonstration of his device on 29 November and patented it the following February. Within two decades it had spawned an entire industry built around the recording, distribution and sale of sound recordings.

Edison's original phonograph was developed as a result of experiments that aimed to record telegraph messages. He had worked with diaphragms during his work developing the carbon microphone for telephones, and was aware that if he could find a way to inscribe the movements of the diaphragm he could effectively 'record' sound.

The phonograph's first recording medium was a grooved cylinder covered with tin foil. As the cylinder rotated, an arm attached to a diaphragm would make an indentation of the movement into the tin foil. The arm moved up and down the cylinder, embossing the recording. By adjusting the machine, the arm could then be used to play back the recorded sound through a horn. The first machine was hand-cranked, but it worked well enough to impress everyone who heard it. Within six months it had been demonstrated to both scientists and politicians.

Although heralded as a 'genius' by the *Washington Post*, Edison did very little with his invention. Within a few years, however, other inventors developed engraved wax cylinders and flat disks to record sound.

NOVEMBER

22

1963

United States President John F. Kennedy was fatally shot as his motorcade passed through Dealey Plaza in Dallas, Texas, at 12.30pm.

Kennedy's trip to Dallas was part of a wider 2-day tour of Texas through which he hoped to bring feuding Democrats in the state together. Having arranged to attend and speak at a luncheon, Kennedy's team arranged a meandering 10-mile route to the venue in order to secure maximum exposure before the Dallas crowds. This route was released to the press a number of days beforehand so that the public had ample time to plan their viewing location.

The morning was wet but, by the time the motorcade set off, the rain had cleared enough to enable the roof to be left off the presidential limousine. When it was barely five minutes away from its destination, the convoy drove through Dealey Plaza and gunshots rang out as it passed the Texas School Book Depository. Lee Harvey Oswald allegedly fired three shots from the sixth floor of the building. A rifle was later recovered from the scene and ballistics experts matched bullets found in the limousine to that gun.

Having been rushed to the nearby Parkland Hospital, the 46 year old President was declared dead half an hour later. Although forensic, ballistic, and eyewitness evidence overwhelmingly points to Lee Harvey Oswald as the lone gunman, the assassination has since become the focus for numerous conspiracy theories regarding the identity of the killer.

Oswald was later captured and charged with murder, which he denied. He was himself fatally shot two days later by nightclub owner Jack Ruby who shouted 'You killed the president, you rat!'

The first ever episode of cult science fiction television show
Doctor Who **was broadcast by the BBC.**

Doctor Who was originally conceived to bridge the gap in the Saturday evening television schedule between the adult-oriented sports program *Grandstand* and the more teenage-focused music quiz *Jukebox Jury*. The idea of a time-travelling science fiction series appealed to Sydney Newman, the BBC's new Head of Drama, who came up with the idea of a time machine that was bigger on the inside belonging to 'the Doctor'.

An Unearthly Child was the first of a four-part serial that saw actor William Hartnell take the role of the time-travelling Doctor – a character he played for three years. Produced by Verity Lambert and directed by Waris Hussein, the episode was taped 'as live' on 27 September. On viewing the material, Newman was unhappy with many elements such as technical problems and performance errors that included fluffed lines. Consequently a second version was taped on 18 October.

The show received a generally positive reception, even though its launch was affected by a power cut in parts of the country as well as being significantly overshadowed by the assassination of John F. Kennedy the previous day. These factors led to the first episode being shown again directly before the second episode the following week, and resulted in increased viewing figures.

The popularity of *Doctor Who* skyrocketed with the second serial. *The Daleks* both mesmerised and terrified viewers, although the storyline had originally been initially rejected due to it featuring so-called 'bug-eyed monsters'.

English naturalist and geologist Charles Darwin published *On the Origin of Species*, the book that is considered by many to be the foundation of evolutionary biology.

Darwin's book was based on work conducted during his voyages aboard HMS *Beagle*, in addition to further scientific research and experiments in the subsequent two decades. The book presented evidence for the process of natural selection, and its publication sparked a seismic shift in the study of science.

Although Darwin was not the first to propose evolution, his book was the first to present the idea outside the scientific community. The idea of a fixed species had become a central part of scientific thought as a result of the Protestant Reformation, in which a literal interpretation of the Bible meant that the Genesis creation narrative was understood to be an exact historical account.

This belief began to be challenged from the middle of the 18th Century. In the 1790s Darwin's own grandfather, Erasmus Darwin, proposed a hypothesis on the transmutation of species in which he argued that slight genetic mutations are passed on to subsequent generations. His grandson's theory built on such prior academic work and led him to infer that, although populations have the potential for infinite growth, this is avoided due to limitations in the availability of the basic requirements for survival such as food, water and shelter which means that only the fittest survive.

Although Darwin's book barely hinted at the issue of human evolution it was, and continues to be, controversial. Despite this, Darwin's theory of evolution by natural selection now forms the core of modern life sciences.

NOVEMBER

25

1936

Nazi Germany and the Empire of Japan signed the Anti-Comintern Pact.

The idea for an anti-communist alliance had first been suggested in late 1935, as Hitler and Mussolini sought to present themselves as upholding traditional values in the face of Soviet communism. However, the plan stagnated while the German foreign ministry weighed up the advantages and disadvantages of an alliance with the arch-enemy of their traditional Chinese ally.

By summer 1936 the military were an increasingly dominant force in Japan's government. Meanwhile Europe was beginning to fear the implications of the Franco-Soviet Alliance that went into effect at the end of March. As a result Hitler pushed ahead with the Pact in the hope of securing an Anglo-German alliance as a result.

The Pact didn't result in Hitler's desired alliance with Britain, but did later expand to include Italy. Mussolini's decision to join with Germany and Japan on 6 November 1937, two years after the collapse of the Stresa Front with France and Britain, led to the formation of what was to become known as the Axis Alliance.

Although directed against the Communist International, the organisation that sought to create a worldwide communist republic, the Anti-Comintern Pact was in reality against the Soviet Union. The terms of the agreement specifically stated that the signatories would not make any political treaties with the Soviet Union but, on 23 August 1939, Germany signed the Nazi-Soviet Pact, also known as the Molotov-Ribbentrop Pact. This caused a rift with Japan, but the relationship began to heal following the later Tripartite Pact in September 1940.

NOVEMBER

26

1922

Howard Carter and Lord Carnarvon entered the tomb of Tutankhamun in Egypt's Valley of the Kings.

Having taken part in his first Egyptian excavation in 1891, Carter secured financial assistance from Lord Carnarvon to lead his own expedition to the Valley of the Kings in 1907. Five years later, the American lawyer and excavator Theodore M. Davis declared in his book *The Tombs of Harmhabi and Touatânkhamanou* his conviction that the valley contained no more treasures. Despite this dour assessment, Carter continued to search for the tomb until the outbreak of the First World War in 1914.

Carter resumed digging again after the war but he continued to make few finds. The situation was so bleak that at the start of the 1922 season Carnarvon warned him that he would only provide one more season of funding.

Having decided to focus on an area of the valley containing a series of huts that had been used in previous digs, Carter's crew cleared debris until they hit bedrock. On 4 November they found a flight of steps that led to a doorway stamped with indistinct oval seals, called cartouches. Carter ordered the stairway be refilled, and waited for Carnarvon to make his way to Egypt.

On 26 November, with access to the tomb cleared again of debris, Carter made a tiny hole in a doorway and used the light of a candle to peer inside. Carnarvon asked if he could see anything. Carter replied with the famous words 'Yes, wonderful things!'

Although Tutankhamun was one of the minor Pharaohs, the discovery of his tomb is significant for it being the most complete example of a royal tomb ever uncovered.

NOVEMBER

27

1095

Pope Urban II launched the First Crusade with an impassioned speech at the Council of Clermont.

By the 11th Century, Christianity had secured a stable base across most of Europe. However the Byzantine Empire was on the very periphery of Christendom and faced continuous threats from Muslim conquests.

The city of Jerusalem had been in Muslim hands since 638, but ongoing wars between different Arab dynasties had resulted in it being captured by the Seljuks in 1076. When their army began threatening to attack Constantinople, the Byzantine Emperor Alexios I Komnenos appealed to the Pope for assistance. Many historians have since argued that Urban II took advantage of the situation as a way to reunite Christendom under his papacy, which was facing a threat from the Antipope Clement III.

No accurate record exists of how many people responded to the Pope's call, but estimates suggest anywhere between 60,000 and 100,000 people joined the First Crusade. A large number of these were ordinary peasants. Exactly why so many people chose to 'take the cross' is also a question subject to fierce debate. Some nobles probably went in the hope of seizing riches along the way, but a large number of Crusaders almost certainly did so out of Christian piety.

Although Pope Urban had intended the Crusade to depart on 15 August 1096, large numbers of peasants and low-ranking knights set off earlier on what became known as the People's Crusade. This group of Crusaders were generally poorly disciplined and had been given little to no military training. They killed thousands of Jews in the pogroms of 1096 before they have even left Europe.

Portuguese explorer Ferdinand Magellan led the first European ships from the Atlantic Ocean into the Pacific as part of his planned circumnavigation of the globe.

By the early 1500s it had become evident that Christopher Columbus' voyages had not found a westward route to the Indies. However, Balboa's discovery of the Pacific Ocean in 1513 had renewed Spanish hopes that a westward spice route could be found. This was particularly important as the eastward route around Africa had been reserved for the Portuguese under the terms of the Treaty of Tordesillas signed in 1498. Magellan's voyage was therefore funded by the Spanish king, Charles I, who is better known by his subsequent title of the Holy Roman Emperor Charles V.

Having first crossed the Atlantic, Magellan's fleet searched the South American coast for a channel that would lead them through the land mass. On 21 October they concluded that they had found the passage at Cape Virgins, and entered it on 1 November. The channel was named the Strait of All Saints but is now known as the Strait of Magellan.

Three weeks later, Magellan and three ships emerged on the other side. He called the new ocean *Mar Pacifico,* or the Pacific Ocean, due to the calmness of the waters. The fleet soon made landfall at the archipelago of Tierra del Fuego which was given the name due to the fires lit by the inhabitants to ward off the low temperatures.

The fleet reached South East Asia the following spring. Magellan was killed a few weeks later at the Battle of Mactan on 27 April when he and his troops faced 1,500 warriors under the command of native chieftain Lapu-Lapu.

The crew of the slave ship *Zong* threw the first of at least 132 African slaves overboard in a massacre intended to allow them to cash in their insurance policy.

Zong was originally a Dutch slave ship that had been captured by a British gunship in February 1781. Having been sold to a syndicate of Liverpool merchants, it departed from Accra in modern day Ghana on 18 August. 442 slaves were on board the ship at this point – more than twice the number that it was capable of safely transporting.

By the third week of November drinkable water was running low, but this was not identified until after a navigational error led to the ship sailing 300 miles past its destination of Jamaica. With death from thirst a high likelihood, the ship's crew voted to purposefully drown some of the slaves in order to ensure the survival of the ones remaining on board.

The massacre began on 29 November and continued for two more days. Due to deaths from disease and malnutrition, in addition to the wilful mass murder, the ship arrived at Jamaica with only 208 of its original 442 enslaved people on board.

The ship's insurers refused to pay out for the deaths of the slaves and the ensuing court cases found that the killing of slaves was legal in some situations. In the case of *Zong*, however, the court ruled that the crew of the *Zong* were at fault and found in the insurers' favour.

The massacre and subsequent legal rulings had little immediate impact. Within just a few years, however, the *Zong* massacre had become a central example of the horrors of the Middle Passage and stimulated the abolitionist movement.

NOVEMBER

30

1982

Michael Jackson released the album *Thriller*, which went on to become the best-selling album of all time.

Michael Jackson had already secured enormous global success as a member of the Jackson 5 and The Jacksons. He followed this by releasing his first solo album, *Off The Wall*, in 1979. Despite its critical and commercial success, Jackson felt that *Off The Wall* did not gain the recognition it deserved and complained that 'it was totally unfair that it didn't get Record of the Year and it can never happen again'. Consequently he set about making an album on which 'every song was a killer' and which would help him achieve his aim of becoming the biggest star in show business.

Quincy Jones, who had previously worked with Jackson on *Off The Wall*, reunited with him to produce the new album. Recording started at noon on 14 April 1982 at Westlake Recording Studios in Los Angeles, California. The album was released just three weeks after mixing was finished and proved so popular that it was selling a million copies a week at its height. Seven of the nine songs on the album were released as singles, with the music videos for 'Billie Jean', 'Beat It', and the title track itself becoming MTV staples.

The music video for 'Thriller' was directed by acclaimed film director John Landis and has since been described as 'a watershed moment for the [music] industry' due to the way in which it merged filmmaking and music. The video went on to win a raft of Grammy and MTV awards.

Thriller has been certified 29x platinum in America and has sold in excess of 20 million copies internationally. It continues to sell over 100,000 copies every year in the US alone.

DECEMBER

DECEMBER
1
1955

Rosa Parks refused to give up her seat on a bus in Montgomery, Alabama after the white section of the bus became full.

Rosa Parks was already active in the Civil Rights movement, having been elected secretary of the Montgomery chapter of the NAACP at the end of 1943. Outside this role she worked as a housekeeper and seamstress to Clifford Durr, a white lawyer with a history of taking cases that challenged the government.

At approximately 6pm on 1 December Parks boarded a bus on her way home from work and took her seat, as required by law, in the segregated 'colored' section. Before long the white section of the bus filled up with passengers. The driver, James F. Blake, moved the 'colored' sign to the row behind where Parks was sitting and insisted that the black people sitting on the row give up their seats for the newly-boarded white people.

Although the three other passengers got up, Parks remained in her seat. After Blake asked her again to move she reportedly replied, 'I don't think I should have to stand up'. In response he called his supervisor before then calling the police.

Parks' refusal to move led to her being arrested for breaking a city code that specified passengers had to obey the driver's seat assignments. This simple act of defiance led to her quickly becoming a symbol of the Civil Rights Movement. That evening, the Women's Political Council became the first group to endorse a boycott of the city's buses. Three days later, plans for the Montgomery bus boycott were announced. The boycott lasted until December 20 1956, when the buses were desegregated after the Supreme Court upheld a judgement that segregation on buses was unconstitutional.

DECEMBER

2

1804

Napoleon Bonaparte crowned himself Emperor of the French at Notre Dame Cathedral in Paris.

Napoleon had risen to prominence during the French Revolution as a result of leading a number of successful military campaigns in the Revolutionary Wars. He returned to France in 1799, where the coup of 18 Brumaire resulted in him becoming First Consul. Having secured the Senate's agreement that he could rule by decree, Napoleon then began extending his political control over the French Republic.

In January 1804 the secret police exposed a plot supported by the deposed Bourbon royal family to assassinate Napoleon. He used this as an excuse to reinstate hereditary leadership under his own family, as a way to avoid a return of the Bourbons. This was supported by a constitutional referendum in November that year, in which over 99% of voters cast their ballots in favour. Notably 52% of the eligible population abstained.

Napoleon's coronation was a lavish affair that referenced various elements of Carolingian tradition, the *ancien régime*, and the French Revolution. The event was attended by Pope Pius VII, but significantly he did not place the crown on the new Emperor's head. Napoleon did that himself.

Napoleon's self-crowning is sometimes presented as a snub to the Pope by the new Emperor, but there is evidence that it was agreed in advance. Despite this, the move didn't please everyone. The composer Ludwig van Beethoven, who had originally dedicated his 3rd Symphony to Napoleon, reportedly exclaimed, 'Now, too, he will tread under foot all the rights of Man, indulge only his ambition; now he will think himself superior to all men, become a tyrant!'

DECEMBER

3

1910

The first neon light went on show at the Paris Motor Show.

Frenchman Georges Claude's neon lighting at the Paris Motor Show was only used to light the front of the large exhibition space at the *Grand Palais* with red lighting. Although his invention gained positive responses at the Motor Show, Claude was frustrated that the red light emitted from the straight 35m long tubes meant that the new technology couldn't be used to replace conventional home lighting.

Claude's friend and associate Jacques Fonseque persuaded the inventor to instead market his lights for advertising as they could be bent into any shape. The first such light was apparently sold to a Parisian barber and, after other successful early purchases by individual shops, a large sign for the alcoholic drink Cinzano became the first use of neon to actively advertise a product.

Claude patented his invention in 1915, and this gave him a virtual monopoly over the production of neon lights for the first few years of their existence. However, it wasn't until he sold the first neon lights to a Los Angeles-based car dealer in 1923 that he really began to benefit from his creation. In some places the new 'liquid fire' signs became even more popular and famous than the businesses they were advertising. Large neon signs such as Vegas Vic at Las Vegas' Pioneer Club have since become cultural icons in their own right.

Despite the development of other light technologies, neon remains a popular form of advertising. It has also made its way into many homes, since the same technology forms the basis of plasma televisions.

DECEMBER

4

1956

The Million Dollar Quartet featuring Elvis Presley, Jerry Lee Lewis, Carl Perkins, and Johnny Cash were recorded during an impromptu jam session at Sun Record Studios in Memphis, Tennessee.

The four recording stars had not planned in advance to meet at the studios. Carl Perkins and his backing band had gone there to record some new material to follow up the success of the song 'Blue Suede Shoes', while the still relatively unknown Jerry Lee Lewis had been invited by studio owner Sam Phillips to come along and add some piano to the tracks.

Elvis Presley had been signed to Sun Records until November the previous year, when his contract was bought out by RCA Victor. By chance he dropped into his former label on 4 December 1956 to catch up with Phillips. Having listened to the playback of the Perkins sessions, Elvis decided to enter the studio and begin jamming with the band.

Before long another Sun artist, the country musician Johnny Cash, arrived and joined in the jam. The quartet primarily played snippets of old gospel and spiritual songs that they had grown up with, including at least one request from Elvis' girlfriend who had joined them in the studio.

Studio engineer Jack Clement, who had discovered Jerry Lee Lewis, was in the control booth and decided to record the session. At the same time Phillips called a local newspaper to photograph and report on the impromptu meeting. The subsequent article was the first use of the name 'The Million Dollar Quartet'. It was the only time that these pop music pioneers would ever record together.

DECEMBER

5

1934

The Walwal Incident took place and laid the foundations for the Abyssinia Crisis.

The Italo–Ethiopian Treaty of 1928 had set an agreed boundary between the territories of Italian Somaliland and Ethiopia. However, in 1930 Italy built a fort approximately fifty miles inside the Abyssinian side of the border at the Walwal oasis in clear contravention of the agreement.

At first the Italian presence was tolerated by the Abyssinians whose only response was to increase their numbers of military personnel in the area. The situation only escalated in November 1934 when a force of approximately 1,000 Abyssinian soldiers arrived at the fort and demanded it be handed over. The demand was refused by the commander of Walwal's Somali garrison.

The following day, a group of British and Abyssinian surveyors arrived at the fort and found themselves caught up in the dispute. The British withdrew in order to avoid any bloodshed, but the Abyssinians stayed and joined their countrymen in a face-off with the troops inside the fort. Over 150 soldiers from both sides died in a two-day skirmish that began on 5 December. Although the exact reason the standoff became violent is unclear, it is generally accepted that neither side tried particularly hard to avoid it.

Both Italy and Abyssinia protested the actions of the other. Abyssinia went to the League of Nations and sought a ruling on the situation, but the League's findings were inconclusive. Meanwhile Italy forcefully demanded compensation from Abyssinia. The diplomatic crisis that ensued eventually led to the Italian invasion of Abyssinia in October 1935.

The 'Blood in the Water' water polo match took place between the USSR and Hungary.

The match was a semi-final at the 1956 Melbourne Summer Olympic Games and became famous as a result of the violence that ran throughout the game. It gained its nickname, and abruptly ended, after a Hungarian player was punched so hard by one of the Russians that it drew blood.

The match was played just weeks after the USSR's violent crackdown of the Hungarian Uprising. At the time of the uprising the Hungarian team, who were reigning Olympic champions, were training outside Budapest but were able to hear gunshots and see smoke in the city following the arrival of Soviet tanks on 1 November.

Having been moved to communist Czechoslovakia to avoid being caught up in events at home while they completed their training, the Hungarian team only became aware of the scale of the USSR's response to the uprising after their arrival in Australia. Facing the Soviet Union in the semi-final, they quickly realised that this provided an opportunity to regain some national pride against their oppressors.

The game was violent from the start with verbal abuse, kicks and punches being thrown by both sides. The Hungarians were leading 4-0 when Russian Valentin Prokopov punched Hungarian Ervin Zádor in the final quarter. As he climbed out of the pool with blood streaming down his face, the pro-Hungarian crowd went wild.

Hungary went on to win gold against Yugoslavia, but many of the Hungarian team didn't return home after the Games as they instead sought asylum in the West.

DECEMBER

7

1941

The Imperial Japanese Navy launched a surprise attack against the United States' Hawaiian naval base at Pearl Harbor.

Japan chose to attack Pearl Harbor in order to prevent the US Pacific Fleet from becoming involved in Japan's advance into Southeast Asia, particularly British-controlled Malaya and the Dutch East Indies. Although the United States was not involved in the Second World War at the time, it had previously provided financial support to the Republic of China in the Sino-Japanese War and stopped selling equipment such as aeroplanes, parts and aviation fuel to Japan in 1940. Remaining oil shipments to Japan were stopped in July 1941.

Japan's military commanders became convinced that the USA would eventually intervene as they advanced further into Southeast Asia. On 26 November the main Japanese attack fleet left port for Pearl Harbour and Emperor Hirohito gave final approval for the attack on 1 December. By this point most Americans expected imminent war with Japan, but the attack on Pearl Harbour caught everyone by surprise.

At 7.48am on 7 December the first wave of Japanese planes began their attack. The entire assault was over within 90 minutes. Sixteen US Navy ships were sunk or damaged by 353 Japanese fighter, bomber and torpedo planes. Nearly 2,500 American servicemen were killed, with another 1,000 injured. The Japanese lost just 64 men.

The following morning, President Franklin D. Roosevelt described the day of the attack as 'a date which will live in infamy' and called for Congress to declare war on the Empire of Japan. They did so less than an hour later.

DECEMBER

8

1980

Former Beatle and political activist John Lennon was murdered outside his New York apartment block by Mark David Chapman.

John Lennon lived in the Dakota, one of the most prestigious apartment buildings in New York. He had moved there in 1973, and was known to willingly interact with fans that waited outside the building for autographs or pictures.

Chapman arrived at the Dakota in the mid-morning and approached Lennon for his autograph when he left the building at 5:40pm. Lennon and Yoko Ono then got into a waiting limousine and drove to the Record Plant Studio to mix a new song.

Chapman remained outside the Dakota until Lennon returned at 10:50pm. As he walked from his limousine to the building's front entrance, Chapman fired five rounds at his back, of which four hit him. Lennon, bleeding profusely, staggered up the stairs into the reception.

The Dakota's staff called the police, who arrived just two minutes later. By this point the doorman had shaken the gun from Chapman's hand, who then waited calmly with a copy of J.D. Salinger's novel *The Catcher in the Rye*.

Lennon was rushed to hospital in the back of a second police car, where he arrived within minutes of the assault. He had no pulse and was not breathing. Despite attempts by the medical staff to revive him, he was declared dead on arrival at 11:15pm.

A number of witnesses noted that at the exact moment he was declared dead, the Beatles song 'All My Loving' began playing on the hospital's sound system.

American television network CBS first broadcast the animated cartoon *A Charlie Brown Christmas*.

By the mid-1960s, the *Peanuts* comic strip by American cartoonist Charles M. Schultz had become an international phenomenon. Ideas for an animated special had already been proposed, but it wasn't until the influential *Time* magazine featured the *Peanuts* gang on the cover that sponsorship was secured. Coca-Cola agreed to finance the cartoon as a vehicle for Christmas advertising. The simple pitch promised 'winter scenes, a school play, a scene to be read from the Bible, and a sound track combining jazz and traditional music'.

The team behind the animation took what were seen to be a number of risks with the special. As well as exclusively casting children to voice the characters, Schultz opted for an unconventional jazz music soundtrack and refused to have a laugh track to accompany the animation. Combined with the necessarily simple animation and relatively slow pace of the story, network executives expressed reservations about whether the special was even worthy of being shown.

The cartoon took six months to produce and was completed just ten days before its network premiere, meaning the executives didn't have any choice about whether to broadcast it or not as they had no alternatives. They needn't have worried, however, as both popular and critical responses to the cartoon were universally positive.

A Charlie Brown Christmas went on to win both a Peabody Award and the Emmy Award for Outstanding Children's Program, but more importantly captured the imaginations of the 16 million people who tuned in to watch it that evening.

DECEMBER

10

1901

The first Nobel Prizes were awarded in Chemistry, Literature, Peace, Physics, and Physiology or Medicine.

Alfred Nobel was a Swedish scientist and arms manufacturer who held patents for a number of inventions, of which dynamite and gelignite are probably the best known. These inventions earned him enormous amounts of money, but little respect from the press. When his older brother Ludvig, who was a leading oil producer, died in 1888 a French newspaper erroneously published an obituary for Alfred instead. Featuring the headline 'The merchant of death is dead', the obituary stated that he 'became rich by finding ways to kill more people faster than ever before'.

The obituary left Nobel distressed at how he would be remembered, and resulted in him seeking a way to improve his legacy. As a result, having never married or had any children, he rewrote his will. This stated that 94% of his total assets would be used to fund an annual prize in his name. The Nobel Foundation was established in 1900 to manage the finance and administration of the Prizes, while separate Nobel Committees were created to collect nominations and award the actual prizes.

The first Nobel Prizes were awarded for Wilhelm Röntgen's discovery of X-rays, Jacobus H. van 't Hoff's work on chemical thermodynamics, Sully Prudhomme's poetry, and Emil von Behring's development of a treatment for diphtheria. The 1901 Peace Prize was shared between Henry Dunant and Frédéric Passy.

The Nobel Prizes continue to be presented on the same date every year, since it marks the anniversary of founder Alfred Nobel's death.

DECEMBER

11

1936

King Edward VIII of the United Kingdom announced his abdication in a worldwide radio broadcast.

Edward abdicated in order to marry American divorcee Wallis Simpson. Simpson had divorced her first husband in 1927, and was married to a second when her relationship with the then Prince of Wales began. Edward was already in a serious relationship with her when he became king following the death of his father on 20 January 1936, but as the head of the Church of England he faced a crisis. This is because the Church of England forbade divorced people from remarrying if their ex-spouses were still alive, as was the case with Wallis.

Wallis Simpson filed for divorce from her second husband in October 1936, which led to speculation in the American press that marriage to Edward was imminent. Although the British press remained silent on the matter, the king was warned that this wouldn't be the case for much longer and that he needed to address the issue. In the middle of November he told Stanley Baldwin, the British Prime Minister, of his intention to marry. Baldwin gave Edward three options: give up the idea of marriage, marry against his ministers' wishes, or abdicate. He chose the latter.

Edward signed the Instruments of Abdication on 10 December, but the change only became official when he gave royal assent to His Majesty's Declaration of Abdication Act 1936 after it was passed by Parliament the next day.

Edward's younger brother Albert became King George VI while Edward was given the title of Duke of Windsor. He and Wallis were married on 3 June 1937.

DECEMBER

12

1935

The *Lebensborn* registered association was established in Nazi Germany by the SS.

Nazi ideology was centred on belief in the racial superiority of an Aryan master race. Social policy was consequently built around the biological improvement of the German population, through a eugenics programme that promoted the breeding of so-called racially superior individuals and the forced sterilisation or murder of those identified as 'life unworthy of life'.

Literally translated as 'Fount of Life', *Lebensborn* was designed to harness apparent racial purity through the birth of children conceived between Aryan women and members of the SS, often as a result of extramarital relationships. It also selected 'racially worthy' orphans for adoption by the families of SS members. As the war progressed, SS troops under command of Himmler – who also oversaw *Lebensborn* – kidnapped desirable children from occupied countries and moved them to Germany where they underwent an aggressive process of Germanisation and re-education.

Historians estimate that around 8,000 children were born under the programme in Germany, with a further 12,000 in other countries. The majority of these were born in Norway. The number of foreign children who were kidnapped and Germanised is unknown due to destruction of the relevant files.

Lebensborn children and their mothers were often ostracised and mistreated by their communities after the war. In Norway, many so-called 'war children' consequently moved to Sweden to escape the abuse. Probably the most famous of these is ABBA-member Anni-Frid Lyngstad.

DECEMBER

13

1937

The Nanking Massacre began at the end of the Battle of Nanking during the Second Sino-Japanese War.

Troops from the Imperial Japanese Army arrived at Nanking, which at the time was the capital of the Republic of China, on 9 December. Despite attempts by a group of foreigners in the city to negotiate a peaceful handover, Chinese Generalissimo Chiang Kai-shek ordered that the city be defended 'to the last man'. Meanwhile, Japanese troops were ordered to 'kill all captives'.

The Chinese defence collapsed on 12 December, and the victorious Japanese army entered the following day. According to eyewitness accounts, the next six weeks saw them engage in numerous war crimes including rape, murder, theft and arson. Captured Chinese troops were the victims of extrajudicial killings by machine gun or by being used for live bayonet practice. Meanwhile children, the elderly, and approximately 20,000 other women of the city were raped. Many were killed immediately afterwards.

Japanese General Iwane Matsui expressed his regret at the behaviour of his troops just a few days after taking control of the Nanking, but the atrocities didn't end until the start of February 1938. At the end of the Second World War, the International Military Tribunal for the Far East convicted only two people for their role in the massacre.

While both China and Japan have both publicly acknowledged and expressed regret over a number of atrocities committed during the war, the Nanking Massacre remains a highly contentious historical event. Although accurate figures are impossible to establish, most scholars estimate that between 40,000 to over 300,000 people died as a result.

DECEMBER

14

1911

Norwegian explorer Roald Amundsen led a team of four others to become the first to reach the South Pole.

Amundsen had planned to become the first to reach the North Pole, but changed his target to the South Pole after he learned of the now-disputed claim by rival American explorers that they had already reached it. Keeping his new plan secret, even from his crew, his ship departed Norway on 9 August. He only revealed their destination a month later, shortly before they left their final port on the island of Madeira.

Amundsen's ship arrived in an Antarctic inlet known as the Bay of Whales on 14 January 1911, where the crew established a base that they called *Framheim*. They spent the next three months preparing depots across the Ross Ice Shelf, prior to the onset of Antarctic winter.

As soon as the sun returned at the end of August, Amundsen attempted to reach the pole but was forced to turn back due to the harsh conditions. A second attempt that began in mid-October was much more successful, seeing them arrive at the pole almost 2 months later.

Amundsen's team arrived five weeks ahead of British explorer Robert Falcon Scott's Terra Nova Expedition, and successfully made it back to their basecamp whereas Scott and his team famously did not. On hearing the news of Scott's fate, Amundsen remarked that it was 'horrible, horrible.'

As well as being the first expedition leader to reach the South Pole, Amundsen is also the first person to be universally recognised for reaching the North Pole as a result of his 1926 air expedition, making him the first person to reach both poles.

DECEMBER

15

1933

The Twenty-first Amendment to the United States Constitution came into effect, repealing the Eighteenth Amendment which had made the sale, manufacture, and transportation of alcohol illegal.

Prohibition was introduced in 1920 as a result of the Eighteenth Amendment. This ban on the sale, production, importation, and transportation of alcoholic beverages was greeted with delight by members of the temperance movement. Meanwhile many law-abiding Americans who had previously been drinkers were angry at the government for criminalising what they saw as a harmless activity.

Some members of the public were consequently willing to break the law, and this ushered in a period of criminal activity focused around the production of illegal bootlegged alcohol. Al Capone, one of prohibition's most famous gangster bosses, made around $60 million a year from bootlegging alcohol and selling it in so-called 'speakeasies'.

Izzy Einstein, one of the government's best-known prohibition agents, demonstrated the scale of the problem facing the authorities who were trying to enforce the ban on alcohol. When visiting New Orleans it took him just thirty-five seconds to obtain liquor after his taxi driver offered him a bottle of whisky.

Combined with the problem of police officers being paid by the criminals to turn a blind eye to illegal activity, prohibition brought lawlessness and corruption to America. In the wake of the Wall Street Crash, repealing prohibition also made sound economic sense as alcohol taxes created a new revenue stream for the government. However, the introduction of the Twenty-first Amendment ensured that individual states were still able to enforce their alcohol laws.

DECEMBER

16

1914

The German Imperial Navy attacked the British seaside towns of Scarborough, Hartlepool and Whitby.

The German High Seas Fleet, which was numerically smaller than the British Grand Fleet, had been ordered to avoid direct engagement with the enemy. Instead they focused on targeted attacks to draw out smaller portions of Royal Navy that could be confronted by U-Boats. After a successful raid on the seaside town of Yarmouth, use of such tactics was increased.

The German leadership had determined that an attack on Scarborough, Hartlepool and Whitby would be possible after a U-17 returned from a reconnaissance mission. It found that there were very few mines in the vicinity and no coastal defences, which made the towns an especially easy target since they were within a comfortable distance of Germany.

British intelligence officers had already decoded messages that indicated the German fleet would be mounting the raid. However, British Admiral John Jellicoe opted to allow the raid to happen and then intercept the German ships on their return. This decision proved catastrophic as the British underestimated the size of the German attack. Over a thousand shells were fired, resulting in 137 deaths and a further 592 people being injured. Most of the casualties were civilians. To make matters worse, the British fleet failed to engage the enemy on their return.

The British public was outraged firstly that the Germans had attacked civilians, and secondly that the Royal Navy had failed to stop them. 'Remember Scarborough' soon became a key message of the British propaganda campaign, and revenge was used as an incentive for recruitment to the armed forces.

DECEMBER
17
1903

American brothers Orville and Wilbur Wright successfully made the first controlled, powered and sustained heavier-than-air human flight.

The brothers originally went into business selling, repairing and designing bicycles. However, by the end of 1899 they had developed a keen interest in flight and began to devise control systems that could be employed on manned gliders.

The Wright brothers' justification for developing systems for gliders was that it was pointless to create a powered aircraft before a reliable control system had been designed. Their research led them to develop three axis control that used wing-warping to control the roll of the aircraft, a moveable rudder to control yaw, and elevators to control the pitch.

Successful testing of these controls on a glider in 1902 led the brothers to build an engine to power their flying machine, along with a pair of specially-designed propellers that were refined under testing in their own wind tunnel.

The aircraft, which was first known as the *Wright Flyer* but was later named *Flyer I*, made its historic flights about four miles south of the town of Kitty Hawk in North Carolina. After a number technical delays, the brothers tossed a coin to decide who would be the first to fly on 14 December.

Wilbur won the coin toss but stalled the engine on take-off and crashed the plane after just a three-second flight. After repairing the aircraft, Orville became the first to pilot it on its first true flight three days later although the first flight lasted for just 12 seconds over a total distance of only 36.5 metres. Each brother successfully flew the aircraft twice that day.

DECEMBER

18

1892

Russian composer Peter Ilyich Tchaikovsky's ballet *The Nutcracker* received its première performance at the Mariinsky Theatre in St Petersburg.

Tchaikovsky wrote *The Nutcracker* as a commission for Ivan Vsevolozhsky, the Director of the Imperial Theatres, following the success of his previous ballet *The Sleeping Beauty*. The story chosen by choreographer Marius Petipa was an adaptation of an 1816 story by German author E. T. A. Hoffmann called *The Nutcracker and the Mouse King*. It is widely recognised that Tchaikovsky wasn't particularly keen on writing the ballet, but accepted the commission anyway.

Composed in the Romantic style, the ballet features a number of widely recognised pieces of music. One of the most famous is the *Dance of the Sugar Plum Fairy* which was specifically written to make use of a new instrument Tchaikovsky had discovered in France called the celesta. He also incorporated toy instruments into the Christmas party scene.

Although the score received good reviews, responses to the ballet itself were mostly negative. Tchaikovsky therefore chose to extract eight pieces of music to form *The Nutcracker Suite* which could be performed in a formal concert setting. Standing apart from the ballet, the suite garnered hugely enthusiastic reviews and became a popular feature in concert performances.

Although the ballet itself continued to be performed on occasion, it wasn't until the New York City Ballet presented George Balanchine's new staging in 1954 that it secured wider popularity. Performances of *The Nutcracker* are now said to generate 40% of ticket revenues for American ballet companies.

DECEMBER

19

1843

Charles Dickens' novella *A Christmas Carol* was published in London by Chapman & Hall.

A Christmas Carol was written in just six weeks from September 1843. Although released by an established publisher, Dickens was unwilling to take a lump-sum fee for the story and so instead published it at his own expense. It has never been out of print since but, despite the first run selling out within 6 days, high production costs due to his very specific requirements meant that the profits were smaller than Dickens had hoped for.

Despite this disappointing financial return for its author, *A Christmas Carol* is said to be responsible for establishing much of the modern interpretation of the Christmas holiday. Historian Ronald Hutton comments positively on the book's theme of 'social reconciliation', and views the story as establishing the link between individuals, families and their place within the wider community. He also links the tradition of charitable giving at Christmas to the story due to Scrooge's actions following his redemption.

Dickens' tale is also responsible for introducing words and phrases into the English language. The name 'Scrooge', now used a noun to describe a person who is ungenerous with their money, and the phrase 'Bah! Humbug!' are among the most obvious. However, *A Christmas Carol* is also said to be responsible for popularising the phrase 'Merry Christmas'. Although this greeting had been in use since the 16th Century, by 1843 the meaning of the word 'merry' was changing – originally it simply meant 'pleasant', but by the time of Dickens' book it had begun to mean 'cheerful' or 'jolly' and it is within this context that Scrooge uses the term extensively at the end of the story.

DECEMBER

20

1917

The Russian Bolshevik secret police known as the Cheka was established.

Established following a decree by Lenin on 19 December, the Cheka's focus was on defending the revolution by removing internal threats to the communist regime. Lenin's decree was purposefully vague, and this enabled the Cheka's leader, Felix Dzerzhinsky, to recruit and direct his Chekist agents in whatever way he saw best. With virtually unlimited powers, the growing number of agents soon began rounding up anyone identified as an 'enemy of the people'. Although often referred to as the Bolshevik secret police, the Chekists were easily identifiable from their long leather coats, and a number of their activities were reported in official Soviet newspapers *Pravda* and *Izvestia*.

The organisation's name was derived from the Russian initials for its original full name – The All-Russian Emergency Commission for Combating Counter-Revolution and Sabotage. Hundreds of Cheka committees were formed across Russia, and these went on to arrest, torture or execute many thousands of dissidents, deserters and other enemies of the state.

Known as the Red Terror, the Cheka's campaign of mass killings, torture, and systematic oppression grew more fierce as the Russian Civil War progressed. Its activities included a number of atrocities using torture methods that respected historian Orlando Figes says were 'matched only by the Spanish Inquisition'.

Official Soviet figures placed the total number of Cheka victims at 12,733. However, in reality the figure is probably significantly higher. Some historians place the actual number of people killed by the Cheka at 200,000 or more.

The first modern crossword puzzle was printed in the *New York World* newspaper.

Although examples of crossword-like word puzzles had appeared throughout the mid-19th Century, British-born journalist Arthur Wynne was the first to include a variety of features that we associate with modern crosswords such as separate boxes for entering each letter and a symmetrical design.

Wynne's first 'word-cross puzzle' was shaped as a symmetrical diamond with a hollow centre, but he soon went on to create other designs. Wynne was also the first to incorporate shaded black squares to allow the creation – and separation – of rows and columns of words that allowed more and more complex designs to be created.

Due to a typesetting error the name of the 'word-cross puzzle' was accidentally changed to a 'cross-word puzzle' and the name stuck. Surprisingly, it was just one of a number of puzzles developed by Wynne for the 21 December issue of the *New York World*'s 'Fun' supplement. It caused a sensation and, before long, crossword puzzles had spread beyond the *New York World* to other newspapers in the United States and beyond.

Within less than a decade the crossword puzzle had become part of everyday life. As well as appearing in comic strips such as Clare Briggs' cartoon 'Movie of a Man Doing the Cross-Word Puzzle', in 1924 the first collection of crossword puzzles was published by Simon and Schuster. This is also the same year that the first crossword appeared in a British newspaper. The *Sunday Express* was the first to do so when it printed an adapted Wynne puzzle in November 1924.

DECEMBER

22

1989

Romanian Communist leader Nicolae Ceausescu was overthrown.

Five days before his overthrow, Nicolae Ceausescu had ordered the military to put down a revolt in the western Romanian city of Timisoara. Triggered by government's attempt to evict an ethnic Hungarian pastor who they accused of inciting ethnic hatred, the Timisoara uprising quickly became a broader anti-government demonstration. News of the government's crackdown was not shared in the heavily-censored press, but quickly spread through western-operated radio stations such as Radio Free Europe.

With unrest increasing, Ceausescu addressed a staged demonstration from a balcony of the Central Committee of the Romanian Communist Party in Bucharest on 21 December. Despite the presence of the secret police known as the *Securitate*, the crowd began to heckle him with chants of 'Ti-mi-soa-ra! Ti-mi-soa-ra!'

Having failed to calm the crowd, Ceausescu was moved back inside the building by his bodyguards. The speech had been televised around Romania and the video feed was only cut after the start of the crowd's protest. It was clear to anyone watching that something monumental was unfolding in the capital.

Over the next few hours the streets of Bucharest filled with protesters. Unable to regain control, the following morning Ceausescu and his wife fled the Central Committee building by helicopter. Their pilot soon faked a threat of anti-aircraft fire and landed, leading to the later arrest of the Ceausescus. They were subjected to a show trial on Christmas Day and found guilty of crimes including genocide and illegally gathering wealth. Having been sentenced to death they were quickly taken outside and shot.

The poem *A Visit from St Nicholas,* more commonly known as *The Night Before Christmas* was published anonymously in the *New York Sentinel.*

The poem is significant for being the first source to give the names of Santa's reindeer, as well as establishing the image of the jolly fat Santa that we know today. Reprinted a number of times in subsequent years, the poem later became attributed to the academic Clement Clarke Moore who eventually acknowledged authorship in 1844. However, debate over the authorship continues to this day with Major Henry Livingston, Jr. often being put forward as the potential writer.

Legend says that Moore was inspired to write the poem while on a shopping trip, and then read it to his children on Christmas Eve 1822. A year later a copy found its way to the offices of the *New York Sentinel* who published it along with a message in which the editor expressed 'his cordial thanks to whoever had sent him these Christmas verses'.

Moore's reluctance to be associated with the verse apparently stemmed from his career as a professor of ancient languages, since he didn't want the poem to undermine his academic credentials. It was his friend, Charles Fenno Hoffman, who first publicly attributed the poem to him in the Christmas 1837 edition of the *Pennsylvania Inquirer and Daily Courier.*

One interesting aside relates to Santa's reindeer in the poem since Rudolph and his famous red nose are not included. This is because the first mention of Rudolph wasn't until a story by Robert L. May that was published in 1939.

DECEMBER

24

1955

The Colorado Springs' Continental Air Defense Command first began giving children the current location of Santa as he made his way around the world delivering presents.

The CONAD military facility was founded during the Cold War as an early warning system against aerial enemy attacks, with the aim of providing Strategic Air Command with the opportunity to retaliate. However, on 24 December 1955 an advertisement for a Sears store in Colorado Springs encouraged children to call the facility for the chance to speak to Santa Claus.

This was, of course, a mistake. The phone number had been misprinted in the advertisement and so presumably hundreds of Sears staff were left to sit by silent telephones while military personnel started receiving calls from excited children who wished to speak to Santa.

Colonel Harry Shoup was in charge when a call came through on one of the top-secret telephone lines that only rang if an imminent attack had been identified. The child on the end of the line must have been terrified as the confused colonel demanded to know who was calling his secret number. However, as more calls came in he instructed his staff to give a 'current location' for Santa when children rang the number.

CONAD was replaced by NORAD (the North American Aerospace Defense Command) in 1958, and *NORAD Tracks Santa* has reported Santa's location ever since. Thousands of volunteers continue to man the phones to provide information to anyone who calls. You can also visit *NORAD Tracks Santa* on the internet at www.noradsanta.org.

DECEMBER

25

1066

William of Normandy was crowned King of England at Westminster Abbey.

William defeated the English king Harold II at the Battle of Hastings on 14 October 1066, but was forced to fight on after a number of English nobles nominated Edgar the Ætheling as the new king. When William led his Norman troops across the Thames at Wallingford in early December they were met by Stigand, the Archbishop of Canterbury, who just a few weeks earlier had elected Edgar as king. However, he immediately abandoned Edgar and submitted to William, who soon marched to Berkhamsted where Edgar himself gave up his claim to the throne.

William's coronation in Westminster Abbey on Christmas Day saw both Norman and English nobility in attendance. Norman troops were stationed outside the Abbey and in the surrounding streets in case of trouble while the coronation itself was conducted by Geoffrey, the Bishop of Coutances, and Ealdred, the Archbishop of York. The account of Orderic Vitalis, the Anglo-French chronicler of Norman England, tells how the assembled nobles 'shouted out with one voice' when asked if they agreed to William becoming King of England.

The troops outside mistook these cheers for a fight between the Normans and English inside the church and set fire to some of the English houses nearby before charging into the Abbey itself. The arrival of the troops panicked the coronation guests, many of whom fled the Abbey while the bishops frantically finished the ceremony amid the commotion. After Edward the Confessor and Harold Godwinson, William became the third person to wear the crown of England that year.

The Supreme Soviet of the Soviet Union met for the last time to formally dissolve itself and the Soviet Union.

The origins of the dissolution of the Soviet Union can be traced back to the election of Mikhail Gorbachev as General Secretary of the Communist Party on March 11 1985. He came to office intending to revive the USSR's economy but his reforms, of which the policies of glasnost and perestroika are probably best known, laid the foundations for the enormous popular demands for change that were to follow.

By August 1991, the Iron Curtain had fallen as a result of the toppling of Communist governments in former satellite states. This increased the pressure on Gorbachev to grant greater autonomy for republics within the Soviet Union. A failed coup by hard-line members of the government who wanted to oust Gorbachev and reverse his reforms failed to derail the independence movements within the republics.

With some having already declared their independence from the USSR, a further ten republics did so between August and December. As it became obvious that the USSR was falling apart, on 25 December Gorbachev resigned as President. That evening the Soviet flag on the Kremlin was replaced by the Russian tricolour. The USSR was formally dissolved the next day.

Declaration no. 142-H formally recognised that the Supreme Soviet announced that the Soviet Union had ceased to exist as a state and subject of international law. It further stated that the former Soviet republics were independent, and established the Commonwealth of Independent States.

DECEMBER
27
537

Hagia Sophia was inaugurated by Byzantine Emperor Justinian I and Patriarch Menas of Constantinople.

The current building is the third church of Holy Wisdom to be built on the site since the first two were destroyed in separate riots and revolts. The third church's long history saw it serve as both a Greek Orthodox cathedral and a Roman Catholic cathedral, before Constantinople was conquered by the Ottoman Turks under Sultan Mehmed II in 1453. He ordered it be converted into a mosque, which it remained until being secularised and reopened as a museum on 1 February 1935.

The architects of the enormous basilica were the physicist Isidoros of Miletos and mathematician Anthemios of Tralles. Anthemios was the first to put together a comprehensive compilation of the mathematical theories of Archimedes and his work was clearly influenced by the Greek academic.

The two architects devised a series of complex vaults and semi-domes surrounding a high central dome with a diameter of over 31 meters. Supported by four marble-clad arches, this dome is probably the most immediately recognisable part of the building although the one in place now is not the original structure. The first dome collapsed during an earthquake on 7 May 558 and was rebuilt over the next four years.

Mehmed II's victory in 1453, in what became known in the west as the Fall of Constantinople, led to him ordering the basilica to be converted into a mosque. This involved stripping it of Christian iconography and building the four minarets surrounding the central dome that are now a major part of the Istanbul skyline.

DECEMBER

28

1972

Kim Il-sung became the first President of North Korea.

Kim Il-sung's early life and rise to prominence is widely disputed due to the personality cult that developed around him after the creation of North Korea. Some commentators even claim that he was an imposter. However, such claims are unlikely to be true as contemporary Japanese sources acknowledge King Il-sung as a popular and effective guerrilla leader in the Second Sino-Japanese War. His family had moved to the Chinese region of Manchuria in 1920 where the young Kim Il-sung joined, and then later led, a division of the Chinese-controlled Northeast Anti-Japanese United Army.

After the defeat of Japan in the Second World War, Korea was divided between Soviet and American control. The USSR installed Kim as chairman of the North Korean branch of the Korean Communist Party where he quickly began to consolidate his control. As well as proclaiming the northern Democratic People's Republic of Korea, with himself as the Soviet-supported premier, Kim also established a highly effective cult of personality through which he began to be known as 'Great Leader'.

Having secured totalitarian rule at home, Kim maintained a course of independent communism that saw him establish Juche, or 'self-reliance', as the official political ideology of North Korea. This increasingly isolated North Korea from the rest of the world, and it is in this context that the new constitution of December 1972 established Kim as President of North Korea. He was already the country's Prime Minister and the First Secretary of the Workers' Party of Korea. Four years after his death in 1994 he was made Eternal President of the Republic.

DECEMBER 29 1170

Thomas Becket, the Archbishop of Canterbury, was murdered in front of the altar of Canterbury Cathedral.

Thomas Becket was appointed Chancellor by Henry II in 1155. In this job he proved himself to be a faithful member of the king's court. When Theobald, the existing Archbishop of Canterbury died, Henry seized the chance to dominate the church by appointing the trustworthy Becket to succeed him.

Having a loyal friend in the most senior religious position in England made sense to Henry. However, as Archbishop of Canterbury, Becket's allegiance quickly switched to siding with the church. This frustrated Henry who asked Becket to sign the Constitutions of Clarendon in 1164 to extend the king's authority over the clergy. Becket refused and, shortly after being summoned to the king to explain his actions, fled to France.

Becket returned to England in 1170, but not before excommunicating two senior members of the clergy for supporting Henry. This act led to him being the target of an angry outburst by the king. It is highly unlikely, however, that Henry screamed out the words 'Who will rid me of this troublesome priest?'

Whatever Henry said was enough to encourage four knights to travel to Canterbury and kill the Archbishop inside the Cathedral. The event was recorded in a later history by the monk Edward Grim. He claimed that the fatal blow split Becket's skull as he knelt in front of the altar.

Becket was canonised by Pope Alexander III barely two years after the murder, and in 1174 the king himself walked barefoot to Becket's tomb in Canterbury in penance.

DECEMBER

30

1922

The Union of Soviet Socialist Republics, better known as the USSR, was founded.

The constitutional basis for the Soviet Union had been agreed on 29 December. The Treaty on the Creation of the USSR and the Declaration of the Creation of the USSR was approved by delegations from all the founding countries. It officially came into force when it was confirmed by the 1st Congress of Soviets and signed by the heads of each republic's respective delegation.

In 1922 the Soviet Union consisted of just four Soviet republics – the Russian SFSR, Ukrainian SSR, Byelorussian SSR and Transcaucasian SFSR – although it's important to note that the Russian and Transcaucasian SFSRs actually incorporated a number of separate Soviet Socialist Republics. The creation of the USSR therefore effectively created a centralised federal government.

This was an important step for the Bolsheviks who, having won the Russian Civil War, needed to consolidate their gains into a formal political entity. Stalin in particular argued that the New Economic Policy that followed War Communism required centralised control, which threatened some national groups. At the same time, some Bolsheviks hoped for a world revolution that would overthrow capitalist governments around the globe.

The USSR's founding documents therefore allowed Soviet republics to withdraw from the Union at any time, even though none actually did so before the collapse of the Soviet Union in 1991. New members were able to join the union at any time, which allowed the USSR's membership to grow from four republics in 1922 to sixteen by 1940.

DECEMBER

31

1935

The board game *Monopoly* was patented by Philadelphia heating salesman Charles B. Darrow.

Although the patent for the game was awarded to Darrow, who had lost his job during the Great Depression, it is now widely recognised that he was just one of many people who developed the complex design and rules that we now know as *Monopoly*.

In 1902 an Illinois-born writer and engineer called Elizabeth Magie had created a board game called *The Landlord's Game* which bears striking similarities to *Monopoly*. She patented this game in 1904 and approached Parker Brothers with the idea in around 1910. Although they declined to publish it, her self-produced copies became popular with Quakers, university students, and members of the public who supported Georgist economics.

Magie, by now married and with the new name Phillips, re-patented an updated version in 1924 and was again turned down by Parker Brothers. The updated version spread widely through word-of-mouth, and Charles Darrow's wife eventually learned this version. Darrow began to distribute his own version of the game, and in October 1934 was himself rejected by Parker Brothers who said that the game was 'too complicated, too technical, [and] took too long to play'.

Successful Christmas sales of Darrow's self-produced version led Parker Brothers to reverse their decision and buy the game from him in March 1935. Before the end of the year they learnt that he was not the sole inventor, but pressed ahead with the purchase and helped him secure a patent. Meanwhile they bought up the patents to similar games, including *The Landlord's Game*, to ensure that they had definitive ownership of the idea.

INDEX

Daily Mail, 155, 310
Daladier, Édouard, 297
Dallas, 356
dancing plague, 192
Darrow, Charles B., 397
Darwin, Charles, 358
Davis, Jim, 187
Davison, Emily Wilding, 172, 310
Day The Music Died, 39
D-Day landings, 174, 181
de Coubertin, Pierre, 108
de Gaulle, Charles, 16
De Havilland Comet, 136
de Launay, Marquis Bernard-Rene, 214
de Lisle, Claude Joseph Rouget, 230
de Molay, Jacques, 86
de-Christianisation, 141
de-Stalinisation, 7, 61, 254
decimalisation, 51
Declaration of Independence, 262, 353
Declaration of Right, 49
Deep Blue, 145
Deep Throat, 243
Defender of the Faith, 311
Democratic Kampuchea. See Cambodia
Democratic Party, 63, 243, 353, 356
Denmark, 93, 347
Derby County, 276
Detroit, 295
diary, 165, 180
Dickens, Charles, 385
dictatorship, 83, 109, 319, 326
dictionary, 117
Directory (French Revolution), 336
disease, 79, 107, 148, 246, 279, 296, 363
Disney, Walt, 149
Dissolution of the Monasteries, 91
divine right, 6, 20, 32, 175
divorce, 44, 89, 377
Doctor Who, 357
doctors, 83, 106, 176, 205, 264
dogs, 187, 206, 337
Dom Pérignon, 238
Domesday Book, 314
Dominican Order, 25, 109
Doncaster, 203
Dönitz, Karl, 142
doodlebug. See V-1 flying bomb
Douglas-Hamilton, Douglas, 144
Dow Jones Industrial Average, 208
Dracula, 160
Drexler, Anton, 280
Dubček, Alexander, 7, 254
Dylan, Bob, 87, 225

Dzerzhinsky, Felix, 386

Eagle (lunar module), 220
Earhart, Emilia, 155
Earth, 115, 119, 190, 211, 213, 337
earthquake, 25, 393
East Anglia, 161, 210
East India Company, 235
EastEnders, 55
Eavis, Michael, 287
Ebert, Friedrich, 17, 245, 294
Eden, Anthony, 329
Edgar the Ætheling, 391
Edison, Thomas Alva, 78, 355
Edward the Confessor, 8, 288
Edward II, 191
Edward III, 260
Edward IV, 256
Edward VI, 89, 210
Edward VII, 46
Edward VIII, 377
Egypt, 52, 110, 152, 173, 178, 197, 219, 221,
    227, 285, 306, 329, 350, 360
Egypt–Israel Peace Treaty, 306
Eichmann, Adolf, 113
Eiffel Tower, 185
Eisenhower, Dwight D., 5, 142, 259, 272
Elba, 62, 186
election, 104, 159, 205, 208, 243, 303, 348, 392
Elephant Island, 126
Elizabeth I, 44, 153, 210, 229, 351
Elizabeth II, 112
Elm Farm Ollie, 54
Elstree Studios, 55
emancipation, 81, 202, 235, 262
Emmy Awards, 344, 375
Emperor Hirohito, 373
Enabling Act, 63, 236
Endurance (ship), 126
Engels, Friedrich, 57
England, 6, 8, 14, 21, 27, 32, 42, 44, 48, 49, 57,
    89, 91, 107, 117, 137, 144, 147, 148, 156,
    161, 164, 175, 183, 191, 203, 205, 209,
    210, 212, 222, 229, 238, 249, 250, 256,
    260, 270, 275, 276, 282, 288, 289, 311,
    314, 321, 323, 325, 339, 347, 351, 353,
    358, 385, 391, 395
English Civil War, 6, 32, 175
Enlightenment, 141, 215
Enola Gay, 240
Entente Cordiale, 99, 110
Epsom Derby, 172, 310
ergotism, 116
Essex, 23, 91

Gorbachev, Mikhail, 162, 253, 392
Gore, Spencer, 209
Göring, Hermann, 22, 354
Grammy Awards, 169, 344, 364
Grant, Ulysses S., 111
Grantham, 203
Gray, Elisha, 78
Great Depression, 75, 114, 208, 249, 261, 286, 294, 324, 397
Great Exhibition, 38
Great Fire of London, 165, 270
Great Rum Debate, 231
Great Sioux War, 193
Great Train Robbery, 242
Great Yarmouth, 21
Greece, 93, 108
Greenwich, 41
Gregorian calendar, 304
Gregory XIII, 304
Gresley, Sir Nigel, 203
Grotius, Hugo, 90
Guernica, 128, 226
guerrilla warfare, 105, 178, 309, 394
guillotine, 23, 58, 127, 316
Guinness World Record, 187
guitar, 56, 169, 206, 225
Guizot, François Pierre Guillaume, 60
Gulf of Aqaba, 173, 329
Gulf of Mexico, 132
Gulf of Tonkin Resolution, 241
Gulf War, 19, 136
gunpowder, 48, 214, 270, 339
Gunpowder Plot, 339
Gutenberg, Johannes, 59

Hagia Sophia, 163, 393
Haig, Field Marshal Sir Douglas, 352
Halsbury Committee, 51
Hamburg, 162
Hardrada, Harald, 288, 314
Harold I. *See* Godwinson, Harold
Harrison, George, 284
Hartlepool, 382
Hartnell, William, 357
Harvard University, 277
Hautvillers, 238
Hawaii, 182, 373
helicopter, 84, 131, 274, 388
heliocentrism, 190
Hendrix, Jimi, 56, 169
Henry II, 395
Henry III, 183
Henry IV of France, 90
Henry V, 325

Henry VI, 156
Henry VII, 229, 256, 275
Henry VIII, 44, 89, 91, 117, 153, 210, 311, 339, 351
Henson, Jim, 344
Herculaneum, 258
heresy, 89, 109, 164, 190, 192
Herschel, William, 228
Heseltine, Michael, 348
Hess, Rudolf, 144, 218
Heydrich, Reinhard, 22
High Seas Fleet, 189, 382
Hill, Octavia, 14
Himmler, Heinrich, 29, 378
Hindenburg (airship), 140
Hindenburg, Paul von, 63, 236
hippies, 76
Hiroshima, 114, 240, 263
Hitler, Adolf, 15, 22, 58, 63, 75, 76, 103, 140, 142, 144, 198, 218, 226, 236, 245, 249, 257, 259, 269, 280, 283, 297, 315, 319, 342, 345, 359
HMS Beagle, 358
HMS Dreadnought, 46
HMS Endeavour, 121
HMS Victory, 321
Hoare-Laval Plan, 319
Hoban, James, 313
Hobbit, The, 289
Hogarth, William, 317
Holly, Buddy, 39
Hollywood, 65, 305
Holy Land, 86, 152, 302
Holy Roman Empire, 129
Honduras, 64
Hoover, Herbert, 208
Hoover, J. Edgar, 82
Hopper, Grace, 277
Horn, Gyula, 278
Horse Shoe Brewery, 317
hospital, 29, 176, 246, 264, 279, 306, 374
hostages, 274, 290, 338
House of Commons, 6, 175, 231
House of Lords, 175, 339
House of Representatives, 72, 241
Houston, 115, 122, 220
Howard, Catherine, 89
Howe, Geoffrey, 348
Hundred Days, 62, 177, 186
Hundred Years War, 164, 260, 325
Hungarian Uprising, 184, 372
Hungary, 61, 99, 223, 254, 278, 343, 388
Hunt, Henry, 250
Hussein bin Ali, Grand Sharif, 178

Nutcracker (ballet), 384

ABOUT THE AUTHOR

Scott Allsop is an experienced history teacher and graduate of the University of Cambridge. He writes and presents the daily www.HistoryPod.net podcast and runs an award-winning educational website for history students at www.MrAllsopHistory.com.

He currently lives in Romania with his wife and two children.

Made in the USA
San Bernardino, CA
07 January 2018